29

I Couldn't Possibly Comment...

Also by Matthew Parris
and available from Robson Books

Look Behind You! Sketches and Follies
From the Commons
Great Parliamentary Scandals

and with Phil Mason
Read My Lips – A Treasury of the Things
Politicians Wish They Hadn't Said

I Couldn't Possibly Comment...

Sketches and Follies from the Commons Again

MATTHEW PARRIS

Robson Books

First published in Great Britain in 1997 by Robson
Books Ltd, Bolsover House, 5–6 Clipstone Street,
London W1P 8LE

Copyright © 1997 Matthew Parris
The right of Matthew Parris to be identified as author
of this work has been asserted by him in accordance
with the Copyright, Designs and Patents Act 1988

British Library Cataloguing in Publication Data
A catalogue record for this title is available from the
British Library

ISBN 1 86105 095 X

Typeset by Columns Design Ltd, Reading
Printed in Great Britain by Butler & Tanner Ltd.,
Frome and London

To my father and mother

Acknowledgements

Except where otherwise acknowledged, articles included in this collection appeared first in *The Times*, to whose successive editors, my patrons, Charles Wilson, Simon Jenkins and Peter Stothard I am grateful.

For all her help in keeping and filing my work, her occasional praise, occasional criticism and constant common sense, I am indebted to my secretary and friend, Eileen Wright. She and Julian Glover helped me choose and edit these sketches.

In *The Times* room at the Commons, Ivan Barnes, Robin Oakley, Peter Riddell, Phil Webster, Nick Wood, Bob Morgan, Sheila Gunn, Jill Sherman, Arthur Leathley, Jonathan Prynn, Andrew Pierce, Alice Thomson and James Landale helped me write them. *The Times*'s sub-editors at Wapping have silently corrected hundreds of stupid errors, and otherwise left me alone. Thanks to all.

Introduction

The journey for which this book is really just a series of travel notes began, for me, in the autumn of 1988. As presenter of London Weekend Television's *Weekend World* I had led the programme to an early grave in the spring of 1988 and – out of work – had accepted the suggestion of Charles Wilson, *The Times*'s Editor, that I try my hand at Parliamentary sketchwriting. I told Charles that a year or so was the longest I would want to be a Commons journalist.

That was nine years ago. There seemed no reason to stop. As I write, I still believe, as I have believed at every point in this nine year journey, that another year or two will be about right.

What makes this servitude so wonderfully bearable is that, unfashionable as it now is to say so, I'm rather fond of MPs. They can be dreadfully silly, of course, and there are days when they irritate beyond measure. Whole weeks pass during which it is not possible to take them seriously. Occasionally, even, comes a moment when an MP's speech or behaviour arouses genuine anger, goading me into an attempt at lofty condemnation.

But I always regret it. It rarely reads well the next day. There are other journalists to ride high horses and my mission, I think, is to remind readers that their MPs are often more laughable than they are wicked and that, through the laughter, we may discern the outlines of ideas, arguments, ambitions, even principles.

British Members of Parliament are mostly human, rarely scaling the heights nor often touching the depths to which the Caesars, Tsars and Kaisers of history fly. Only a handful among them are of unusual intelligence but many are effective and most are hard-working. Like us, really.

What distinguishes them is an almost child-like desire for attention. Writers who think themselves clever wink at us and confide that an MP must be noticed to get on. The reverse is true. Most successful politicians are remarkable for having avoided notice until the last moment: ambushing us unawares. Our most noticeable politicians – take Dennis Skinner or Edwina Currie, for instance – have generally wrecked what might have been a serious political career by their craving for attention. Both are, incidentally, brighter than many of their more career-minded senior colleagues.

Why do so many MPs want to be noticed so much? To this I turn in the first sketch in this book, only partly in jest. And that phrase 'only partly in jest' hangs in the air above a fair sample of what follows. The jester's role is enviable. He is not being serious and may therefore be as serious as he likes. He is never called to account, not supposed to be fair, never obliged to justify. In observing the passing scene – and the scenes ahead begin during Margaret Thatcher's last days, end during what may or may not be John Major's, and encompass the rise and fall of Neil Kinnock, the rise and death of John Smith, and the rise and rise of Tony Blair – a little sly judgement here and there has proved possible: more, I think, on character than on policy. Challenge me on any of this – and I couldn't possibly comment.

A reader writing to the Editor of the *Spectator* was kind enough to describe me as being on my low horse. On this unelevated saddle, then, join me in a canter through some interesting times ...

Matthew Parris, *Times* Room, Westminster, March 1997

One Day I'll Show Them

Why are all those MPs – those, that is, who are not called Norman – called Reggie, Ronnie or Stan; Cyril, Cecil or Archie? Why are people with ludicrous names driven by some unseen force to stand for election?

As with so many great discoveries the answer came to me by chance, while pondering another great question of our time. Why can so few politicians pronounce their rs?

In a flash it was all clear. Both questions have the same answer: MPs were desperately unpopular at school.

They were the boys and girls who got teased in the playground. Some had funny names. Some had speech defects. Some had squidgy little faces, awful freckles, or problems with girls. And the whole of their lives since have been a desperate attempt to compensate. Plump little Kenneth hid in the loo from the other boys, sobbing silently: '*I'll* show them. One day, I'll be Secretary of State for Education. I'll wear flashy ties and be popular with all my mates.' Correct Miss Margaret-Hilda flinched at classmates' taunts: 'Snobby-Roberts!' Inwardly she vowed to work even harder, to be even *more* superior, and – one day – to be the first woman prime minister in the Western world, *and* end up a duchess.

Thin, shy, studious young Michael Meacher ('Meacher, Meacher, suck-up to the teacher') knew he'd grow up to be a working-class hero. Oh yes! They'd be sorry they'd bullied the bloke they now needed to protect *them*! He'd stand at the Opposition dispatch box championing the unemployed.

So he did yesterday, at Employment Questions. Opposite him was the Secretary of State. Who is called Norman. And cannot pronounce his rs. When he was Minister of Transport his Labour opposite number was called Albert (really!) and couldn't pronounce rs either. The repartee on 'redundant British Rail rolling-stock' was richly rewarding.

Someone called Conal from York wanted to know why some tourist information centres were closed in winter. Then Cyril from Rochdale spoke. But soon Cecil from Barrow-in-Furness was on his feet, worried

1

lest Norman's relaxing of the rules about employing teenagers might usher back chimney-sweeps.

Norman from Chingford looked in. Dale, Derek and Kenneth (Workington, Leeds and Blackley) intervened.

Then on to a Mr Rooker's question ('Rooker! Rooker! You're a silly ...') where Bernard from Castle Point came to Norman's aid. Alistair's exchange proved interesting to Dafyd, so there was hardly time to hear Irvine. And none for Dudley, Archy or Spencer. As for Hugo and Trevor, there was no chance at all of questions 79 and 80 being reached.

For it was time for Prime Minister's Questions with Hilda. The first was from Keith of Manchester; the second from a Ms Walley. Hugh from Hornsey was away, but a freckled person called Neil seemed especially agitated, while a chap called Robin Maxwell-Hyslop was furious about a girl called Edwina.

With Hilda sat Tristan (a whip, or class monitor). In garish tie was Kenneth who (since our story started) has become Education Secretary. Still waiting at the back was Sydney from Barnet. Standing at the Bar of the House, yet another Kenneth, next to a Miss Fookes and a Mr Brandon-Bravo.

We never reached Humphrey's question.

The Liftman   *10.5.89*

After seven years of being punished for impertinence, it is an exhilarating experience to find myself paid for it. But the Press Gallery presents special problems for an ex-Member, gamekeeper turned poacher. When debate gets heated, the temptation to join in is almost unbearable.

'Faced by this dilemma,' I heard a frontbencher declaim, the other day, 'what should I do?'

'Resign!' I swear the cry was only a micro-second from my lips before, in the nick of time, it struck me that I was no longer a Member. Think of the ignominy. Hauled out of the Gallery by policemen, to the growls of my old colleagues and the titters of my new.

Still, it's nice to be recognized by erstwhile fellow MPs, a couple of whom (I suspect) have not registered the change either. Alistair

Goodlad has only recently stopped sending me those 'Have you any spare PM's Questions Gallery tickets?' notelets.

Keith Joseph used to make the opposite mistake, as became clear during a strange ride in the lift from the Special Gallery (East) during my first year as a Member. Keith, who was in the same lift, mistook me for a lift-attendant.

'Take me to the Members' Lobby,' he said, courteous but brusque. Then a worried look crossed his face. Perhaps, I thought, he has realized his error. Better for me to say nothing.

'East–West trade,' he muttered, half to himself and then, turning to me, the only other occupant of the lift, 'By cutting the link, would we gain strength, or simply lose a potential lever?' I stammered out some half-baked reply.

Sir Keith looked at me intently, listening. 'Yes. Quite possibly … Ah, we're here. You can let me off. Thank you. Goodbye. I shall think about what you said, and perhaps discuss it further, next time I am in your lift.'

I suppose the story could be cited as unintended discourtesy, a testimony to Keith's absent-mindedness. To me it serves better as testimony to his intellectual openness – an unintended courtesy. Keith addressed his colleague as a lift-attendant, but was as interested in a lift-attendant's views as he would have been in a colleague's. Other ministers would address you as a colleague, and be as interested in your views as in a lift-attendant's.

6.12.89   # Taking No Part

Sir Anthony Meyer challenges Mrs Thatcher for the leadership …

The staircase outside our Westminster room has a dustbin-alley air. Overshadowed by the black metal caging of an ancient lift, it is cluttered with bins of old papers. You don't expect to meet the Prime Minister there.

So, walking to the stairs just as a colleague asked me how many rebels would surface today, I flung open the door with a confident declaration. 'Sixty,' I said. And stared point-blank into Mrs Thatcher's eyes.

I felt myself blushing. What do you *say*? I was seized with an absurd desire to sing 'green bottles, hanging on a wall, sixty green bottles … – Oh! Good afternoon, Prime Minister. Fancy seeing you here!' … but suppressed it, and stood mute.

Mrs Thatcher glanced at me for a micro-second, and – almost on the instant – addressed her Parliamentary Private Secretary: 'Ah, Mark, I think it's one floor further down.' I heard her voice trailing down the next flight of stairs: 'It's *such* a labyrinth …'

She was on her way from casting her vote in the Committee Room above.

Denis Healey passed me on his way there, eyebrows beetling famously: 'I want to vote in the Tory leadership election. Where can I apply to join? *You* should remember.'

I returned to the *Times* room. 'How would you have voted?' someone asked me.

I wonder.

Happy Ever After?   *21.2.90*

Once upon a time, children, there was a place called Hamelin in Germany. It was 'twinned' with somewhere called Westminster.

And, in this place, they had a terrible problem. An infestation of rates. Rates were everywhere: huge rates, rates with sharp teeth, slinking through people's letter-boxes and ruining their lives. The citizens begged their leaders to get rid of the rates; but the problem was, nobody could think how.

Then a man called Mr Baker with silver hair and a big smile came forward. He wore flashy wide ties and they called him the Wide-Tied Baker of Hamelin.

'I know a way of eradicating rates,' he said. 'Trust me. But if I do this, I want you to reward me. I want to be the next Leader of Hamelin.'

Not *everybody* did quite trust the Wide-Tied Baker but they were frantic to get rid of the rates, so they agreed to let him try.

He was as good as his word. He passed a law, saying that 'from 1 April, all the rates are abolished' and – hey presto! – they were.

But it was at about this time that the Wide-Tied Baker noticed that the people were unlikely to make him Leader. Frankly, the elders were not giving him the nod. Younger citizens were pointing at him and snickering about some of his other schemes, like Student Loans, GCSE and the National Core Curriculum.

And, though he continued to smile, the Wide-Tied Baker grew rather impatient and slightly bitter, for he was a clever man and had really meant well, underneath. Yet there was no sign that the present Leader was planning to retire and no sign that, when that day came, Baker would be the favoured one.

And a very evil idea came to him. He called everyone together. 'With the rates gone,' he announced, 'I'll take you all somewhere really fantastic. It's a magical mystery tour to the Polltax Mountains. Not an easy journey but it'll be great when you get there; and, to lead you, my young friend Christopher Patten will dance ahead and play sweet music all the way. You'll love it, honestly.'

At this, young Chris looked a bit nervous as he wasn't at all sure he knew the way, or that people would like it when they got there. But the Leader of Hamelin told him it was his duty.

And off they all set. The Wide-Tied Baker had detached himself, now, from the throng and sat on a rock at 32 Smith Square, watching them stumble towards the horizon. A thin smile played upon his lips. 'Have fun!' he called.

As night falls, and they still don't seem to be getting anywhere, and the ground grows stonier, the path steeper, and the wind colder, cries of distress fill the air. Yet still they stumble forward ...

Children, there is a logical flaw in the plot of this story. Can you spot it? Yes – correct, David Wilshire. *The people didn't have to go to the Polltax Mountains in the first place. They still don't. They could just turn round and go home again.*

Do you think they will?

21.6.90   **Hallowed Be Thy Name-calling**

The rancour started as the echo of prayer died away in the Chamber.

Newspapermen are excluded from the religious ceremony. It is only after 'Prayers for the Parliament' in which Mr Speaker's chaplain leads the MPs at 2.30 every afternoon, that we journalists are allowed in. Crowding at the oak doors, pressing our ears to hear the murmured devotions, we might just pick out the words:

'Almighty God, the Fountain of all Goodness ... by whom alone Kings reign and Princes decree justice ... we, thine unworthy servants ... do most humbly beseech thee to send down thy Heavenly Wisdom from above, to direct and guide us in all our consultations; and grant ...' Or so I recall.

'Questions to the Secretary of State,' the Speaker cried. All fell at each other's throats.

'... that laying aside all private interests, prejudices, and partial affections ...'

'There are a number of unpleasant features about the hon gentleman.' Junior minister Douglas Hurd was referring to Labour's industry spokesman, Gordon Brown. 'Discreditable,' said Hogg.

'... the result of all our counsels may be to the glory of thy blessed Name, the maintenance of true Religion and Justice, and tranquillity of the Realm ...'

'This arrogant little shit has not answered one question!' shouted Labour's George Foulkes (Carrick, Cumnock and Doon Valley). He was talking about Mr Hogg. Screams of protest rose from the Conservative benches.

'He will withdraw that word immediately. And do not repeat it,' said Mr Speaker, his colour rising ...

'... the uniting and knitting together of the hearts of all persons and estates ...'

'Which word?' Foulkes shouted back: 'Arrogant, little, or shit?'

'The last word,' snapped the Speaker.

'... in true Christian Love and Charity one towards another ...'

Now it was Hogg's turn: 'This whingeing and whining from the Opposition benches is amusing and pathetic ...'

'Further us with thy continual help, that in all our works begun, continued, and ended in thee, we may glorify thy Holy Name ...'

'Humbug!' roared Nicholas Ridley, the Industry Secretary. 'Humbug!'

'... and finally by thy mercy obtain everlasting Life through Jesus Christ our Lord ...'

The Chair has the last word, here, too. Amid the hurling of abuse, Mr Speaker rose, shaking his bewigged head wearily. 'Some rough things are said in this Chamber,' he sighed. 'That's what it's all about.'
'... Amen.'

28.6.90 # Portillo Mk II Shines

When a new minister is taken out for road tests, it is a privilege to be among the observers.

Fresh from the showrooms, the air-cooled Portillo Mark II – 'Poll Tax Turbo GTI' – was driven round the circuit for the first time yesterday. Results were promising. A discreetly lively performance, road-holding good.

Over at the Department of Transport, the machine had been put through extensive trials as 'Rail minister', and reports were positive. The sleek Latin lines have, of course, been widely admired; but the Portillo's performance had been restrained. Backroom boys were impressed by this minister's information system; but the Portillo always seemed to be operating below design specifications. Answering for BR sandwich quality hardly tested this minister to the limit. This machine had still to win the hearts of the public and the plaudits of the trade press.

To do so under the 'Poll Tax' badge was never going to be easy. This is a troubled marque with a history of horrendous teething problems. Preceding the Portillo in this niche, the David Hunt (or 'Wirral Wonder') had been a smooth performer, but criticized as lacking kick. The challenge facing the Portillo was formidable.

They wheeled him in at 2.30. While a trusty Trippier raced up and down the tarmac at Question 1, final checks were made to the Portillo's paperwork and exterior trim. The minister was ready.

Performing the bump start at Question 2 was an able young mechanic, Tim Devlin (C, Stockton S). Devlin chose a safe stretch of track.

'Is it not remarkable that my hon friend has not received the promised policy paper from the Opposition?'

That was more than enough. The minister fired first time. Brm, brrm, brr ... The Portillo was away.

'Yes, I think it is truly remarkable that they have not come up with an alternative ...'

Into a gentle bend: 'They have no "reasoned policy document" ...'

A touch on the throttle: 'There was no background paper.'

Easing up a gear now, needle creeping up nicely: 'Indeed, I suspect there was no background.'

On the straight – maybe a taste of burning rubber? 'Labour have no idea what to do about local government ...'

'Hear, *hear*!' came approving growls from the grandstand. There was an angry whine of Opposition engines, revving in the pit. Their wheels – 'alternatives to the poll tax' – long promised from Walworth Road, had still not arrived. The Portillo purred past, first lap complete.

It was time for a fast run through the S-bends. Richard Tracy (C, Surbiton), an experienced race official from the back benches, flagged the Portillo away: would the government look at the standard community charge and the iniquitous suggestion by some local authorities that it must always be applied at the two-times multiplier?

'Of course I will look at the point.' The minister moved silkily up through the gears. 'This is an area where the government wishes local government to be local.' Rubber bit into asphalt now, as the minister tried a boost to the turbo: 'They can apply multipliers on the standard community charge up to a maximum of two.'

Chrome flashed in the afternoon sun as the minister coasted past the grandstand. The Portillo Mark II 'Poll Tax Turbo GTI' was making an auspicious debut.

First Ballotah   *10.11.90*

The leadership questioned ...

Tory leaders used to 'emerge' but now we have democracy. Democracy among Tory MPs, as Julian Critchley has explained, is the system under which the common will is least likely to triumph. Events of the past week prove it.

Half the Tory backbenchers you talk to subject you to a private harangue about how much nicer it would be if Mrs Thatcher could be surgically removed and somebody cuddly put in her place quickly, before the next election.

'But would you vote that way?' one asks.

'On the second ballot, yes,' they reply.

'What about the first ballot?'

'Ah.'

Ah. We could summarize the problem as the 'first ballotah' dilemma. How to get from here to the second ballot without passing through a first ballot on the way.

I can guess what you are thinking, but you are wrong. In the first ballot, MPs do not need to know for whom they are voting: they only need to know for whom they are *not* voting. The ballot paper should say '1: Mrs Thatcher; 2: Not Mrs Thatcher; 3: Another Not Mrs Thatcher ... etc.' If No 1 did not gain an overall majority there would be a second ballot and numbers 2, 3 etc. (who would have been voted for randomly) would be invited to say who they were. If we hadn't guessed already.

Mild Turns to Bitter

Sir Geoffrey Howe resigns ...

All along the rabbit warrens inhabited by journalists at Westminster, a tannoy system crackles occasionally into life with urgent information. At ten to four yesterday came a warning hiss ...

'Attention! Attention! In view of Sir Geoffrey Howe's personal statement, there will be no four o'clock.'

What a pity the word 'devastating' has been drained of meaning by journalistic overuse, for it was never so apt as yesterday. When can so much powder have been kept so dry for so long? Outsiders sensed, as much in the gasps of the packed Chamber as in Sir Geoffrey's words themselves, how much greater was the impact on a House which knows the unvarying low-key style this man has adopted over the last twelve years. The urgency of feeling reminded your sketchwriter how seldom the quality of earnestness is sensed these days in the parliamentary performances of any but the mad, or impotent.

Mrs Thatcher started with a look of tense composure and a faint smile. The composure held, the tension grew, and the smile disappeared.

That will teach her to take a fellow's country house away. If this wasn't Mrs Thatcher's Waterloo, then it was undoubtedly her Clapham Junction.

Hear Hear, Perhaps   *22.11.90*

One after the other they rose. Members of the party which, beneath the cloak of anonymity and in the shadows of Room 12 the evening before, had plunged in the knife, stood now in the light of the afternoon to congratulate their leader. With one voice they cheered her to the rafters as she entered the Chamber.

'Hear, hear, *hear*!' they bellowed.

One hundred and fifty open mouths in round faces; one hundred and fifty expensive suits; three score waistcoats covering three score plump stomachs; gold watch-chains, gold tie-pins, silk handkerchiefs billowing from top pockets ... the Tory party was marching behind its leader, every shiny shoe in step. It was a magnificent sight.

Of course 'hear, hear' has a certain anonymity. 'Hear, hear' is a noise, not an undertaking. 'Hear, hear' is not contractually binding and does not constitute an offer. So there was no shortage of mooing and yelping and growling in Mrs Thatcher's support yesterday.

Getting up to speak is rather different. You are all on your own, then. You have stood up, and you will be counted.

So when the Prime Minister had finished her statement, reporting the CSCE summit in Paris ('hear, hear!'), what could be seen differed strangely from what could be heard. The usual crowd – the place-men, job-seekers and fair-weather friends – sat motionless. And in their place rose a small and eccentric platoon: the men still willing to be numbered in her company.

They are best not named, for there were some brave supporters, careless of their own advantage, but there were also fools, ignorant of danger, and creeps so inured to creeping that they have forgotten the purpose of sycophancy.

More depressing to Mrs Thatcher even than the sneers of her enemies must be to observe the calibre of much of the band that still count themselves her friends.

For each, the Prime Minister had a word of gratitude. If we had not known that she was facing political death, nothing in her manner would have suggested it. Dressed in a mustard suit edged in black and pinned with a brooch shaped like a panther leaping, Mrs Thatcher's own expression was not unpantherlike. She looked as ready as ever to leap.

She delivered her statement like a robot, as usual, but sprang to life under hostile questioning, most notably from Tony Benn about war in the Gulf. Mrs Thatcher has never been comfortable dealing with the new 'moderate' Labour party, and flew at this representative of the old, familiar enemy with practised passion. They would miss each other, if she had to go.

28.11.90   # The Tribe

The fall of Mrs Thatcher …

There will be people who will portray what has passed in recent days as an embarrassing lapse. Such people speak of chaos and confusion, of panic and self-destructive anger. Soon they will be referring to these past few weeks as an awkward wobble, when the Tory party temporarily took leave of its senses, then recovered its nerve.

Nothing could be further from the truth. As in some tribal folk-mystery, the Conservative party has suffered a great internal convulsion, triggered as much by the collective unconscious of the tribe as by any conscious plan to contrive its survival. They have not, as individual men and women, known what they were doing, but the tribe has known what it was doing, and has done it with ruthless efficiency. The instinct to survive has triumphed.

Not that they were aware of that. All they knew was that they were heading for disaster. Each had his own opinion as to why. What they concurred upon was the imminence of danger; and when they concurred on that, the convulsion began.

At their conference in Bournemouth, a strange, flat despair gripped the occasion. We all noticed it, but none of us knew how to interpret it. Then they began to fight. They lashed out at the media, they lashed out at Europe, they lashed out at the Opposition, and they lashed out at each other. The tribe was in turmoil.

Michael Heseltine – as much, by now, a totem of dissent as a person – found members of the tribe dancing around him and chanting. He responded. The media took up the chant. Michael Heseltine started a teasing dance: was it a war dance? Nobody knew. He did not know himself.

At this point their leader took on the dervish character. Saddam Hussein said she was 'possessed'. In a series of sustained rants she stunned the Chamber, alienated half her party and scared hell out of most of us.

There followed a short silence, and then the murmurs began. They grew until an extraordinary thing happened. One of the elders of the tribe, Sir Geoffrey Howe, began to speak. He spoke almost in tongues: he spoke as he had never spoken. He poured down imprecations upon the head of the leader.

Around Mr Heseltine the dance now reached a pitch of excitement that demanded answer. He rose, took the dagger and stabbed her.

What happened next is folklore. With the leader now wounded, but still alive, her own senior tribesmen drew back with one accord and left her. Suddenly alone, she hesitated a moment, then staggered from the stage.

The tribe mourned her departure. Not falsely or without feeling, they wept. Then, last night, the final twist occurred. The tribe fell upon her assailant, Michael Heseltine, and slew him, too – with many shouts of anger. Real anger.

All drew back, and the new leader, already blessed by the old leader, clean, apart, and uninvolved, stepped forward. With cries of adoration, the tribe gathered around him.

It could have been done as a ballet. It had all the elements of a classical drama. Like Chinese opera or Greek tragedy, the rules required that certain human types be represented; certain ambitions be portrayed; certain actions punished. Every convention was obeyed: every actor played out his role. The dramatic unities of time, place and action were fulfilled. It started in autumn 1990, and ended in the same season; it started in Committee Room 12 at Westminster, and ended there.

It started with an old leader, who was assassinated as she deserved; then her assassin was assassinated, as he deserved. Then the new leader stepped forward; and here the ballet ended.

And the tribe danced. As I write, they are dancing still.

30.11.90 # Mr Major Begins to Bore

A group of reporters and political sketchwriters sipped tea yesterday in a Commons cafeteria. Despair gripped us. It was 3.40, just after Prime Minister's Questions. One spoke. He voiced the mood of all.

'If people are going to be moderate, reasonable and fair-minded, they have to be got rid of. They are no use to us.'

Yesterday was John Major's debut.

Mrs Thatcher had arrived first, in papal purple.

Opinion divided sharply among the press corps as to whether she was early for Prime Minister's Questions (3.15) or late for Prayers (2.30). One faction among us noted that waiting until other MPs had arrived (and the public gallery had filled) guaranteed the cheers she got.

The other faction speculated that she would not have wanted her new life to start with devotions. Missing Prayers might arise from having been caught in her first traffic jam for eleven years. Now she knows what all those stationary cars are doing.

When she came in, Mr Heath's front seat was empty.

'Don't let Heath get that place!' came the helpful call from Labour's Dennis Skinner. Mrs Thatcher smiled and shook her head, occupying a more modest position near the back. She sat next to Mrs Elizabeth Peacock (Batley and Spen), a known second-ballot 'Heseltinista'.

Next, at 3.11, came Mr Heseltine himself. He strode in to scattered cheers from both sides and plonked himself down next to Chris Patten, who gave him an encouraging pat on the arm – as well might a minister who had just handed his successor 'an unexploded time bomb' (if Mr Patten's description of the poll tax is to be believed).

Then, thirty seconds later, in walked the Prime Minister.

There was a huge cheer from the government benches. Mrs Thatcher smiled – her face a tug-o'-war between pride and anxiety: like a gym mistress watching her young star pupil approaching the vaulting-horse in his new leotards.

3.15. They were away – with a planted question from Roger King (C, Birmingham, Northfield) of a type of which we all fervently hope Mr Major's fixers do not intend to make a practice.

And what, you ask, of the main event?

What indeed! It was dull. Mr Kinnock asked a routine question about the poll tax, Mr Major gave a holding reply about the need for 'refinements' and Kinnock (luckily for Major) did not enquire how exactly you do refine an unexploded time bomb.

A series of the usual crawling questions from the government benches, and the usual insults from the Opposition left both the strengths and the weaknesses of their target untested.

Apart from the intriguing hint of an underlying petulance, Major kept a cannily straight bat. He looked intelligent but nervous and sounded like the whine of a chainsaw in a distant forest. He does not, yet, command the Chamber naturally. Achieving that took Mrs Thatcher years.

'Resign,' shouted Labour hecklers at him, without enthusiasm. 'Resign,' came the returning shout back at Neil Kinnock from some Tories. From others, more interestingly: 'Don't resign.' It was, in short, a day like any other. If this was Thursday, that must be John Major. If this was Prime Minister's Questions, that must be the Prime Minister.

Tactical Baby Seals   *29.1.91*

Yesterday, Michael Heseltine told the House what Saddam was doing to 'fish, sea mammals, and shellfish'. MPs were the angriest they have yet been, in this war.

So far as is known, there are no baby seals in the Persian Gulf. This is a pity for Hussein. It deprives him of the ultimate weapon against the British public and its outraged House of Commons: to target Scud missiles on to seal nurseries. Short of this horror, all that is left to the evil Iraqis is to breed seals in one of their secret biological establishments and engage in low-level baby-seal-bombing, dropping their furry bomblets straight into the greasy sludge. To judge from yesterday's performance, the psychological blow here would be devastating.

None of the atrocities so far committed by Baghdad against humans has unleashed a thesaurus of parliamentary shock of anything like the intensity we heard yesterday. It was no particular expression (any of which, alone, could be justified) but the sheer scale of accumulated adjectival outrage which impressed.

'Abomination,' said environment secretary Michael Heseltine, 'outrage', 'calamity', 'catastrophe'.

This was mild. 'Monstrous,' thought the Father of the House, Sir Bernard Braine – one of those few with the grace to mention (in passing) the mass murder, by gas, of Kurdish people. 'Blackmail,' said Heseltine. 'Vicious' (Jonathan Aitken), 'evil and reckless' (Peter Shore).

'Desperate act,' said Labour's spokesman, Ann Taylor, 'war-crime'. Each one of us, she added poetically, was the poorer for this. She did not quite say 'Any oyster's death diminishes me/Therefore never send to know/On whom the oil spills: it spills on thee …' But she nearly did. Mrs Taylor was concerned about the 'eco-system'. Or it may have been 'echo-system' – a reference, perhaps, to the Opposition's response to government policy in the Gulf.

Has military science yet developed a sea-cow-seeking missile? Such a weapon would give Saddam a key advantage in the war of nerves. There was concern at Westminster about the loss of human life: that was bad enough. But to threaten *sea-cows*!

'Absolute inhumanity of this repulsive regime,' was Gravesham's Jacques Arnold's phrase; 'despicable ecological devastation' came from Simon Burns (C, Chelmsford).

I wonder whether Saddam has considered taking a group of cormorants hostage? To judge from yesterday's anxiety, this would unnerve our elected representatives a good deal more than the holding of British journalists. I had not thought of cormorants as an endangered species, but yesterday, plummy voices – voices able to report the most harrowing of news at the tensest of cheese-and-wine parties, and still stay steady – trembled with horror. Even Mr Heseltine's grammar deserted him ('deliberate act of environmental appalling consequences') as he thoughtfully carved out for himself a post-war role in organizing a 'working party' for permanent international preparedness.

'Appalling and uncivilized' (Norwich's Patrick Thompson), an 'evil man,' thought Anthony Beaumont-Dark (Selly Oak), 'vicious and brutal' (Phillip Oppenheim, Amber Valley) ... 'Eco-terrorism' was what Henry Bellingham (Norfolk NW) called it.

The Liberals' Simon Hughes wanted environmentalists to enjoy the same privilege as the Red Cross in war zones. Tony Banks (Lab, Newham NW) wanted to go there himself ('I'll go!' he shouted) to assist.

Nobody has yet tried 'Saddam Hussein ate my hamster' on the House. But they will.

Poll Tax: The Final Curtain   *22.3.91*

Any keynote speech, any poem, novel, story, *career*, of any consequence, turns upon a fulcrum. Somewhere concealed within it will be found a word, a passage, an episode, upon which the centre of gravity of the whole thing rests. In logic or in passion, every argument has a heart.

Yesterday's statement by the Secretary of State for the Environment was no exception. Michael Heseltine, though back on cracking form, could not escape a single phrase, buried in paragraph 40 on the fifth page of his long and closely argued statement. He had been building up to it for years. It lay there, waiting for him. He knew it was coming.

In a sense it was the sentiment for whose expression the whole of the Opposition had been cat-calling at Prime Minister's Questions, minutes earlier, when they shouted, 'Say you're sorry! Say you're sorry!' over and again.

It was the thing which every Tory MP dreads facing in the long months ahead at a hundred 'any questions' sessions and a thousand cheese and wine parties. It was the rock which scuppered Mrs Thatcher.

As his ship approached those straits, the minister's voice was lowered and the Chamber hushed. 'The public,' said Mr Heseltine, 'have not been persuaded that the charge is fair.'

'Say it again!' someone shouted. There was an enormous cheer from the Opposition. Most Tories grinned, foolishly.

The first half of Mr Heseltine's statement had been a gingerly approach to this sentence. What now remained was the painful climbing down which it entailed. He carried this off with aplomb. He almost seemed to be having fun.

For Labour, Bryan Gould had fun with his reply. To the gourmet of mixed metaphor, Mr Gould is a feast. He approaches the table of possible imagery rather as one who has paid a fixed price for a plate of salad under one of those 'all you can eat for £3.95' schemes and, starting with the potato salad, finds the sauerkraut equally attractive and the bean shoots hard to resist. The dinner loses coherence.

Mr Gould rose, and approached the table. This, he said, was a 'complete capitulation and a startling U-turn' as well as 'the most shameless abandonment of principle in modern political history'. It was a 'flagship, fatally holed below the waterline' but still 'afloat, the hulk a danger to shipping'. It 'refused to lie down and die'. It had taken the Prime Minister 'through the revolving door,' whereupon he had been 'bounced by a leak'. Still 'in thrall to the monster it had created,' it was now mutating into 'a pig in a poke' which 'put a price on the right to vote'. The pig in the poke was 'in the driving seat', a 'debacle', 'born of arrogance', and 'spreading its malign influence'.

But the pig, debacle, chauffeur, mutant monster or floating hulk, having completed its capitulation, shamelessly abandoned principle and accompanied Mr Major through the revolving door: and having then avoided the bouncing leak, refused to lie down.

It was, said Mr Gould, 'a bloodstained statement'. It was a pretty bloody reply, too.

27.3.91   **Lego Man Takes on Bendy Doll**

Wilde defined fox-hunting as 'the unspeakable in pursuit of the uneatable'. At PM's Questions yesterday, Mr Major, tackled again on the subject of the poll tax, gave a passable impression of the improbable in flight from the unsaleable.

There was another 'row' between Mr Major and Mr Kinnock. Lego Man meets Bendy Doll. If either of them had anything to say, it would matter less that neither has the gift of language. If either had the gift of language, it would matter less that neither has anything to say. Here were two men saying nothing, badly. It was unspeakable, uneatable, improbable and unsaleable.

The Vulcan and the Donkey   *14.6.91*

John Redwood has unusual origins …

The finest thoroughbred horses are often accompanied by a favourite donkey, goat or sheep. Some racehorses will travel nowhere without such a beast. Animal psychiatrists report that the pedigree is relaxed by the presence of its plebeian pal.

Sitting behind the junior industry minister, John Redwood, yesterday was his new parliamentary private secretary, David Evans (Welwyn Hatfield).

A PPS, who is unpaid, is a backbencher appointed to mind the backbench interests of a minister. The PPS keeps the boss in touch with feeling and acts as his eyes and ears in bars and tearooms where ministers do not go. If there are ruffled feathers, a PPS will let his master know. If a minister seeks to plant a question, a canny PPS will find the mug to do it.

It is up to ministers to choose. Redwood has chosen Evans. Not since Noddy and Big Ears has a more odd couple been seen.

Though Evans trades shamelessly on his humble origins, loves to play the buffoon and boasts of failing his 11-plus, he is no fool. A shrewd businessman and ex-chairman of Luton Town football club, Evans's braying interventions at PM's questions shock and delight. Beneath his superficially vulgar populism lies … well, a profoundly vulgar populism. To say that the member for Welwyn Hatfield is no intellectual is more than fair: it is your sketchwriter's best hope of avoiding a black eye. Yet the Evans family crest bears the motto *Ne me minoris face* ('do not underestimate me') – or would, if Evans could be doing with Latin. 'Watch yer step, sonny' says it all.

John Redwood could hardly be more different. Possessed of a supersonic intellect, this slim young ex-investment manager with Rothschilds, philosopher of the new right and Fellow of All Souls, is a lean, mean thinking machine. But he is dry, apparently cold, and has an emotionless manner which sometimes spooks his colleagues. This column was the first to tumble to the fact that Redwood is not in fact a human being at all, but a Vulcan, recently landed from the planet of the same name, where merciless logic rules. Redwood now passes as human, engaged in the covert task of assembling a team of Vulcans to take over the Conservative party.

The plot thickens. Redwood has employed Evans. Why? Evans is human!

I shall tell you why. Colleagues have advised Redwood that his only serious bar to upward mobility is his apparent lack of a sense of fun: he should show more warmth, a more roustabout quality, towards fellow MPs. To see what they mean, he has tapped the words 'fun', 'warmth' and 'roustabout' into the secret computer package of 'handy phrases for travellers to Earth' they gave him when he left Vulcan, but it flashes up only synonyms, equally unfamiliar. How can he cultivate emotions alien to him?

'I know,' he has concluded, 'I'll get a PPS. Somebody with all these qualities, to act as a bridge between me and the humans. I'll key the words for every vulgarian quality into my computasearch program, and see which MP the screen throws up.' Tap, tap, tap ... 'rollicking', 'rough', 'roustabout', 'rude' ... finally, he presses EXECUTE.

Oh dear. 'Evans, David John'. The computer has overdone it. Human, yes. All too human, but there is no way a Vulcan can know that. Operating according to strict binary logic, the computer has produced the optimum solution. Reacting with utter rationality, Mr Redwood has accepted it.

The best of luck to both!

13.9.91

A Dead Spider Reaches for the Skies

The Liberal Democrat Conference in Bournemouth ...

Paddy Ashdown has four famous poses. His favourite is staring, commando style, flinty-eyed into the middle distance: hand to chin, one finger up the side of his face, three fingers under the jaw, with neck jutting forward. In a previous era he would have chewed a pipe. Male models like this used to advertise knitting patterns in ladies' magazines. 'Paddy looks to the future.'

He enjoys too his 'come into my parlour' pose. Looking the front row straight in the eyes, he leans softly forward on to the lectern and, resting on elbows, lowers his voice. 'Paddy tells it straight,' or the 'frankly, my dear' stance.

For the 'agony and the ecstasy' pose – careworn yet compassionate, eyes narrowed to slits with suffering – the face is raised heavenward as the Ashdownian features grow taut with pain and passion. Sometimes the arms are outstretched. 'Would that this cup were taken from me.'

Finally, the 'I see angels!' pose. Arms wide open but chest now thrown forward; and on his face an expression of powerful optimism. '*Believe* me, friends! Come into my world! If only you could see how beautiful it is!' Parachutists call this the 'freefall position'.

To these four poses, Mr Ashdown yesterday added a fifth. It is new: designed to accompany moments of intense and very personal conviction. For this the body is hunched slightly, the shoulders rounded, the right hand held out, tense, at chest level. Palm facing upwards, extended fingers and thumb are clawed into an upturned cage, cradling – as it were – some sacred flame, or pearl of unknown price. The face is racked with urgent certainty. 'O fellow Britons! This is wisdom! This is truth! What treasure have we here!' I call it the 'dead spider' pose.

It was a huge hit yesterday. As the Liberal Democrat leader rallied the faithful at the end of their conference and the beginning of their march to glory, I counted more than 37 dead spiders from the lectern: two for each page of his interminable speech.

It was a dreadful speech and most effective. It was corny, it was hammed, and we would never have tolerated it from Kenneth Baker – yet, perhaps because he has still to be undone by office, from Mr Ashdown we somehow do.

They say George Bush is plagued by an inability to rise to what he despairingly calls 'the vision thing'. Reviewing speech drafts, friends mutter 'where's the vision, George?' Paddy has the opposite affliction. His problem was the reality thing. The speech was *all* vision.

It was vision in paragraph one, vision in paragraph two, and vision right through to the end, at paragraph 270. Within seconds of kickoff and only moments after we had been confronted by 'a new spirit abroad' – this following 'a new era of democracy and liberalism and peace and democratic renewal in our continent' – it was, said Paddy, 'a time for optimism' (*dead spider*) and 'a moment for democratic renewal' (*freefall position*). Those of us who felt it might also be a moment for a cup of tea were dismayed to hear that now came 'the hour of the free citizen'. The *hour*? He wasn't exaggerating. Page three (and 14 pages still to go) found modern liberal democrats (like Martin Luther) concluding 'here I stand. I can do no other' (*knitting pattern pose*). Aagh.

By page 13 ('words are not enough!') words were too much. One grew desperate. By page 15 – (*frankly my dear stance*): 'I give the people of our country this clear undertaking' – one knew it must end. It did. Mr Ashdown swept upwards through the raked galleries towards the ceiling and the Bournemouth sky, allowing the populace to touch him as he passed.

'Let this,' cried Charles Kennedy, 'be a metaphor for the ascent of our party!'

After the agony. After the triumph. The ascension of Paddy.

10.10.91 # The Lady's for Returning

The Conservative Party Conference in Blackpool ...

The appearance on the platform yesterday of the top half of Mrs Thatcher – mute and nodding, her smile too broad – was like those videos of hostages. Along with the audience, I wanted to storm the rostrum to see whether her legs were in irons, she had been forcibly injected with sedatives or Chris Patten was twisting her arm behind her back.

For days we had been promised by the Tory high command that they were going to show us Mrs Thatcher. We would see for ourselves that she was well treated and in good spirits. She would appear on the platform in Blackpool.

Appear? How? Wild speculation gripped devotees and the media. Roadside reporters were posted all around the hall but, as helicopters chopped the wind, rumour had it she might land from above. A story circulated about a tunnel: she could pop up from the rostrum floor. Others pictured a figure in an azure tutu, abseiling from the wings.

One Tory MP speculated unattributably that she might materialize in mini-hologram form, a tiny blue image shimmering, like Princess Leia in *Star Wars* on the chairman's palm, endlessly repeating the same message: 'There is no such thing as society ...' The hall waited. Then the platform party parted like the Red Sea awaiting the most important Israelite of all. Leaving a 50 yard gap at its centre, ministers cowered to each side as though to receive in their midst a radio-active rod.

And she simply walked on, with Mr Major.

A conventional entrance, an unconventional welcome. The conference erupted, leaping to its feet. If there were any doubts for whom, the Prime Minister settled it: modestly bowing to the obvious, he stood, and clapped. Immodestly bowing to the obvious, she sat, and acknowledged it.

Now that everyone applauds everything, you have to cheer too. There was a huge cheer for Mrs Thatcher, she stood, waved, sat, stood, waved, and sat again. Shouts continued. But still she did not speak. Brows furrowed. Was she all right?

'Speech!' someone shouted and soon everyone was shouting 'Speech'. This had not been scripted. The podium mafia looked worried. Mr Patten scowled. And on it went. 'Speech'.

I cannot report that Mrs Thatcher shook her head, wrote a note, or did anything to indicate unwillingness to speak. Her face showed only rapture. But around her the men in dark suits were frowning and growling to each other. Suddenly the chairman took the initiative.

'I have received a message,' he shouted. 'I have received a message from Mrs Thatcher' ... the crowd fell silent '... and she has asked us to continue with the programme.'

Had she? We looked at her, the Woman in the Iron Mask. Her face now was expressionless, the men in dark suits were smiling. Mr Patten pushed out his hand to stop the applause.

All through the debate she peered forward, sometimes smiling a little, sometimes clapping, but silent. At 12.30 they took her away. She was not dragged, but always there was a little knot of big men around her. Outside, helicopters beat the air, car engines revved and blue lights flashed. She was gone.

17.3.92   **The Lady Sails Proudly Away**

Mrs Thatcher attends the Commons for the last time ...

After years of making personal remarks about the former prime minister, perhaps I am permitted to say that yesterday she looked lovely. She wore very dark green with black collars and a diamond star on one lapel. She seemed quite composed. John Major was absent. Mrs Thatcher made for the government front bench, which was empty. What, we wondered rather nervously, had she in mind?

The table on which the dispatch box sits – where she had stood so many thousands of times – was littered with papers. Mrs Thatcher walked up and tidied the mess. She put the documents together into neat little piles, glanced at her handiwork, and left.

I remembered how, when she was Leader of the Opposition, she would climb on to chairs to check for dust on top of the picture frames in the shadow cabinet room. 'Its the way a woman knows that a room's *really* been cleaned,' she once told us.

MPs trooped off to the Lords to hear the prorogation. Neil Kinnock being absent, Mrs Thatcher paired up with Frank Haynes, the retiring Labour MP for Ashfield. His booming and good-natured interruptions have always made her laugh.

When they returned, it was time for Mr Speaker to send us home. It was his final duty. 'I have to acquaint the House ...' he began – and read out the completed bills: 'Still Birth Definition Act, 1992, Traffic Calming Act, 1992 ...' Then 'by virtue of Her Majesty's command', he prorogued the Commons.

Mrs Thatcher, who had sat with her long-time supporter and friend, Gerald Howarth (C, Cannock and Burntwood), was almost the first to say goodbye. To a huge cheer she walked down the gangway, shook Mr Speaker's hand, and sailed proudly out. It was sublime.

Cuddly Green Mammals   *20.3.92*

The Green Party launch their election manifesto …

'To be Green in Britain in 1992 … is like being a small mammal watching the last two dinosaurs engaged in a struggle to the death. On the one hand, there is a deep inner sense of personal fragility. On the other, there is a deep inner confidence that the future does not belong to the dinosaur.'

That prefaces the Green party manifesto, launched yesterday. The small mammals had gathered in a modest burrow near Covent Garden. The hounds of the press had gathered to bait them. The London Ecology Centre, 21 Endell Street, lacks the pretensions of a great conference hall. Squeezed between Johnsons' outfitters ('Closing Down') and the Carrie Awaze II Deli and Sandwich Bar, a simple room awaited. At one end was a table with a green tablecloth and three chairs.

Into the three chairs filed a mouse, a grey dove and a rabbit. The mouse was called Richard Lawson: a small man with a kind, slightly anxious face, and very bright eyes. The grey dove told us her name was Sara Parkin. She had a finely chiselled beak and, though quite young, striking grey hair worn long and unadorned. There was a sort of handsome serenity about her, like a Quakeress. The rabbit, Jean Lambert, was a little shorter with round face and nervous movements. Fur and feather neatly brushed, the small mammals had come to present their survival plans.

Manifestos were distributed. There were two. One was called *The Path*, the other *The Policies*.

The grey dove spoke first. The double manifesto was 'a special treat' for us. She and her fellow mammals were 'in very high spirits'. They were 'the fastest growing political movement the world has ever seen'.

Some Greens from Czechoslovakia had come to stay with some of the Green candidates here. 'Greens from Prague to Portsmouth are inspired by exactly the same concerns.' The grey dove urged the dinosaurs to stop 'fiddling with a penny on income tax, while the planet burns' and handed us over to the mouse. The mouse made an arresting speech, in an offbeat sort of way. Peering intensely at us with his shining little eyes, he took a risk for a Green: he adopted a military analogy.

He and his fellow mammals were, he said, a tiny posse fighting huge and brutal invaders: the forces of extinction. The dinosaurs, Tories and Labour, seemed blind to the threat and collaborated with the wreckers of our planet. The Liberal Democrats were 'wimps'.

Green politicians deal in a different sort of prediction from the forward figures for interest rates or GDP. Last week Mr Lamont said the economy will grow by 1 per cent. This week, Mr Smith said the recession would continue, under the Tories. Yesterday, the mouse said that humans will end up alone on the planet except for cockroaches and rats. The householder canvassed in quick succession by all three parties may need a stiff drink.

Outlining the 'five screaming injustices' of modern politics, the mouse called Mr Kinnock 'Tweedledum' and Mr Major 'Tweedledee', and sat down. The rabbit told us it was acceptable, even desirable, to have no children. Pressed on this, she admitted that Greens are not proposing to legislate for it. She quoted Gandhi, proposed a tax on packaging, and denied that Greens were 'anti-car'. Their manifesto undertakes to cancel road-building schemes and offer 'incentives to those able to use the canal network'. The rabbit did not expand on that.

Finally, the mammals took questions from the hounds. The mouse got into a muddle about why the apparent £75 billion cost of his scheme for a basic wage was an exaggeration, and the grey dove inveighed passionately against the word 'other'. Greens object to the way pollsters lump their supporters under 'other' parties. In Sweden, she said, Greens sue people who use the O-word.

The hounds of the press restrained their savagery. These little creatures seemed to believe their own message and care little what we make of it. Small mammals which roll over on their backs and offer the jugular are confusing to scavengers. The mouse, the grey dove and the rabbit were not playing our game. We left: by taxi, there being no canals.

Hubris

2.4.92

Labour holds a rally in Sheffield ...

It is at times of retreat that an army's strengths can best be observed. It is in moments of triumphalism that we first see the seeds of its downfall. It was when Margaret Thatcher employed a train-bearer to carry her gown that we knew her day was done. It was in the slick, sick, cynical image-manipulation of Labour's spectacular at Sheffield last night that we first sensed the contempt into which they too must come.

'Any dream will do,' sang the children, as Neil Kinnock played king of the kids in a Leeds school yesterday. He was preparing for the Sheffield Arena. He took their song to heart. Any dream would do.

Something about the very instructions printed for backstage operators last night chilled the soul. It was entitled 'Running order for Mega Rally'. *17.30: Doors open: party bus; band, etc, arrive. Street entertainers will be working the audience outside.*

The days when candidates would have worked the audience themselves, treading the streets in person, are gone. The candidates were in helicopters.

18.00: Dave Blunkett does welcome. DB to Royal Box. 'Will Mr Blunkett sing?' asked a reporter, 'And is it true his guide dog's gone sick? Will he sing "How Much Is That Doggy in the Window?" ' *Regional contingents with banners and bands. 18.42: Neil Kinnock's arrival in helicopter shown on video screen.*

After speeches by Roy Hattersley and John Smith came the *first endorsement, 2 mins.* 'That's Mick Hucknall of Simply Red,' said the aide. 'No, he won't actually be there. He's in Marseilles working on his next LP. He'll be signing his postal vote and singing "Something's Got Me Started" and this will be intertwined with his message. The message will say (and she began to dictate): "On 9 April I'll be voting Labour ..." (she paused for us to take this down). "It's time for a government that invests in skills ..." '

And we were promised 'Sarah Jane Morris, ex-of the Communards'. Now of Democratic Socialards. I expect. This item was to appear in the *Top-Slot, 15 mins* preceding the *second endorsement* after which came *Opera-Slot, 15 mins*, except that it wasn't opera, but a lady singing 'Summertime'. Normally, as John Cole observed, 'You know it's over when the fat lady sings,' but this was a thin lady and it was far from over: for next came *20.05: NK speech*. This was printed in advance. It was entirely devoid of content. *20.35: NK finishes; 20.40: Jerusalem; 20.45: finale, NK and Shad Cab leave. 20.55: All out, Goodbye music.*

I spoke to a press photographer who has been following the Kinnock campaign. Photographers are normally mute and I have no reason to think this one was a Tory: his frustration was professional. 'The manipulation has been crushingly successful,' he said. 'This has all been done for television: it goes against a video cameraman's instincts to show the props holding things up and all the minders marshalling the crowds.

'All we're shown is Kinnock with smiling kids, Kinnock in hospitals – happy faces, young children ... the image control has been total. The TV bosses need a few minutes of Kinnock every day to balance their few minutes of Major and if all he gives them is sanitized pap, that's all they can use. That's all anyone sees.'

As an ideal matures into a crusade and a crusade translates into a government, there comes a point when, throttled by the very apparatus set up to project it, the ideal begins to choke. This point has come early with Labour. Last night in Sheffield, image throttled intellect and a quiet voice in every reporter present whispered that there was something disgusting about the occasion. Those voices will grow. Peter Mandelson has created this Labour party and, on last night's showing, Peter Mandelson will destroy it.

'We will govern,' Neil Kinnock said, opening his speech, 'as we have campaigned.' Oh I do hope not.

13.4.92   **Underdogs Get the Bone**

The Tories win ...

'This pig does not weigh as much as I believed,' an Irishman once observed, 'but then I never thought it would.' This General Election, too, has turned out contrary to what we predicted: but then we rather thought it might. The losers have won. The day of Floppism has dawned.

You raise an eyebrow? Let me explain. Floppists maintain that the nation will vote for the party it believes most likely to lose. The Floppist analysis was vindicated last Friday when the party everybody had expected to triumph flopped. The party everybody had expected to flop triumphed. The pundits found this surprising.

But the lady in the newsagents opposite Wilko's in Matlock did not find it surprising. 'Never take anything for granted,' she said, smiling like a sphinx. Back in my kitchen I pondered that smile. My mind moved to three self-evident truths.

First, it is undoubtedly true that the nation had no desire for another Tory government. Second, that the nation did not want a Labour government. Third, that nobody wanted a coalition with the Liberal Democrats.

Whichever outcome, then, emerged as the most likely was the one that would fill the electorate with the most horror. Special hatred settled upon whomever began to look like the winner because, the prospect being more immediate, it was more odious. No party being admired, the sight of *any* of the three possible victors cock-a-hoop with certainty of impending victory was sure to prove especially detestable.

Picture each in that condition. Picture, first, a Labour party so confident that John Smith could summon us to an oak-panelled room and, standing in front of a big bowl of roses, unveil his 'budget'; so puffed up with importance that Jack Cunningham could discuss his forthcoming Queen's speech with commentators while yobs pelted Mr Major with eggs; so vainglorious that, before the mere formality of Thursday's vote, Labour could stage the biggest political rally since Nuremberg, at which the poor of Sheffield paid £1 each to sit in a stadium and watch a video of a pop star in the south of France telling them to vote Labour, and another of Mr Kinnock, getting out of a helicopter. Yuk. From that point the polls began to slide towards a hung parliament ... so ...

Picture next a boastful Paddy Ashdown prancing before us and telling us who might, and who need not bother to, 'pick up the phone'. And after the passion, the piety. Mr Ashdown stares tenderly into his autocue and confides the intimacies, the dreams, the little hopes and fears of Liberal Democracy. We can almost feel the manly stubble pricking on the pillow beside us. Ugh. Over breakfast on Thursday, the needle edges a little further towards ...

... Yes. Picture, finally, not the Tory party we saw, but a Tory party that had realized it was winning easily. That smug look on Mr Major's face, the tongue-in-cheek Princess Di smile, the braying Timothys and shrieking Amandas, the champagne and laughter, the young men who hardly need to shave, the triumph of vanilla, the jubilation of the jelly babies. Picture the two-fingered gestures from the honking Porsches making a quick circuit of the nearest council estate, the portable phones, the wine bars, the wing collars and the clutch of Kinnock jokes zapping round the computer network of the Square Mile. Spare us.

... But of course we *were* spared. The Tories never did believe it, so they behaved. Instead of triumphalism, we saw a poor chap on a soapbox, jostled and shouted down, a coach that went to all the wrong places, and the bungling of 100 photo opportunities. I heard that women were rushing from the pavements and flinging their arms round Mr Major, telling him never mind and not to be sad, poor lamb. He looked completely harmless. Naturally we voted for him. His winning margin came from votes intended to console him for losing.

Does John Major realize, even now, that it was the *failure* of his campaign that took him to Downing Street? That the cock-up that caused his final victory rally to miss *The Nine O'Clock News* saved him from defeat? Does he know how lucky he is that, when he said he was winning, nobody believed him?

7.5.92   # Defying Gravity with Gravitas

The Queen's Speech is delivered to parliament ...

In the Commons a spring chill has blighted the roses. Labour lapels were bare.

Over in the Lords, a quick tiara-count suggested that the recessionary chill blights even peers. Economic slump has taken its toll upon headgear. Diamonds were smaller. My *Guardian* colleague saw green shoots of recovery among Lady Wakeham's emeralds; but the Baroness Strange's tiara had shrunk from last year's TV aerial diamanté, to a small lozenge on her big blonde bun.

Lady Porter, of Tescos and Westminster, combined the commercial and the dignified aspects of her career by appearing as a large Easter bunny, her blue hat dwarfed by an enormous pink bow.

The men were duller, but the ambassadors' paddock offered relief from the wastes of ermine. One Arab envoy wore a sheikh's robes over what appeared to be an M & S woolly. The French ambassador, who resembles Maurice Chevalier, appeared in a waistcoat of gold brocade and looked ready to entertain us with an old-time song-and-dance act. The peers' wives' benches – all stoles and lorgnettes – put us more in mind of the props department of an amateur dramatic society; the diplomats' wives – saris, turbans and sarongs – of a Nigerian Sunday market.

But it was Lady Renwick who drew all eyes. Well, *parts* of Lady Renwick. An attractive middle-aged woman, hers was the lowest neckline I have ever seen in an upper chamber. Her tiara went quite unnoticed. She could have been an extra from *Fanny Hill*. With black cloak tugged insecurely around shoulders as she leant low to talk to Lady Granville of Eye, the effect upon the press was of fascination tinged with alarm. At any moment something dreadful could have happened. We might have another Wimbledon – a first, surely, during a Queen's Speech? Physics textbooks illustrate a London bus tipping sideways on a special machine to determine the point at which gravity takes over. Could a simulated peers' bench be constructed, then tipped progressively forward with the ladies buckled in, to establish when containment fails and catastrophe strikes?

It never did. I moved my gaze to the new Lord Cecil, Lord Salisbury's son, who was Viscount Cranborne until last week. A 'writ of acceleration' has transformed him into a peer capable of sitting in the Lords while his father is alive. Looking suitably accelerated, noble ermine flattened against noble chest by the force of 3G, he chatted animatedly to Lady Strange. Lord Waddington, now subjected to a writ of deceleration and sent to be governor of Bermuda, reminds us that velocity in politics is a wayward mistress. Over in the Commons, Andrew Mitchell (C, Gedling, Accelerating) was preparing an excellent speech. Kenneth Baker – a case of sudden velocity-loss – was to speak with him.

A trumpet fanfare disturbed the reverie: and in came Her Majesty.

It was a dull speech. There was a moment of tension when the Queen's remarks about monetary convergence prompted Lady Renwick to breathe heavily and slip her cloak, but without mishap. Field Marshal Lord Carver, a soldier of severely practical intellect, looked forbearing rather than ecstatic in his role as The Sword of State. The sword was heavy, the speech long. After it, The Cap of Maintenance (Mrs Wakeham christened him John) bumped into Silver Stick in Waiting (friends call him Jeremy), which is not surprising as both were walking backwards. Has it struck peers that forwards is quite a good way to walk?

22.5.92

My Word! Did I Really Say That?

As the new parliament heads for a break, here are verbatim extracts from a speech by John Prescott in the House of Commons earlier this week. In the right-hand column is the official version of what he said according to *Hansard*.

They tried to make up for the loss of income British Rail in their financing by on the one hand sacking personnel at 6 and 7,000 a year which had the consequences on those that remained in the employment of British Rail of working in a rather exhausted way. Indeed the signalman in Clapham as it came out in the enquiry was working months on end without a day off because there were fewer left to do the job after you'd cut back on the manpower requirements.

British Rail tried to make up for the loss of income by sacking 6,000 or 7,000 personnel, which resulted in those employees who remained having to work very long hours that left them exhausted. According to the enquiry, the electrician at Clapham who made that fatal mistake had worked for months on end without a day off because, manpower requirements having been cut, fewer personnel were left to do the work.

I accept readily the argument the Secretary of State says that 1 per cent of road transport is a small

I accept the Secretary of State's argument that a 1 per cent growth in road transport is a amount to the kind of growth we see that it will always be about 80 per cent of the traffic but that 1 per cent represents hundreds of thousands of lorry movements which is important down in the South-East [if you haven't got a decent rail network to take you to Europe our roads in the South-East are not going to be able to take that traffic and even if you was to double their capacity would not be able to take that kind of increasing amount of capacity].

small amount, compared with the overall growth in road traffic. However, that 1 per cent represents hundreds of thousands of lorry movements which will be relevant in the South-East if it does not have a decent rail network to Europe. Even if the capacity of roads in the South-East were doubled, they would not be able to take that traffic.

And even in the gas and electricity he talks about governments and Treasury particularly have always imposed a kind of energy tax on them, forced them to charge more through the external financial limits the negative role he talks about which is a tax on those industries.

The Treasury has always imposed a kind of energy tax on the gas and electricity industries, forcing them to charge more through a negative external financial limit.

The Heathrow Paddington seems to be falling about because British Rail can't get the money for the 20 per cent required to get in with the private sector. The Olympia & York now seems to be in serious difficulties because of possible bankruptcy situations in these matters and can't raise the money.

The Heathrow to Paddington link is collapsing because the government cannot get its 20 per cent with the private investment that is required. Olympia & York appears to be bankrupt and cannot raise money.

I mean that's an example of this government that believes in the private sector and is in fact

The government's insistence on private sector terms has damaged the public sector.

damaged the public sector's handling within the public sector in a number of these areas and you can go on with them in another areas.

So I think the basic point that it is necessary in order to have private capital in our industries to get the extra resources that we do want, that you have to be privatized is not borne out by the facts in other countries and neither we should we have it here also and if he's any doubts about that go and have a look at the reports that talk it.

This passage is not reported at all. *Hansard* gave up.

3.7.92

A Midsummer Day's Dream

Lady T makes her first speech in the Lords …

It was mischief: but it was delicate mischief. 'As gently,' said Lord Callaghan, 'as any sucking dove.' The sucking dove, in blue and pearls, smiled, her talons sheathed.

Callaghan put it best. She had sung sweetly to her new audience, he told us. Patronizing her, as he did in those far-off seventies when he was PM, he advised her that their lordships do not take kindly to being hectored, so she had been wise to avoid the histrionics. Observing her, he added, he was reminded of Bottom. Lord Callaghan paused.

Eyebrows raised. Callaghan explained. In *A Midsummer Night's Dream*, he said, Bottom says to his co-conspirators 'I will roar … but I will aggravate my voice, so that I roar you as gently as any sucking dove; I will roar you as 'twere any nightingale.' Peers chuckled.

The nightingale had been there from the start, looking nervous. From time to time she fiddled with a sheaf of notes, conscious that she was being observed. When the Earl of Onslow (something of a card) rounded on a nervous, bespectacled junior viscount, Lord Goschen (who was defending the government's record on homelessness) and told him that spending £96m on 464 'rough sleepers' was extravagant – 'it would pay my Lloyd's losses several times over' – she took care not to smile. When Baroness Chalker, foreign office minister, rose, Lady Thatcher took her glasses from a small black crocodile-skin case and put them on.

Lady Chalker spoke of 'the vision of a wider community that I know my Right Hon friend [Lady Thatcher] so much shares'. The dove took off her glasses, impassive. When Chalker, in episcopal drone, sailed into a peroration about 'special events' in the British presidency, 'a theatre, arts and business programme ... wide range ... full agenda ... whole community ... busy and interesting ... firm basis for success ...' Lady T fumbled in her pocket, pulled something out, and popped it into her mouth. A mint? Or a painkiller? She took off her glasses.

Roy Jenkins spoke before her, offering John Major 'my un*way*vawing support' but explaining that he would have to leave for dinner by 8.15. Prodding Lady Thatcher gently, he advised her not to pull her punches. Prodding a little more, he warned that the European vision was not a meal to be taken à la carte, picking through the menu. Lord Jenkins looked in lip-smacking form, and ready to sign up for olives, canapés, all six courses, pudding, savouries, cheese, biscuits, port and petits fours – and then to await the cigars. Lady Thatcher, lips pursed, looked ready for a small green salad. Before sitting down, Lord Jenkins was kind enough to read extensive sections of his Jean Monet lecture delivered in 1974, to refresh our memories.

The nightingale rose. She thanked Jenkins, complimenting him on his speech, which she took à la carte, approving (she said) of 'parts of it'. She looked forward to the tranquillity of her new nest 'after 33 testing years before the mast'. The humour worked, and, when she reminded their Lordships that 214 of them had been sent there under her premiership, they decided to take it as a joke. She was sorry to come so early to controversy, she said, but she simply couldn't wait. They took that as a joke, too. Behind her, Geoffrey Howe, who knew it was no joke, lowered his head like an irritable bear.

Lady T then treated us to a light skip through the meadows of her scepticism. 'I had some *great* budget battles in my day,' she breathed,

'I *always* found that the most *effective* weapon was No.' A chilling smile. 'And sometimes No, No, No.' Lord Howe gripped his jaw in his hands.

And soon the sucking dove finished her serenade, and yielded to Lord Callaghan, who yielded to Shakespeare.

But he did not finish that quote. After promising to start as a nightingale, Bottom arranges to meet his pals again, in a wood ...

'And there we may rehearse more obscenely and courageously. Take pains. Be perfect. Adieu.'

The dove's lieutenants, crowded at the door to watch, understood.

15.7.92   Kinnock's Sun Sets with Dignity

... Then came Neil Kinnock. He rose. Jocular shouts of 'resign!' The mood changed. Mr Kinnock wanted to know where the economic recovery that the PM had promised had gone.

It was a simple, serious question, simply and seriously put. It was one of his best. It struck me that asking a serious question, without 'spin', is one of the few tacks Mr Kinnock has never really tried. He has tried gravitas, which is quite another thing, and inspired only giggles. He has tried humour, and provoked only scorn. He has tried long questions, and been mocked for long-windedness; and he has tried short questions, and been dismissed as gimcrack. But yesterday he indicated to the PM what everyone knew was a real problem, and played it straight.

Mr Major commenced his reply with a graceful tribute. 'Generous,' the press will call it, but of course it costs a PM nothing and goes down well. It was nicely done. John Major is a foxier fellow than at first we knew.

Kinnock replied that it had been an honour to serve his country in this way, and repeated his question about the economy, reinforcing it with examples. Major remarked that he and Kinnock shared common goals but differed as to means. By now the goodwill was becoming tiresome. MPs fidgeted.

Kinnock reminded Major that he was equally sincere, and Major gently suggested that at least they could agree about that. MPs began looking towards doors and windows for escape routes ...

And it was over, very dignified. Nothing became his office like the leaving of it. One remembers with similar affection Mrs Thatcher's marvellous exit. Like a glorious tropical sunset, a resigning politician is a beautiful sight.

Sniggering MPs Denied Their Fun

26.9.92

David Mellor makes his resignation speech from the back benches ...

The fun – *Mr Mellor: A Personal Statement* – was scheduled for 11 am: a civilized time for a lynching.

Just before 11, Mr Mellor arrived for his ritual humiliation. Tory numbers had doubled. They had come for the usual show: pale figure of minister – head bowed – old school tie – restrained regrets concerning own folly – delicate references to nature of folly – heartfelt thanks to colleagues for support during difficult time – sit down – 'hear-hear' from all sides – shoulder-pattings from pals – dignified exit, to kindly buzz of 'poor David', 'there but for the grace of God ...' etc from outwardly mournful, inwardly sniggering colleagues.

By 11, the Tory benches were full: a charcoal waste of Tories, one of whom has a new wig.

From back benches where he was a stranger, Mellor rose. Something within him said 'stuff the lot of you'. The speech was not an outburst: more a shrug of the shoulders, a brave grin, and two fingers fidgeting to make a rude sign.

'Having become heartily sick of my private life myself,' he said, 'I cannot expect others to take a more charitable view.' It was an eccentric statement, by degrees chatty, defiant, funny, menacing and bitter: but devoid of self-pity. His colleagues had come to reward a show of regret. But of regret there was little, so sympathy was tinged with bemusement.

A fortnight of total cock-up ended yesterday with just one resignation: a man agreed on all sides to be good at his job.

Tories with Attitude

In America, militant groups like the self-styled NWAs and QWAs ('Niggers with Attitude' and 'Queers with Attitude') shake fists. Now, on British back benches, appears a variation – TWAs: 'Tories with Attitude'.

This breed, almost extinct, has revived. Fed by Euro-sceptical resentment and miners' anger but mostly by the slimness of the prime minister's majority, your Tory backbencher can smell fear as dogs can. He has seen the terror in the chief whip's eyes, noted the pits' reprieve, anticipated the Jubilee line rescue. He is emboldened.

Yesterday at transport questions, Tories with Attitude sprouted from every bench. Matthew Carrington (Fulham) wanted a new station on a new Tube line through Fulham. He did not actually *say*: 'You missa my constituency, I smasha your face,' but the implication was clear.

Taking note, a minister, Steven Norris, almost bowed. John Bowis (Battersea) wondered with menacing courtesy whether this line might extend under the Thames to Battersea. Before he could add 'or I'll send the boys round', Norris was on his feet to 'take your suggestion on board'.

By now other Tories were leaping up and down, no doubt with new Tube lines and stations of their own to propose. Norris was fascinated by each suggestion.

As questions proceeded the prospect grew of a vast new Underground network in London, through which gleaming modern trains conveyed mollified electors to and from brand new Tube stations constructed in the constituencies of every London Tory with Attitude.

The handful of government backbenchers still willing to bowl soft balls at their ministers looked uneasy. Might they have sold at too low a price? Your sketchwriter remembers a time, under Mrs You-know-who, when a backbencher would return to his constituency at weekends to be asked what he had done to help the government. But today's TWAs are asked: 'What did you threaten to rebel on this week, Sir Bufton? Only the agriculture bill? And what have you brought back? Only a couple of hill-livestock premiums and a turnip subsidy? No new railway? No airport? No six-lane by-pass?'

Finally came Peter Brooke, the new heritage minister, with news of 'restoration of important national monuments', of which the return to office of Mr Brooke is a fine example. Asked about sites English Heritage might relinquish, he offered a hypothetical example in Wales, then, to heckles, quickly withdrew it.

'Does he know Wales isn't in England?' I asked a colleague, later. 'He does know,' replied my friend, 'much of the time. But short periods occur when he does not know.'

Mr Brown's Bullets   *13.11.92*

Shadow Chancellor Gordon Brown replies to Norman Lamont's Autumn Statement ...

In vain did Gordon Brown spray the Chancellor's getaway car with a hail of bullets. These bullets you can see among the paragraphs which follow. In Fleet Street a 'bullet' is one of these: •. Many years ago Mr Brown abandoned ordinary English prose and began to speak entirely in lists prefaced by bullets. His speech yesterday was composed of fourteen lists, strung together with angry conjunctions.

He said that Mr Lamont had caused:
- unemployment to rise
- the deficit to worsen
- greater poverty
- cuts in the aid budget
- more bankruptcies.

Britain was, furthermore, bottom of the EC league in:
- growth
- investment
- output
- employment.

Yet he had promised he would:
- stay in the ERM
- not devalue
- get unemployment down
- bring recovery.

Now he planned to:

- break up training schemes
- tear up promises
- scapegoat home-helps.
  This would:
- add to unemployment
- prolong the recession
- damage productivity
- hit the poor and weak.
  At one point Mr Brown fumbled in his pocket and we began to fear he would bring out a crumpled list and declaim:
- bread
- tea-bags
- 1lb tomatoes …
  But no. He stuck to the economy. It was a tragedy, he said. Millions faced:
- cuts
- joblessness
- starvation.
  … Pencil poised, I waited to continue:
- impetigo
- beri-beri
- rickets …
  But he omitted these, predicting:
- tragedy
- disaster
- catastrophe
  … and sat down.

Cheerful Chappie in Parliamentary Pantomime

26.1.93

It seemed somehow fitting that the first two Tory backbenchers to speak in support of the national lottery bill were Kenneth Baker and David Mellor. Something in the demeanour of both has long proclaimed 'Roll up! Roll up! Wonderful prizes!'

And some instinct in us has demanded we check that the tickets were not forgeries and the prizes were real.

Mr Baker's great delight, he told MPs yesterday – his whole aim in life, we gathered – 'the cause of cheering us all up'. Cheering us up! He grinned. Mr Baker does not have (as peacocks have) a many-splendoured tail, nor does he have painted wings (as butterflies have) to spread in the sun.

But he has a way of pausing during a speech, holding himself still and beaming gently, which suggests that were he a peacock this would be the moment for the tail to quiver while we marvelled; and were he a butterfly this would be the time to pause upon some honeysuckle blossom and fold and unfold his wings in the sunshine while his little feelers waved. One looked back on Mr Baker's record as education secretary, home secretary, environment secretary, industry minister, campaign manager, Chancellor of the Duchy of Lancaster and Conservative party chairman, and remembered the troubled history of his areas of responsibility, the self-destruct tendency of so many of his intriguing initiatives. There were the prison riots, the national core curriculum and 'Baker days' at school. There was the poll tax, the infotech revolution, the CTCs, the Dangerous Dogs Act …

And suddenly one grasped the key to this puzzling charade of a life. *It was all a joke*! Mr Baker's whole career has been an elaborate trick designed to cheer us up: a sort of exploding cigar writ large. The self-sacrifice leaves you breathless.

Forbidden Fruit in Garden of Eden

11.2.93

In the Beginning, there was Nicholas Soames; and the MP (C) for Crawley was without form, and void. And the Chief Whip recommended that he be made food minister; and Soames was given dominion over the fish of the sea, and over the fowl of the air and battery farms, and over the cattle, and over all the earth and large sections of the agriculture ministry, and over every creeping thing on the Tory backbenches that taketh an interest in food.

And it was all going pretty well. Unfortunately, however, Mr Soames had reckoned without Gavin Strang. Labour's principal agriculture spokesman is, as the Good Book says of the Serpent, 'more subtil than any beast of the field', but his role in yesterday's parliamentary drama differs sharply from Genesis, 3. Strang had come to the Commons not to commend the apple, but to denounce it.

Strang warned MPs about toxicity in apple juice. He took Soames to task for failing to alert the nation earlier. The problem was a substance called patulin, present in certain apples.

'Patulin,' cried Soames, 'is a naturally occurring toxicant which has been with us since the Creation. It is produced by moulds.'

'Good heavens!' said John Carlisle (C, Luton N).

Of course, Deadly Nightshade is also naturally occurring. As Strang put it, 'the fact that a substance occurs in nature does not mean it is not dangerous.'

'Like socialism,' shouted Tory wags.

'It is to top independent scientists that the government looks for toxicological advice,' Soames protested. Fruit was 'a natural product which has been with us since Adam ate the apple and thus made a career decision.'

MPs scratched their heads. Which career decision had Adam made by eating the apple? Soames seemed to be suggesting that upon leaving the Garden of Eden, Adam and Eve had gone straight into the cider industry, perhaps in partnership with the Serpent.

Speaking for the Serpent, a number of Tory backbenchers with constituency commercial interests to defend arose and said that they drank apple juice themselves, and behold it was very good. Glamorous Emma Nicholson (Devon W and Torridge) managed a prime-time plug, in husky contralto tones, for Inch's Cider. A few pints of this, she cooed to Soames, would produce 'a wonderful result'. The thought of Miss Nicholson in fig leaves was as pleasant as that of Mr Soames without them was alarming.

Jacques Arnold (C, Gravesham) advised Soames to 'ignore the chattering classes'.

Glenda Jackson (Lab, Hampstead), who represents them, rose. We remember her without fig leaves in *The Music Lovers*. She wasn't touching the apple. Pregnant women in Hampstead had drunk of its juice, she said, and behold they were sore afraid. Mr Soames said that they weren't to worry.

You would have to drink 140 litres of apple juice a day, said that doughty defender of the orchards of Kent, Andrew Rowe, to be in danger. Rowe (C, Kent Mid) had addressed the wrong man; the enormous and *bon-vivant* Soames is the one minister whom we can imagine achieving this level of consumption.

With shouts of 'What about bananas?' and 'Let's have a windfall tax!' ringing in my ears, I left the Gallery. Teresa Gorman (C, Billericay), in cerise with five medallions, was advertising herself as proof that drinking apple juice produced no harmful effects. MPs rushed from the Chamber to destroy every carton they possessed.

After the Black Eye   *10.3.93*

The government had suffered a defeat during the passage of the Maastricht bill …

John Major entered the Chamber of the House yesterday to the most enormous cheer.

There is something blood-curdling about the Conservative party cheering. It is more chilling than their enmity. Resonating within it is the folk-memory of a thousand treacheries. In recent months the cheering has been growing louder. Yesterday it approached the pitch accorded his predecessor in the weeks before her followers knifed her. If Tories carry on cheering Major like this, he would be wise to bring bodyguards.

The Prime Minister arrived in the final minute before he was to take the floor. As the digital clock flicked to 3.14, and still no Prime Minister, faces on the government front bench tightened. None who knows Mr Major ever *quite* discounts the possibility that he might just send a note saying he had gone back to mother.

He did turn up, and great was the cheering. What remained of defence questions was inaudible as late arrivals jostled to find a place. Jabbering filled the air.

It was like the atmosphere at sunset at an African water hole as the animals come down to drink. Jackals sniffed the wind, hyenas giggled among themselves, and smaller scavengers sneaked their way to ringside seats. On the front benches, big cats stretched or snarled in a desultory way, while monkeys chattered. Here and there a crocodile lifted an inquisitive eye about the surface of the pond. I cannot say the mood was grave: it was excited. Back-bench life is usually so dull.

11.3.93 # Blair Evades Roadblock

As the Prevention of Terrorism Order passes the House ...

Security dominated yesterday's debate. Tory MPs joined MPs from Northern Ireland and crowded into the Chamber to hear the Home Secretary outline a strategy for dealing with the most insidious danger Her Majesty's government has faced in decades: now a daily threat which every member of the Cabinet, from the Prime Minister downwards, must live with.

Kenneth Clarke was to unveil the centrepiece of the government's defences. It is called the Prevention of Tony Blair (Exclusion of Sound Bites) Bill (1993).

With every month that passes Blair becomes more dangerous. Well-dressed, well-spoken, good-looking and immensely plausible, Labour's principal home affairs spokesman is just the sort of smoothie to lull the British public into forgetting that they are playing with fire. Confronted by the manicured moderation of a man like Blair smiling into the television cameras, it is all too easy for ordinary citizens watching from home to overlook the ruthless tendencies of the underground organization he fronts.

In recent weeks, at the dispatch box and at *Any Questions* sessions up and down the country, Blair has been posing as the policeman's friend, deploring crime and holding himself out as guardian and protector of every little old lady in the land. He has even smooth-talked his way into the *Daily Mail*. 'I'm Tony Blair,' he announces, seldom mentioning who has sent him. Elderly, naïve or confused electors have been inviting him into their living rooms, many quite unaware that he is not a Conservative. Charmers like this must be denied the oxygen of publicity.

Unfortunately, the government has not yet found a way of banning Blair from the Chamber itself. He kept getting up and sounding reasonable. His blue suit was beautifully cut, his shoes shiny and his posture good. His hair was perfect. He made the Tories look like the men of violence. 'It's no good standing up and looking steamy-eyed,' snapped Clarke, plainly exasperated.

But that was the problem. It *was* good. Blair is good. His case against parts of the act was perfectly arguable. To imply that this was unpatriotic was plumb stupid. Clarke was left manning a useless roadblock while, once again, the wily Blair had slipped through his net.

Paleskins and Fuzzy-wuzzies   *15.4.93*

The Conservative party squares up to the Balkan conflict ...

To the Tory backbencher, foreign troublemakers fall into two categories: paleskins and fuzzy-wuzzies. The paleskins are murderous fiends who will stop at nothing and are to be treated with the utmost caution. The fuzzy-wuzzies are troublesome hooligans who must be shown, if necessary with the butt of a British rifle, that aggression does not pay.

Depending on the category, entire armouries of moral and military reasoning must be switched. If the aggressor is Saddam Hussein (fuzzy-wuzzy – the slightest suntan counts, as do turbans, reading from right to left, Greeks, Italians and Argentines), then the vocabulary is of contempt: 'ludicrous', 'madman', 'bully', 'banana republic' etc.

The reasoning is clear. At whatever cost and for however slight an apparent prize, these louts must be taught a lesson: the rule of law must never be flouted with impunity. The military logic is that allies must be defended and important strategic goals (land routes/sea-lanes/exposed flanks, oil, etc) protected. The cost of recapturing Port Stanley or Kuwait can never be disproportionate. Victory over fuzzy-wuzzies is unconsciously assumed.

Dealing with a paleskin aggressor, a wholly different policy framework is wheeled out. Now arises what is called 'traditional British caution' or 'the prudence of a mature and adult European power'.

Thus it was yesterday, when Defence Secretary Malcolm Rifkind upheld HMG's Balkan policy of locking ourselves in the loo. Sage heads nodded along the Tory ranks behind him. Sir Nicholas Bonsor (C, Upminster, defender of the ancient rights of the fox-hunter), in tones as mellow and gruff as an Island malt, rumbled to his feet to 'welcome the caution' of his Right Hon friend. 'Our troops are sitting under Serbian gun-barrels,' he growled.

Was this the same Sir Nicholas who interrupted James Callaghan 11 years and eight days ago, to cry: 'It is imperative that the House now show its united resolution to see the sovereignty of the Falkland Islands returned to our people!'?

David Howell (C, Guildford) admired Rifkind's refusal to yield to 'the emotional heat of the moment'. Edwina Currie thanked him for not 'embroiling our troops in that dreadful conflict', and Shrewsbury's Derek Conway was relieved he had resisted the temptation to 'express emotions and anger' and chosen 'realistic judgement' instead.

With the exception of a small counter-Serbian expeditionary team – Major Patrick Cormack (C), Sergeant Campbell-Savours (Lab) and Corporal Tony Banks (Lab), commanded by Lt-Col Winston Churchill (C) (Lady Thatcher C in C) – nobody was calling for a fight.

Wisely, no doubt. But I cast my mind back to that war with Iraq. Our EC allies took a cooler attitude than Britain. MPs erupted in fury at this 'backsliding'. What in ourselves we call restraint, in the French we called cowardice. Shall we compromise and call it discretion? In the House yesterday it proved the better part of valour.

'The future is grim,' Mr Rifkind said. 'The noose is being drawn tighter. Other weapons are available.' For a moment I thought he meant Lady Thatcher.

21.4.93   # Major Was There

Joe Orton once remarked that the most any boy can expect of his father is that he should be present at the conception.

Somewhat to the astonishment of MPs, John Major yesterday told the House that his own son James had been luckier. James is the only boy in Britain who can honestly say that John Major is the first human being he ever saw.

It was Labour's Michael Connarty (Falkirk E) who elicited the news. During an afternoon otherwise dominated by Bosnia and the public sector borrowing requirement, Connarty asked the PM whether he had known 'the sheer joy of being present at the birth of his children'. Major leapt to the dispatch box to declare 'yes, twice'. It seems his daughter Elizabeth shared with James the surprise of arriving in this world to see the expression of considerable pleasure on Mr Major's smiling face.

Is Mr Major the first Prime Minister to witness the birth of his children? The answer must be no, as his predecessor was undeniably present when Carol and Mark arrived. If there were any way Mrs Thatcher could have pleaded a prior political engagement she would surely have made her excuses and left, so Major may well be the first PM to have been *voluntarily* present at the birth of his children.

Battler Clarke Puts Bruised Blair out for the Count

14.5.93

An event occurred in the Chamber yesterday of the kind we may one day look back upon and say, 'Ah, *that* was the day we first got an inkling ...'

It was the first time anyone had seen it happen. Kenneth Clarke annihilated Tony Blair.

Clarke has always been a prize puncher. A boxer, not a fencer, there is nothing of the weasel in him.

Plenty of aggression but no malice, his manner by turns jolly or belligerent, he is unguarded, intellectually confident and careless whether he knocks things over by mistake.

Who else could have got away with chortling that he hadn't read the Maastricht treaty, or describing the government as 'in a dreadful hole'?

If there remained any doubt that Clarke was a potential Tory leader, it was wiped out yesterday by a single punch.

As to Tony Blair, there never was any doubt that he is a potential successor to John Smith.

While Smith paws the air and frets 'Why on airth?' at the dispatch box, it has sometimes seemed that the Opposition has devised a system for picking each succeeding leader off the shelf just after his sell-by date has expired; and that Blair, still fresh and saleable, has been lodged on the shelf to stale little, while Smith loses the next election.

Talk of Blair's charms has been growing. He is persuasive and nice: a splendid debater.

Middle-class, middle-of-the-road and ideology-free, Blair does not sound as though he ever could have been a socialist, let alone be one now. His hair is perfect. Clarke is Home Secretary, Blair his shadow. Blair has been doing well, fulminating about rising crime, comforting old ladies and looking more like the policeman's friend than any Labour frontbencher has ever done before.

For the first time in their lives, Tories can see law-and-order as a potential vote-*loser*. Blair arrived yesterday as a rising stock.

The Home Secretary, by contrast, was in trouble. His Criminal Justice Act was not working, magistrates were in revolt and he had come to the House to climb down.

Clarke can do this sort of thing frankly and without apology, and his statement sounded confident, but nothing could disguise the retreat. Tony Blair rose – for the kill, we supposed.

He made a fatal mistake. Unable to resist the lure of a headline, or a slot on the six o'clock news, Blair began by ignoring the statement and demanding instead a statement on the 'royal bugging' story.

It was plainly offside. When he did turn to the Criminal Justice Act, his remarks lost force in a shaking of Tory heads, and disapproving clucks.

Clarke arose and gave him the most comprehensive verbal thumping anyone has seen Blair receive.

Pushing aside his notes, and with the Tories cheering behind him, the Home Secretary told him his priorities were utterly absurd: ridiculous allegations promoting a sleazy book. 'A tabloid politician,' he spat.

Would he care to 'turn away from royal scandals and the bugging of matrimonial rows, and turn his mind to something that actually matters to ordinary men and women?'

The Tories, who are feeling bruised, loved it. At last! A champ! ... but – aye, there's the rub. What a contrast with the wooden exchanges at PM's Questions ten minutes earlier.

Labour, who had thought they were on to a winner, hated it. What? Our Tony, bested? ... but – aye, there *was* that compensation: he'd been upstaging the boss too often of late. This should quell the muttering for a bit.

For Labour, then, a cloud with a silver lining. For the Tories an unexpected burst of sunshine: but with a rumble of distant thunder.

Redwood Shows His Human Nature   *15.6.93*

Years ago, this column was first to spot the entry into the Commons, under deep cover, of the only Vulcan ever elected to parliament. John Redwood had arrived on the Tory back benches.

Vulcans come from the planet of the same name. Their most famous expatriate (half-Vulcan) is *Star Trek*'s Mr Spock. They are super-intelligent and utterly logical, resembling humans in every respect except that they have no emotions, and many have pointed ears. The new breed, like Mr Redwood, have their ears straightened in private clinics, so it is very hard to know when you are dealing with a Vulcan, but a giveaway sign is a steady, emotionless voice and chilling stare. They also exhibit gaps in knowledge about the folksier side of life on planet Earth, and will occasionally react to human displays of passion or humour with complete bafflement.

When Mr Redwood became a minister, I recorded this first example of Vulcan penetration into the junior ranks of government. I also recorded doubts as to whether Messrs Lilley, Howard and Portillo were pure-bred humans. It now falls to this sketch, which we may rename *Vulcan Watch*, to announce that a full-blooded Vulcan has for the first time entered the British Cabinet. John Redwood, the Welsh secretary, came to the Commons yesterday to report on flooding in the principality (or 'testing zone' as they speak of Wales on Vulcan).

He was accompanied by his PPS, David Evans (C, Welwyn, Hatfield, human, very), recruited in an attempt to 'humanize' his master, teach him jokes, explain about love, merriment, sin, etc. Mr Evans has been having some limited success. At the weekend,

Redwood's address to the Welsh Tory conference had featured the pseudo-humanoid singing 'God Save the Queen' in Welsh – it is a simple matter, you see, to programme a Vulcan with an extra language, even Welsh. So far so good. Yesterday's statement, his first as a secretary of state, was an important new test.

Alas, attaining power has caused Redwood to revert. Striding in, attempting, mechanically, to swing the arms as humans do, he sat down, then rose in one smooth movement, staring icily into space.

'The – damage – has – been – very – extensive,' he softly droned, in that BT directory enquiries machine voice, 'eighty – five – per-cent – of – eligible – expenditure – over – the – threshold ...' Had he gone on to say 'the – number – you – require – is – Llandudno – 0 – 4 – 9 – 2 ...' few would have been surprised.

Alan Williams (Lab, Carmarthen) decided to test him. The 'Bellwin rule', said Williams (a formula for allowing relief payments) 'is a fig leaf'. Vulcans are weak at imagery; Redwood activated his WordSearch program and established that 'Bellwin rule' does not mean 'fig leaf'. 'No – it – is – not – a – FIG LEAF,' he droned, aware of a need to hit the Indignation Key, but hitting it on the wrong word.

But the performance was not altogether discouraging. Various backbenchers tried to short-circuit his logic system by putting the muddle-headed proposal that uninsured householders should be compensated by the government. At this, I saw Mr Redwood's eyes swivel involuntarily. Through my sound-amplifier I just managed to eavesdrop the interference from his internal circuitry: (*very faint*): 'Il – log – ic – al!' (*crackle-crackle*) 'Il – log – ic – al!' But something (a tap on the shoulder from Evans?) stopped him. He rose. '... appreciate – problem. There – is – mayor's – fund ...' he whirred. Our Vulcan is learning.

Calming Influence of the Voice-over for Every Crisis

29.6.93

Yesterday the Foreign Secretary urged an agitated Commons to support the US attack on Baghdad.

The really terrifying thing about our diplomat turned head of Mr Heath's political office turned Thatcher's Home Secretary turned Major's Foreign Secretary, Douglas Hurd, is the very thing that makes him *at first* so reassuring. Mr Hurd is so completely professional that you have absolutely no idea what he thinks himself. You have a suspicion that he does think himself, but no inkling what.

Whatever the government has done, Mr Hurd pops up (if so dignified a creature can be said to pop up) and explains in the calmest voice that there was simply no alternative. Have appeals been made to reconsider the convictions of the Guildford Four? Mr Hurd is sorry but the most exhaustive review has already been undertaken. The finest intellects have looked afresh. Mr Hurd regrets ...

Are Vietnamese refugees in Hong Kong being dragged into lorries and carted off to the airport? Ah, how Mr Hurd shares your distress, how carefully he has considered every other suggestion, how plain it is that none would be workable. Is some appalling new tangle of Euro-bindweed called the Maastricht treaty threatening our sovereignty? Oh, but you have been deceived! Mr Hurd has read the treaty; please understand that its purpose is to *enhance* our sovereignty. Are Muslims being slaughtered in Bosnia? The pain is written across Mr Hurd's own face. If only he could help, you know he would. It is *almost* vulgar to suggest otherwise. You sit down to hear Mr Hurd, convinced there can be no way of talking our way out of this one. You end up embarrassed that you even thought there was a problem. Such is his relaxed, civilized self-confidence, his evident humanity, that every horror becomes a tragic necessity (or why would he tolerate it?), every accident a part of the plan.

He could be Foreign Secretary, he could be chaplain general to the armed forces, he could be UN secretary-general, he could be Master of Balliol, or he could be the expert voice explaining the cleansing effects of Harpic in your lavatory. He could be the instructions on the wireless after a nuclear bomb, advising us that all was well but would we please whitewash our windows, wait under the table, and not drink the water for the moment – just in case? Mr Hurd's is the ultimate voice-over to video pictures supplied by somebody else.

This weekend the video pictures were supplied by the United States. Yesterday came Mr Hurd's voice-over. We must stand by our US allies; repel state terrorism. We must not be tricked by Iraqi propaganda ...

One had entered the Gallery with hackles raised by this attack, doubtful of its wisdom. But as that calm, decent voice washed, in polite waves, like his hair, over hearers, one's doubts began to seem so adolescent. Maybe we just needed a good night's sleep? Of course the Americans had been right. Of *course* the Iraqis would dissemble. Of *course* the Arab moderates would make a show of displeasure, at first … You don't need to listen to his words: the very cadence of Mr Hurd's voice says 'of course'. We had been making a fuss about nothing, of course.

13.7.93

Flying Visit Gives Beckett a Buzz

As Margaret Beckett harangued media representatives assembled in Christchurch to hear her kick off Labour's by-election campaign, a fly became caught in her hair.

Picture the scene. A crowded room, chairs, hot television lights, foam-covered microphones and a table graced by a plastic rose, the candidate and Mrs Beckett. She was in an arresting outfit of shamrock green and blinding white, with earrings. Nigel Lickley, her candidate, was dressed like a Young Conservative from the early 1980s, smartly suited for the slaughter.

For us, just another press conference in another town. For the luckless Mr Lickley, a bid to save another Labour deposit. For the fly, a whole new situation.

The fly became confused. Initially it had been attracted by the sugared coffee and oatmeal biscuits. Now, disoriented by the television lights and the ringing of portable phones, its compass failed. Spotting the fine, bouffant, blonde soufflé of Mrs Beckett's hair, it thought it had found a place of safety: somewhere soft and fluffy where it could take refuge and snuggle. It flew straight in.

In an instant it was trapped. Contrary to the soft appearance, each brittle, lacquered strand represented, to the fly, a girder: but twisted and crimped into a wrought-iron maze. This was a Margaret Fly Trap. Caged and fenced and struggling to find a way through, the insect clambered and fell further into the interior. Now perilously near the scalp, you could see that it was close to panic.

Then somebody asked Mrs Beckett about the Tories' pension plans. She flew into an agitated state. Eyes flashing, she lashed out: 'Every day brings fresh rumours,' she said, omitting to mention that she was starting them. In a display of contempt for Tory heartlessness, she shook her head fiercely. The fly tumbled straight through to her roots and lay on its back waving its legs. Maybe it was stupefied by the fumes of Spray-'n-Go.

Not far away, Mrs Beckett's striking white earrings waved alarmingly from her lobes. She began a quieter, reasoned assessment of prospects for the welfare state. Righting itself and seizing the chance offered by this temporary lull, the fly began to crawl back from the roots, seeking a passage to the surface. It made headway.

'*Tories* want to *cheat* pensioners,' Mrs Beckett raged, jerking her head with each emphasis. The insect was trampolined to left and right, bouncing between strands, spiralling back down. It lost ground and, almost, hope.

Mrs Beckett moved to NHS dentures, the hottest topic in Christchurch after VAT on pensioners' gas bills. She built slowly to her peroration. A window of opportunity for the fly! It made a final dash for freedom, scrambling through three coiffeured layers in the course of one paragraph of her argument about dentistry. 'When the going was good,' she said, 'they gave money to the richest taxpayers. Now the going is tough, they take from the *poor*!'

On the word 'poor', Labour's deputy leader climaxed, with a sudden wild sweep of the head. The centrifugal force spun the fly helplessly to the surface of her hairdo. 'They *don't CARE*!' she spat, with another neck-breaking jolt.

We had lift-off. Ejected violently into the air, the fly found its wings at last and accelerated to safety, resolving never, ever, to attend a political press conference again. Labour's deputy leader reached her closing remarks, and was still.

For Margaret Beckett, one more by-election. For your sketch-writer, a welcome distraction. For the fly, a nightmare.

Verbal Bulldozer Clears Smith's Path

30.9.93

'I am a typical creature of the movement,' he roared. Terror gripped the faint-hearted. Yesterday in Brighton, John Prescott went 12 rounds with the English language and left it slumped and bleeding over the ropes. Among the collateral damage were thousands of Mr Smith's critics, many trade union dinosaurs, several big composite motions and Margaret Beckett's political career. And all this in quarter of an hour! Such gratuitous violence should be kept off our television screens for fear of frightening old ladies.

Other politicians pre-release transcripts of their speeches. The very thought of a Prescott transcript is laughable. Before his speeches are delivered, Mr Prescott is unaware of what he is going to say; after they are over, nobody has the least idea what he has said. Any transcript would be gibberish – nouns, adjectives and unattached parts of speech lying among the verbal wreckage like a rose garden after a bulldozer. Yet, somehow, everybody guesses what he meant. I dare not offer a summary, any more than I could provide the précis of a multiple pile-up, of which Prescott's speeches are the literary equivalent. His off-the-cuff rendering of the Lord's Prayer would read like this:

'Our Heaven which Thou art hallowed in Be Thy name Father to give us ongoing daily delivery of this trespassing to Kingdom come and will Thy be done on earth for Heaven's sake as it is! And forgive us this day our evil bread likewise also deliver us not into any leading temptations like we do if they do it unto us because Thy power is in the Kingdom of the Glory and ... [stops to pant] Amen! Comrades for ever! (wild cheers and standing ovation).

Prescott's relationship with his mother tongue ranks with *Moby Dick* as one of the great adversarial contests of all time: a life spent pursuing our language with a vengeful fervour. Yesterday he cornered and flattened it. The destruction, simultaneously, of political enemies was incidental.

Diva Delights in Cries of 'Encore'

20.10.93

Lady Thatcher answers questions and signs books ...

The questioner whose chance came almost at the end summoned it up. Offered the microphone, and after a short pause, she said: 'Lady Thatcher, I miss you dreadfully.'

You could feel the groundswell of support for that. It welled up from most of the audience. Those who had come to mock, to take detailed notes, or to make enquiries of a practical sort, sensed the inappropriateness of our presence – like turning up at a revivalist rally in the hope of nailing down the preacher on his claimed healing powers.

This baroness – attired yesterday in imperial purple, diamonds and pearls, and draping herself over the lectern like an operatic diva there mainly to be adored and only incidentally to sing – has long passed the stage of needing to prove anything, or indeed do anything. She needs only to exist, to appear in the flesh, to *be* just what we always knew she was; to recite one or two of those famous sentiments, once more with feeling.

Would she consider setting herself up as an international one-woman political Red Adair? Ah, she replied, Red Adair only put the flames *out*. Did the Conservative party need a period in opposition, to recharge its batteries? '*Never* give up office! Hold on! You might not get back.'

Her voice is an octave deeper than it was: a semi-tone down for each of the 16-odd years since she first led her party. She has gained terrific stage presence, a powerful use of the controlled pause, and a sense of the spectacle she herself is creating which leads almost – but not quite – to self-parody. It teeters on the edge of pantomime. Good fairy? Wicked witch? Cinderella, stepmother or Widow Twanky? She played them all, rolled into one.

Lady Thatcher simply, obviously, unconcealably adores being told that nobody can replace her and she never should have gone. When the first questioner asked if she would consider resigning her peerage and returning to Number Ten, her 'no sir' came somewhere between a purr and a growl. We never heard a lady more capable of saying 'no' when she meant 'yes'.

It is when she speaks of battles that her eyes burn and her voice takes wing. Battles with Galtieri, battles with Scargill, battles with the Wets. All these chapters in her story are well known, but she went over each again, to the delight of her audience. Lady Thatcher has reached that lucky state when it really doesn't matter what she says. She symbolizes things. Her presence, to be seen, touched and to sign books is taken as evidence of the political verities, as might the appearance of some minor saint be evidence of religious truths.

At party conferences they have taken to magnifying the platform speaker on to enormous video screens to each side. But she stood at the Barbican last night, a tiny figure on a vast stage before a huge audience, and all attention was on her. There was no need at all for magnification.

10.3.94   # At Last He Admits It

Mr Waldegrave had told the Scott enquiry that ministers sometimes lie …

It is a mad world into which William Waldegrave has stumbled.

If you want to know why the British public and its news media get liars for their politicians, just look at what we do to those who try to tell the truth. Here we go again, sniffing around our political leaders, picking up the scent of any intellect bolder than the others, and hounding him down. Political commentary seems to consist in ambushing anyone so incautious as to tell us truths we do not wish to hear, shrieking 'gaffe! gaffe!' like parrots, and baiting him into oblivion. We take pot-shots at every head that appears above the parapet, then notice that we are left only with pygmies for politicians. Then we write columns bemoaning our leaders' lack of stature.

We mob, ridicule and finally destroy those who try to refresh our politics, and then complain that our politics is stale. Every time a politician stands up, we break his legs. We end up with those whose only posture is to crouch. And then we rail against timidity! Truly, we are a most hypocritical people.

In the mad world which Mr Waldegrave has described, the man who says he never lies is accounted more honest than the man who admits he might.

A Pocketful of Social Deference   *16.3.94*

We witnessed yesterday one of the last surviving examples of social deference at the Commons. A Tory barked at a Labour MP that he should get his hands out of his pockets. Despite himself, the socialist almost complied.

A century ago the first Labour MPs struggled under a handicap: in class terms the Tories were their 'betters'. Habit of respect for toffs died hard, even in men who had rejected the class structure intellectually. It is said that, before the war, working-class MPs often found it difficult to question Tory ministers with the insolence that Opposition requires. Deference lingered in the second natures, if not the conscious beliefs, of MPs born in Victoria's reign. That has gone.

Or has it? Male readers will know that, though nothing comes more naturally than to put your hands into your pockets, it is almost impossible to *keep* them there after a voice with any hint of social command has told you to take them out. So spare a thought for Labour's Alan Simpson (Nottingham S), a quietly spoken, polytechnic-educated 45-year-old. He had a question for the Prime Minister. Unfortunately none of us can remember what it was, for the occasion was swamped by hilarity.

Mr Simpson rose. More out of nervousness than disrespect he thrust his hands into his pockets. Addressing the PM, he began: 'Would the Right Hon gentleman ...'

'*Get* your hands out of your pockets!' came an officer-rank bark from somewhere on the Tory side. Simpson reacted without thinking. One hand was out of his pocket, the other well on its way, before he remembered the class struggle. Too late to put back the hand! Aborting the withdrawal of the other hand, he thrust it defiantly in. One in, one out. MPs guffawed. The impact of his enquiry was lost. PM's Questions, commanding the premium they do, it may be years before he gets another chance.

Heseltine's Black Day
Swings From Bad to Verse

14.4.94

Something seems to have upset Michael Heseltine. Nobody and nothing pleased him yesterday. Labour questioners received terse, irritated replies, while even friendly Tory poodles were sent away with cursory lists of statistics, sniffily delivered.

Perhaps he was a touch disappointed about something? A little miffed, possibly, still to be there? Like waking up from a dream in which one has become a rock star, a football hero ... a prime minister, even ... one blinks, focuses on the heap of dirty linen on the floor that is yesterday's clothes, and realizes that these, after all, are the circumstances of one's life; and likely to remain so. Mr Heseltine's short fuse and depressed countenance put us in mind of that Tom Jones hit, 'The green, green grass of home':

> I wake up and look around me –
> At four grey walls which surround me.
> And I realize – oh, yes, I realize –
> I was only dreaming.

With no more than a slight effort of the imagination it was possible to imagine Heseltine doing a classic karaoke rendering, from the front bench, of Tom Jones's great hit.

With his frilly lace shirt unbuttoned half-way to reveal a tanned, hairy and medallioned chest, leather trousers far too tight, a toilet roll stuffed discreetly down them to enhance his leadership prospects, the Industry Secretary grips the mike and, belting it out with great intensity, sings:

> Yes, they'll all come to meet me.
> Arms reaching, smiling sweetly.
> It's good to touch the green,
> Green grass of ...

... well, Chequers.

Then, laying down his mike for a moment, he looks around. The Chamber is nearly empty. The television monitor screens say *Industry Questions*.

The tattered file of civil servants' notes on the table before him reads 'Trade & Industry: 13 April 94: supplementary briefing.' To his left sit a junior whip and a junior minister.

Sadly, the prisoner picks up his mike again, and croons soulfully:

> And there's a guard, and
> There's a sad old padre;
> On and on we'll walk at
>   daybreak,
> Again to touch the green,
> Green grass of …

… well, the DoI, 123 Victoria Street, SW1.

The Epitaph Was Silence   *13.5.94*

MPs react to the death of Labour's leader …

For MPs, whose job is so often to express shock or grief when little is felt, real shock and real grief are almost strangers at their gate. They have ransacked the vocabulary of distress for slighter occasions than this. Now, like children in the face of something they cannot understand, they are all at sea. How can they show they mean it? How can they mark the difference they feel?

They tried very hard. Margaret Beckett spoke with real dignity. Struggling to control her voice, she recalled the previous evening and the last time she had heard John Smith speak. She touched a chord among Members on all sides when she said that he was a man 'who knew what he could do'.

He was more completely at ease with himself, she said, than any politician we know.

John Major was kindly and utterly unpompous in his remarks. Departing often from his notes he raised a smile when he remembered how friendly – and lengthy – had been his regular meetings with the Opposition Leader. 'Sometimes we drank tea,' he said, 'sometimes not tea.'

Was there a rueful smile behind the Prime Minister's remark that Mr Smith had been 'an opponent, not an enemy'?

When Paddy Ashdown, in his own tribute, remarked that this was a period 'when the public are not much given to trust politicians' one reflected on the irony that, over the short time when Mr Smith was Leader of the Opposition with Mr Major as Prime Minister, Britain has experienced the coincidence of two more decent political leaders than our political system has thrown together for decades.

But as the tributes continued, the words began to pall. Perhaps because they speak too much and too easily, MPs are curiously incapable of articulating the extraordinary. Even at times of genuine emotion, auto-tribute is an ever-present danger in the Chamber.

The most touching epitaph for John Smith at Westminster yesterday lay not in the tributes which began to roll from MPs at 3.30. It lay in their silence just after Prayers, at 2.30.

The Chamber was packed. For just a couple of minutes, as Madam Speaker suspended the sitting for Members to collect their thoughts, a sort of emotional confusion reigned beneath the watching Press Gallery.

There was no buzz of conversation. Margaret Beckett was very close to tears. People tried to pat her on the back, or put an arm awkwardly on her shoulder. John Major looked simply staggered. Most of the Cabinet were there, Douglas Hurd and Kenneth Clarke at the Prime Minister's side. Between Sir Patrick Mayhew and Michael Portillo sat Nicholas Scott – suddenly yesterday's news.

The Labour front bench was too full to accommodate the Shadow Cabinet. Gordon Brown stood, by the Speaker's Chair. Every face was knotted with tension. Hands twisted and untwisted. David Blunkett's guide dog, stretched indolently on the carpet, occupied a tiny plot of unconcern in a field of tension.

Nobody really knew what to do. It was a moment, suspended in a sudden silence, between an event and the consequences of an event. These would flow soon enough. The speeches would flow sooner.

But, just for an instant, as it faced the unexpected intervention of mortality, the whole House of Commons added up to a strange, awful, uncomprehending pause.

27 Things You Didn't Know About Blair

Tony Blair becomes front-runner for the leadership of his party …

Supporters of Tony Blair (wrote the political editor of *The Times* yesterday) are worried that his leadership bandwagon is racing out of control. There are fears that Tory enthusiasm and media 'hype' for Mr Blair might antagonize traditionalists in the Labour Party.

This is disturbing. Those of us who wish Tony well must act fast. As both an ex-Tory MP *and* a columnist, this sketchwriter must be as close as you can get to an Identikit picture of the sort of supporter Blair can do without.

In fact to improve his street-cred with the appalling types with unwashed hair, CND badges and training shoes who characterize his party's activists, I can best assist him by attacking him. Here, then, is a thoroughly nasty column about Tony Blair: Twenty-seven bad things you didn't know about the next Leader of the Labour Party (*oops! Sorry*).

☐ He has terrible teeth
☐ He looks like a vampire
☐ It is not true that Tony Blair is attractive to women. He's too pretty. He's a *man*'s idea of a man who attracts women. Seven out of nine women in the Westminster Press Gallery do not fancy Tony Blair. Gordon Brown scores four
☐ He went to public school
☐ He went to Oxford
☐ His dad became a Tory
☐ He smiles too much
☐ He cannot possibly be as nice as he seems. All politicians must rise through a nasty political process, work with nasty people in nasty parties, and prosper. He has. He must be pretending to be nice.
☐ He cannot lack a simple ambition for office, as he claims. He must be lying
☐ He has never held down any job in Government
☐ He spends too much time on his hair
☐ He looks like a prototype for something, but nobody is sure what

☐ Nobody had heard of him before 1992

☐ He may be a Vulcan. This man is too good to be true. I believe that military strategists on the planet Vulcan, having infiltrated into Westminster an early attempt at an Earthling politician, John Redwood, have now learnt from the mistakes in this design. They have sent an improved version, with added charm. He has pointed ears

☐ He probably approves of Cliff Richard

☐ He may *be* Cliff Richard

☐ The Tories will say he's a boy sent to do a man's job

☐ Richard Littlejohn supports him

☐ He used to wear flares

☐ He was almost certainly a fan of Peter, Paul and Mary; the New Seekers; the Carpenters; Bucks Fizz; Abba ...

☐ He probably listens to Classic FM now

☐ His father was a lawyer

☐ Tony Blair is the next leader of the Labour Party (*oops!*) but he could just as well have been the leader of the Conservative Party or the Social Democratic Party or the Liberal Party or the Green Party, or Archbishop of Canterbury, or a progressive missionary, or in charge of Bob Geldof's PR, or director of a major charity, or chairman of English Heritage, or general secretary of a small, service-sector trade union, or a management consultant, or King Herod, or the leader of the Dutch Social Democrats, or manager of a small plastics factory in Enfield where he is also sidesman in the local church and takes his daughters to pony classes in a newish Volvo

☐ He wears pastel suits

☐ He reminds us of Bill Clinton

☐ If he had ever smoked marijuana he would *not* have inhaled

☐ He doesn't fool me

Hope this helps, Tony ...

11.7.94   # The Tony Blair ABC

Last week, Tony Blair called for an initiative. Money spent on new police authorities should be diverted, he told the Home Secretary, to a 'drugs initiative'. He did not elaborate. I hugged myself with delight, for 'initiative' begins with the letter I. It filled the final gap in the Tony Blair ABC I have been compiling from the recent speeches and interviews of the soon-to-be Leader of the Opposition.

Here follows a guide not just to the preferred vocabulary of the incoming Blair regime, but to its mood and themes. Labour MPs hoping for a job under the new leader would be wise to draw their speeches and their tone from this lexicon. Get ahead of the pack: get in tune with Tony now!

A is for Achievement. Achievements are one of the main things a Blair government will achieve. A is also for Abstract. Abstract nouns are another Blair achievement. A is for Absolutely, too. 'Absolutely' means 'yes' in Islington.

B is for Beliefs. Politics is about beliefs. B is also for Basic. Basic beliefs. B is for Broader society. And B is for the Battle of Ideas. 'Only by re-establishing its core identity, can the Labour Party regain the intellectual self-confidence to take on and win the Battle of Ideas' (Fabian/*Guardian* Conference, 18 June).

C is for Core identity; also Core beliefs; also Community, Citizenship, Cohesion, Compassion, Confidence, Coalition and Change.

D is for Duty: 'individuals owe a Duty to one another and to a broader society' (ibid). D is also for Direction, new Direction, and Drive in a new direction.

E is for Energy: 'the power and Energy of ideas and vision' (ibid). E is for Equality, too: 'social justice, cohesion, Equality of opportunity and community' (ibid); and for Ethical Socialism, as distinguished from unethical socialism.

F is for Fairness, for Freedom, and for Full employability.

G is for Global: 'First, the economy is Global' (ibid). Labour's foreign and defence policy are also likely to be Global.

H is for Historic mission. Also for Historic opportunity: 'a Historic opportunity now to give leadership' (ibid).

I is for initiative. No minister will be without one. As well as Initiatives, a Blair administration will have Ideas. 'The future will be decided ... through the power and energy of Ideas and vision' (ibid).

J is for Justice and social Justice (see Ethical Socialism).

K is for Key values and also for Key beliefs (see also Core values and Core beliefs). 'Socialism as defined by certain Key values and beliefs is not merely alive, it has a historic opportunity now to give Leadership' (ibid).

L is for Leadership (see Historic opportunity/Key values).

M is for Modern: 'a future that is both radical and Modern' (ibid). M is for Movement, too: 'a popular Movement in this country for change and national renewal' (ibid).

N is for National renewal.

O is for Opportunity. '… the chance to capture the entire ground and language of Opportunity' (ibid. See also Equality).

P is for Partnership. P is also for Purpose, Power, Potential and Pluralism: 'a greater Pluralism of ideas and thought' (ibid. See also Ideas and Thought).

Q is for Quality work. 'Central to my belief about this country is that we've got to give people the chance not just to work, but actually to have Quality work' (interview with Frost 12 June).

R is for Rediscovery, Responsibilities, Realization and Respect: 'We do need to Rediscover a strong sense of civic and community values, the belief that we must combine opportunities and Responsibilities, and the Realization that true self-respect can come only through respect for others' (speech to the CBI 14 June).

S is for Society; and plural Society, and shared Society, and broader Society, and changed Society, and Social … and 'Social-*ism* – if you will' (Fabian/*Guardian* speech).

T is for Tough: 'Tough on crime, Tough on the causes of crime'. T is also for Thinking, Thought, Trust and True self-respect.

U is for Urgency. 'Radical reform … should be pursued by a Labour government with Urgency' (ibid). U is also for United: 'a strong, United society which gives each citizen the chance to develop their potential to the full' (ibid. See also Society and Potential).

V is for Values. For Vigour and Victory too; and, more than all else, V is for Vision: 'a central Vision based around principle but liberated from particular policy prescriptions …' (ibid). You can say that again!

W is for Worth: 'the equal Worth of each citizen' (ibid). W is also for Welfare and Well-being.

X is for Factor 'X'. John Major doesn't have it, according to a survey conducted for Mazda cars. Tony Blair has Factor X.

Y is for Youth. Blair has that, too.

Z is for Zero-sum game. A Zero-sum game is a calculation in which if you add to one thing, you must take away from another. Blair's economics, as he has said, is *not* a Zero-sum game. This means that you can have your cake and eat it.

Comet Tony Hits Earth   *22.7.94*

Mr Blair takes the crown …

As fragments of Shoemaker Levy–9 thudded into the surface of Jupiter, Tony Blair stood up in Bloomsbury and released a barrage of abstract nouns of unprecedented duration and ferocity.

It was awesome. Grown men – hardened journalists – rocked against the walls in disbelief; camera crews – unable to cope with exposure to such sustained levels of intellectualism – staggered from the hall; Tories ran for cover. Even Liberal Democrats winced. Across the nation, TV viewers, watching the event live, shielded themselves as honour, pride, humility, community, excitement, conviction, trepidation, passion, aspiration, gratitude, courage and determination – and that's only the first page and a half – rocketed out of the television sets and across their living rooms, thudding into a million sofas.

Devices tracking Earth from Jupiter will have blown their fuses at the sheer philosophical energy unleashed. Never, even in Islington, have so many generalities been uttered with such passion by a single politician within one lunchtime.

For those inclined to doodle it was interesting to take keynote phrases ('the power of all for the good of each', 'ours is a passion allied to reason') and try swapping their constituent elements, to see whether it made any difference: 'the power of each for the good of all', 'ours is a reason allied to passion', or even 'the power and passion of each, allied to reason, for the good of all'.

The show was well executed: stagey without being vulgar, media-friendly, cunningly lit, pre-scripted, press-released, sound-enhanced, Autocue-supported, video-assisted, and cheap. Seating in the hall was divided into the three sections eligible to choose the Labour Leader: one third BBC, one third print journalists, and one third Labour Party. The trades unions had disappeared: something called 'affiliated organizations' figured on the video-graphics. There were no comrades either. Those present were addressed by loudspeakers as 'colleagues'. Next year we will be ladies and gentlemen. Blue was the predominant colour.

And another Tory feature is creeping into Labour occasions: incessant, fatuous applause. Tony Blair's speech was prefaced by some 15 seconds of applause, interrupted by 27 separate bursts of mostly polite clapping, each lasting about 10 seconds, and concluded with some two minutes' clapping.

Blair delighted most journalists. His skills would serve in those amusement-arcade 'Grand-prix' screen games. His own screen the Autocue screen, and his gaze rigid with concentration, Mr Blair drove at gathering velocity round a track littered with the death-traps of policy-commitments, swerving to avoid every one, fuelled by a tankful of abstract nouns. Meanwhile, in an event which cannot be unrelated to the discovery of Tony Blair, a team of scientists in a remote mountain range in New Guinea have discovered a species of whistling tree-kangaroo: the bondegezou. These kangaroos, held in huge affection by local tribesmen, are soft, furry, and completely unthreatening. They sit amiably on their branches, and when they see a human being walking below, they whistle a friendly greeting.

It remains to teach the bondegezou to intersperse its song with words like 'honour, pride, conviction' and 'passion', and to teach Mr Blair to climb trees. Then, British political life may become interchangeable with that of the New Guinea cloud forests.

Dedicated Spurners of Fashion   *22.9.94*

The Liberal Democrat Conference

Are you a bank manager? Does the name Richard Denton-White ring a bell? He has an account at your bank, perhaps? Then read on. These were Mr Denton-White's words, opening a debate about the City at the Liberal Democrats' conference yesterday morning: 'Bankers are excrement living on increment.'

In case anyone should accuse him of fudging, Mr Denton-White clarified his position. 'The City sucks,' he cried. Happily for the beleaguered Paddy Ashdown, Tim Clement-Jones came to the rescue and persuaded delegates to give the whole motion what he called 'a decent burial'. They did. Liberal Democrats do retain some vestigial instinct for self-preservation. But happily only vestigial. Your sketch writer parts company with other commentators in finding the careless idealism of a Liberal conference not only endearing, but a strength. If at Brighton this week they had adopted what their incoming president called 'the smiling anaemia' of Tony Blair's New Model Labour Party we would all be complaining that there was no need in British politics for *two* bands of vanilla-flavoured pixies. The star-gazing element in Liberal Democracy may be what stops it winning, but it may also be what keeps it breathing.

It is breathing fine by the Sussex seaside. I watched the next debate, on the future of the Western Sahara. Dame Penelope Jessel addressed (to the backs of departing reporters) all the arguments for helping a dispossessed people regain the territory of which Morocco has robbed them. 'We will be criticized for discussing issues that are not mainstream,' said Clive English, 'but *this has to be discussed.*'

Nothing is easier than to mock the use of prime conference time by obsessives who want to rage against skulduggery in the City or injustice in the Sahara. But how many great causes must have started in this way! We need a party capable of seeing things out of the corner of its eye.

Peripheral vision, however, is distracting: hence the invention of blinkers. There will be growing media pressure on the Liberal leadership to tame its party into the sort of beast capable of carrying Mr Blair over the river – whereupon the beast will be summarily shot.

But the highlight of the day was a speech from the new president Robert Maclennan.

It is reported that a growing problem with pheasant-shooting is that the bird declines to fly up and dodge about, sticking instead to its position, staring amiably at the gun and presenting an unmissable target.

As a politician Mr Maclennan resembles these pheasants. A thoughtful man of academic disposition, he lacks cunning and seems oblivious to applause. He is easily and often tripped up. Fair-mindedness blunts his attack. Stammering his way earnestly through arguments whose depth is lost on hearers, he reminds me of a brilliant theology student forced to take a living as a country preacher in a hillbilly community. He should avoid the press conferences, verbal duels and hostile audiences at which his predecessor, Charles Kennedy, who had the manner of a television chat show host, so excelled.

But give Maclennan a pulpit, a cathedral and a hushed congregation and he takes wing. Yesterday his party gave him just that. And he was, by turns, funny, sharp, reflective – and even inspirational. His remark that European politicians look at Michael Portillo 'as children look at their first giraffe', will not be forgotten; nor his comment on Labour's new modernity, which was not healthily rooted, he said: 'All their changes were made in reaction to defeat.'

Delegates rewarded him with a standing ovation, his words – 'chase no fashions, spurn all opportunism and stay true to yourselves.' – ringing in their ears.

4.10.94   # Eau de nil backdrop

The Labour Party Conference

Watching TV pictures of Tony Blair on the Blackpool podium, do you wonder why he keeps his head so still? Well now we know. There is really only one hot topic of conversation here at the Winter Gardens. Tony Blair's face-powder. Nobody has ever seen so much powder on the face of one man at a party conference.

Apparently this is for the TV screen, and on the screen Mr Blair does look radiantly unshiny this year. But photographers, who must cower beneath the podium and take the full blast of the particle-laden wind, are putting in for danger money – terrified by the threat of respiratory disease. Hardened journalists – men who covered the arrival of Liberace at Southampton in 1962 without flinching – wail now.

Outside, it's worse. October in Blackpool is windy, and those who approach the new Labour leader for one of those *mwah-mwah* Islington-style kisses, speak of an encounter reminiscent of meeting a traveller in a violent Saharan sandstorm. Approaching Mr Blair, they say, it becomes increasingly hard to see where he is. As with his policies, everything becomes a pale, sweetly-scented blur. Women have been traumatized by the experience. All in all, this conference is proving a disorientating time for delegates.

And the new stage-set is making it worse. It must have been designed by the Early Learning Centre. The colour is not quite blue and not quite green but something in between: a shade of turquoise which I believe was all the rage in the 1950s, called *eau de nil*. Labour has gone retro-chic. The colour – on one of those Dulux colour-planners it might be called 'Sedgefield' and recommended for bathrooms – looks as though it has been chosen by Sealink's corporate psychiatrist as providing the environment in which you are least likely to want to be sick.

As Evelyn Waugh once put it, this is a shade that behavioural psychologists have tested on animals and found to produce a mood of dignified gaiety in mice. The Littlewoods branch adjacent to the Winter Gardens is using precisely this hue for gigantic window-posters proclaiming the store's victory in the British Sandwich Association's competition for 'Sandwich Retailer of the Year'.

Sandwich retailer of the year, vanilla-flavoured pap retailer of the year: you can take your pick. Delegates, who once were drawn to Labour by heroic tales of the struggles of Keir Hardie stare glumly around, wondering if this is all a bad dream, or whether they really are trapped in a Beckenham bathroom in 1951, face-powder blowing in the wind.

But for television viewers nationwide the nightmare is worse. Do they warn you anywhere in the *TV Times* that Labour has abandoned red as its colour? Millions of lifelong Labour supporters up and down the country must be apoplectic, banging their sets, convinced that their colour-controls are up the spout. We await an emergency motion sponsored by Radio Rentals imploring the party to restore its traditional conference decor.

An early fashion victim yesterday was carrot-bearded Robin Cook. Set against the reds and rose-bunches of previous Labour conferences,

Mr Cook used to look great: very autumnal, a ginger-snap by the fireside. But carrot and jade don't go. Cook's speech never caught fire.

Gordon Brown's did: the most effective of the day – the leader Labour hasn't got – delivered in his best Daddy Bear voice. Delegates seemed unsure how to react.

For a feature of the mood is this audience's confusion about when and whom to applaud. The old key-words shouldn't trigger passion, but do; the new ones should, but don't.

Bill Jordan of the EEUW, a brave man who was Modern before it suited your career in the Labour Party to be Modern, should have been a welcome speaker but faced a palpable *froideur*. Arthur Scargill's rant embraced everything Labour no longer believes – and got the only cheers of the day.

But they were rueful cheers. The mood is not rebellious. It is half-hearted, uncomprehending, and a little sad. Perhaps turquoise is the right colour after all.

5.10.94   # Dashing Captain Blair

A froth of self-satisfaction filled the room … the mood was exuberant, the air alive with the fizz of irrelevant party chatter.

Sorry, that should have been in quotes. It's not a report from the Winter Gardens as Tony Blair paces the podium before his big speech. Nor is it the speech. It is the opening paragraph from another notorious work of fiction: Anna Pasternak's *Princess In Love*. While the dashing young Captain Blair wooed his own fairy princess – the Labour Party – at Blackpool, holidaymakers browsing along W.H. Smith's bookshelves found their thoughts moving towards a different romance.

'Theirs was a love both passionate and full of hope,' wrote Ms Pasternak, 'a love that arose through force of circumstance.' In the conference centre something similar was happening, so I took *Princess In Love* into the hall with me. The speech had its *longueurs*. I mentally channel-hopped between Blair and Pasternak. In what follows, the two have become hopelessly jumbled. *'The minute she saw him standing waiting for her, tall and assertive, she felt at once tense and relaxed … she could not help but be struck by his appearance.*

'*He seemed so pure and uncomplicated … nothing would give him greater pleasure than to help the Princess regain her confidence. Surely the horizon could only be clear? Why, then, did he see intermittent flashes of desperation discolouring her face? … As he watched her and gently stroked wisps of her hair across and away from her forehead, he was overcome by the strength of his feeling, swept away by the vulnerability that lay unguarded in front of him.*'

'We meet in a spirit of hope,' began Captain Tony. '*Holding his breath and scarcely moving his body so as not to alarm her he gently, firmly squeezed the hand that had found its way into his palm.*'

'It means what we share,' said Tony, 'it means working together, it is about how we treat each other … we must protect each other.' '*He stared at her with his slow, full gaze, acutely aware of his own desirability, from time to time flashing the broad careless smile he knew she found so attractive … she knew he would do nothing to dominate her overtly yet would dominate her completely.*'

'A belief in society. Working together. Solidarity. Co-operation. Partnership. These are our words. This is my socialism.'

'*Intuitively he knew both the deceptive crevices and the effortlessness of the plain, untroubled ground; he knew exactly where, and where not, to tread.*'

'I know how important the education of my children is to me. I will not tolerate children going to rundown schools, with bad discipline … If schools are bad, they should be made to be good.'

'*Instinctively he knows how to get his charges to relax, by chatting and issuing gentle commands.*'

'Some of you support me because you think I can win. Actually that's not a bad reason! But it's not enough.'

'*His flirtatious gambit was to chide gently, to couch his flattery in caressing teases, and a warm, ready smile.*'

'I want you with me in that task. I want you with me. Head and heart. Because this can only be done together.'

The speech, now drawing to a close, had gone well. Blair's ideas may not have convinced, but his personality had. Reaching his twentieth use of the word 'new' – 'Our party. New Labour. Our mission. New Britain. New Labour. New Britain!' He inclined his head. His speech over. He knew applause must follow, but there was a moment's pause …

'The split second before you kiss, when you know it is going to happen but at the same time are not quite sure, is a moment of ecstasy that can never be repeated.'

8.10.94   # Lord Snooty and His Pals

Tories? 'I just can't stomach 'em,' bellowed John Prescott, Labour's deputy leader, yesterday. 'So many snouts in the trough that even the pigs are complaining.' The conference loved it. They loved him. He loved them. When Prescott speaks to a large Labour gathering you sense something rarely seen in a modern British politician: real affection for his audience.

Tony Blair is already beginning to snap at them or adopt a tone of baffled rationality, as one might when reasoning with a child. There is also something I have observed in him for the first time this week: a slight haughtiness. Paddy Ashdown seems afflicted by the juxtaposition between himself and his audience of an invisible row of footlights. John Major can look like a head boy keeping order, nervous of his authority. Depending on her mood, Margaret Thatcher might address us either as though we deserved a pat on the head or a jolly good smack.

But Prescott did without needing to say it what Blair had failed to do though he did say it: Prescott implied: 'I'm on your side.' He read out a message from a small businesswoman asking him 'to give a plug for Betty's Pie Shop' as business was not too good. Later he invited the excruciatingly embarrassed Betty on to the rostrum (it was her 40th birthday) and sang – or rather howled – *Happy Birthday to You* while Betty cringed, and tears filled delegates' eyes.

I watched Tony Blair sitting behind him: pale, tense, aloof, his face set and his hands clasped a little primly. He could almost have been wearing a top hat. He on the one hand, Prescott and his fellow-delegates on the other, reminded me of Lord Snooty and his Pals from *The Beano*.

But Mr Prescott was enjoying himself. 'New Labour. New Computer!' he declared, adapting this year's slogan to his appeal for funds. It was a knockabout performance. He joked, at his own expense, about gibes over his command of the English language. 'I'll spell it out in sentences that even I can understand,' he promised. Stumbling once over his speech and coming to a halt, he said: 'I did that on purpose so as not to disappoint you.' Mr Prescott also ventured triumphantly into statistical science: 'If every one of you gets one new member, then we'd double the membership!'

The Winter Gardens warmed to him more than they had warmed on Tuesday to the man now behind him. But I reminded myself that Tony Blair, though he had been heard uncertainly, was applauded to the rafters when he finished.

There was no mistaking that applause. They did not quite understand Mr Blair and they were not sure they liked him but they knew they needed him. It reminded me of a remark of Ann Leslie's, on radio, to Robert Robinson: 'I love it when you talk like that. It reminds me what we lost when they closed the grammar schools.' As Prescott stirred the conference to an emotional finale, it struck me that Lord Snooty needs his Pal: but his Pal needs Lord Snooty, too.

Majestic Vision from the Deep   *12.10.94*

The Conservative Party Conference

'She's coming,' whispered a maid-in-waiting dressed all in white like a temple virgin.

It was 9.30a.m. Down at the Conference Centre the Reverend Geraint Edwards was leading the faithful in prayer: 'We have preferred shadows to reality,' he was declaring. 'Guilt and shame weigh us down.' But we had bunked prayers and were waiting for her. We heard the purr of a Daimler. It ceased.

Up she came, like Aphrodite from the sea, or a monster from the deep, depending on your viewpoint. Assembled above the steps to the Highcliff Hotel, our view out was straight down to the Atlantic. From this Lady Thatcher seemed to rise in a thin mist and imperial purple pecking her way up the steps in that partridge-in-a-hurry style of hers. 'Tense but majestic,' describes her.

'Aren't you distressed at the allegations?' shouted several rude journalists at the celestial being. Lady Thatcher *almost* paused as if to suggest she *might* have heard the question then sailed on – as if to suggest that she had decided not to. She went in, still purple, for coffee. 'Go inside the monster washing machine,' the poster outside the Persil Road Show assembled in the town centre was calling. 'Go through the tunnel of horrible stains!' Hours later she emerged from the hotel in royal blue and made her way down to the conference.

Lady Thatcher had missed William Waldegrave's debut as Agriculture Minister. His intelligent speech met a sort of bemused tolerance from its Tory audience. No rabble rouser, Mr Waldegrave failed to achieve applause for English apples but just managed to prompt a cheer for Cheddar cheese. He sat down. Lady Thatcher, still blue, sailed out onto the rostrum. Where once the applause had been ecstatic it was now sympathetic. It needed to be. She was to hear a speech on local government by David Curry. This new appointment is immensely brainy and rather sensible but talks as might a fridge-freezer granted the gift of speech. On and on he went. I recalled an office memo from Mrs Thatcher's private secretary in 1978: 'MT does *not* like to listen to colleagues' speeches.'

MT gazed, rapt into the blue fuzzy felt of the backdrop, grinding her teeth. No one has ever seen so much fuzzy felt. Everything is covered in it. Those with Velcro fastenings to their clothes should beware of sitting down with the platform party lest, in rising, they are undone. Onto the Velcro are fixed, in letters of expanded polystyrene, the words 'Britain growing stronger' – as though the nation had recently been the victim of a hit and run accident. One suspect, an elderly Lady in blue, was invoking the right to silence.

13.10.94   # Jungle Drums Beat Out a New Rhythm

This weekend *The Lion King* comes to Bournemouth cinemas, but two big cats have already arrived. Yesterday an ageing lion and a frisky cub looked in at the conference centre. In the film the cub succeeds the old lion. The Tory story looks like turning out the same.

Michael Heseltine has been lionizing Tory conferences for decades. He would stride along the seafronts, blond mane blowing in the breeze as he acknowledged the salutations of conference-goers. The Heseltine speech was the highspot of the season. Some people came to hear only it. We would watch those carefully coiffed locks start to shake as he approached the climax; break free as he tossed back his head and snarled out his derision of socialism; and flop all over his face as he roared forth his call to arms. Nobody did it better.

Nobody did it better this year either. The lion king can still roar. Yesterday he roared well enough. There was the lion's joke – there always is – and it was good, very good. There was the lion's attack on socialism, and it was good. There was the lion's call to arms (this year he chose 'the darkest hour is just before dawn') and it was … well, OK.

Or did we cringe a bit to see the old trouper pacing the ring one more time? Did we sense that karaoke *My Way* approaching? A novel and disturbing feature of this speech was that much of it was about his own job: trade and industry. It is unusual for Mr Heseltine to restrict himself to his own responsibilities. Most years we would be lucky if he touched on them at all. Has the lion lost his wanderlust?

The gloomy thought was reinforced by the behaviour of the Heseltine hair – for the mane is the man. It looked flatter, greyer: some of the lustre was gone. As his peroration approached the old lion tried his famous head toss, just like the days gone by. One lock at the front seemed to come loose. 'Hurray!' we thought. 'We have lift-off.' He tossed his head again. Alas, not hard enough. The lock trembled but there was no full-scale break-up of the coiff. That mane used to have a life of its own. No longer.

All the more distressing, then, to report what is happening to Michael Portillo's hair. It is turning into a mane! Yesterday the young cub performed first. Mr Heseltine is claiming not to have read or heard his speech, but we can tell him it was good: clear, if shallow blue water. Pawing the air, he assailed rather than addressed, squeaking intermittently like a pubescent finalist in a school debate: the only recorded squeaked leadership bid. Portillo raises his left palm, fingers clawed upward, to explain; his right palm to associate himself personally with a statement; and both for emphasis. Nothing he said lifted the imagination except perhaps his admiring reference to Calvin Klein, a brand of underwear still unknown to most Tory activists. Next year they'll be wearing nothing else.

He judged his audience shrewdly, and one section was in near-ecstasy. The speech was all about destiny. By the end, I had forgotten what Mr Portillo was secretary of state for. I think he had, too. That old leonine wanderlust was upon him.

On and on the ovation went. The young lion looked thrilled. And as he basked in applause I glanced at his quiff. It seemed to have grown. Standing proudly on its roots, it swept up with a vigour that reminded me of another conference, another mane, another man.

Mr Heseltine never did reach the top, but conferences loved him. This one now loves Michael Portillo much more than before; and the Parliamentary Conservative Party trusts him a little less. Welcome to your cage, lion king.

15.10.94 # Decent Cove Offers Shelter From the Storm

Who says this man's politics lacks a theme? John Major yesterday unveiled as his vision perhaps the most riveting thing a statesman ever encounters in political life. Himself.

Sensibly brushing past such tiresome subjects as monetary union, the future of Europe or income tax, we followed Mr Major into infancy and early learning experiences. We empathized with him over educational opportunities missed and remembered with him what fun school games had been.

We sympathized as he recalled illness in the family. We were told of his motor accident and were sorry to hear about it; sorry, too, that the leg is still giving him trouble. Convalescing with him afterwards, we thrilled with him to the pleasures of Trollope and braced ourselves for the rigours of his textbooks on banking.

He took us abroad and we visited Lech Walesa, but this went on for too long. We wanted to hear more about his earlier life.

We longed for the story of his courtship with Norma – but consoled ourselves that Mr Major may be saving that for next year's conference. If there were gaps in the biography – the chapter on Black Wednesday seemed to have been omitted and rumours of a stormy relationship with a baroness of advancing years were never mentioned – we reminded ourselves that these were, after all, mere political stories.

Our wise PM was sticking to a golden rule: never discuss religion or politics at party conferences.

The speech, though delivered in an often suicidal tone, reassured its audience. Reading the press-released text while hearing the real thing, I made an intriguing discovery. Mr Major has a horror of bald statements.

Any short sentence ending in a full stop discomfits him. Thus, his text read: '... the boom-and-bust cycle that causes so much pain and so many lost hopes' *full stop*. But when Major reached 'hopes' he shrunk from the silence and added 'to so many people'. Then he paused again and added 'up and down this country'. He could have added 'of ours'.

It is strange how one can feel a mood. All week we have sensed among conference-goers an affection for Mr Major and a willingness to accept his judgment. It is a gentle mood, nothing like the adulation Margaret Thatcher used to excite. It is mixed with concern about Tory prospects; nor have those gathered at Bournemouth always been convinced that they agree with their leader.

But they seem content to follow him. They do like him. He seems like a decent cove, does not make a great song and dance about things, and appears to get his way remarkably often in practical matters. A British audience notes especially this last.

There is a feeling that you might enjoy a candlelight supper with Mr Portillo but you would rather have breakfast with Mr Major. He would probably get the eggs right.

Others' claims have met louder cheers this week, but yesterday John Major's received the final nod.

What Colour Are His Socks?   *18.10.94*

The only thing about Viscount Cranborne that was upbeat yesterday was his socks. These were a joyous shade of peachey yellow. The rest of his lordship was the last word in caution.

Poor Lord Cranborne. As he admitted to his peers when opening yesterday's Lords debate on developments in Northern Ireland ('there's no point in denying it') Cranborne is an old-fashioned Unionist. You would expect it of a Cecil. He voted against the 1985 Anglo-Irish Agreement.

Now, propelled to the top as Government Leader in the Lords, his job was to persuade the Upper Chamber of the wisdom of John Major's new moves. And he did manage to toe the line. 'I salute the Prime Minister's courage,' he said, rather as one might to someone about to go over the Niagara Falls in a barrel. But were it not for the promise of a referendum 'I for one would have been most unhappy'. To be safe, Cranborne added that John Major would have been most unhappy, too. It was good to hear that the PM approved of his own proposal.

In the circumstances, Cranborne's was a solid speech, but it could have been made by the Unionists' Jim Molyneaux. By the time he sat down his yellow socks seemed to have taken on a pale orange hue. Our disorientation grew.

One or another of their Lordships seemed to have spoken for almost every cause. It remained to put the Almighty's point of view. This was done by the Belfast-born Bishop of Southwark, a sort of watered-down John Cole look-alike, houndstooth overcoat replaced by a white nightie. Concluding with an assurance of 'goodwill and prayerful support,' Southwark came perilously close to ending with a short prayer.

Foreign students would be assisted in understanding our constitution if speeches in the Upper Chamber were all to end in a collective murmur of '*amen*'.

19.10.94   # New Labour New Leader

Tony Blair takes his place as Labour leader ...

So much for the wonderful new reign of courtesy at PM's question time! It was rather like one of David Owen's Bosnian peace plans: 30 seconds of handshakes and then out they jumped from their trenches and started biffing each other over the head. In the House of Commons, luckily, it is only ever with pillows.

Tony Blair entered the Chamber a full three minutes early (John Smith liked to time it to the second) and paced up to the dispatch box like a nervous greyhound, to prolonged cheers. John Prescott sat beside him with the expression of a pit bull terrier. John Major, who ambled amiably in a couple of minutes later, looked more like a family pooch returning to his favourite corner. Both party leaders were dressed identically: dark suit, light blue shirt and burgundy tie. Blair carried a sheet of cream paper with his question written out neatly in longhand.

The spat was to begin at 3.15. Ever since lunch, backbenchers had been arriving in the Chamber to watch. They scarcely attended to questions to the new Employment Secretary, Michael Portillo, treating the session as one might the short films and trailers that come before the Big Movie. Amid the low, excited conversation you could almost smell the popcorn. Even junior minister Ann Widdecombe's new *Prisoner: Cell Block H* hairdo escaped notice. Only Lady Oppenheim-Barnes, watching lovingly from the Peers' Gallery, had come for Employment questions: it was her son Phillip's debut as a minister. His mother appeared to be restraining herself with difficulty from clapping. And at last 3.15 arrived. The first question – from Labour's Anne Campbell – was the sort of thing Neil Kinnock might have chosen to take up: Mark Thatcher, and arms deals.

John Major doggedly batted it back with a dogged expression of loyalty to Lady Thatcher. Tony Blair did not rise. There was a rustle of interest in the Press Gallery. Would he rise at all? He did, after the next question.

First came the new era of courtesy, which lasted a few seconds: Mr Blair congratulated the PM on his Irish initiative. Then he turned nasty: why were the Prime Minister and his Chancellor saying different things about a referendum on Europe?

Blair put the question succinctly and with clarity. He sounded precise, rehearsed and a little tense – like a middle-ranking barrister with a good mind, a sharp tongue and a careful knowledge of his brief on his first important case: skilled enough to get it right, not quite relaxed enough to swing the big punch.

Major reciprocated the courtesy, treated us to an extended reprise ('these you have loved') from the Northern Ireland section of his Bournemouth speech, then brushed aside the question about Euro-differences with his Chancellor. Blair returned to it: why was the PM singing a different tune from Kenneth Clarke? If the Labour leader had left it there, he would have scored: but, like generations of his predecessors, Mr Blair could not resist the temptation to have a go. Major's Government was weak and divided, he said. Yah-boo sucks.

This of course gave Major the chance to ignore the substantive question and declare that it was the Opposition who were weak and divided. Yah-boo sucks with knobs on. Down came the curtain on Commons New Man, and the pantomime resumed: John Major playing his familiar Buttons, Tony Blair a new Puss in Boots. Another Tuesday, another Labour leader, another honourable draw.

25.10.94   Fearful Minister in Unknown Territory

Even into social security policy has the aura of sleaze now permeated. 'Broken down between sex,' Peter Lilley said yesterday. Madam Speaker looked up, startled. Snoozing journalists stirred in their seats. MPs were mystified. What could the Social Security Secretary mean?

Mr Lilley was being questioned in the Commons after his statement on the Jobseeker's Allowance. Sitting alongside the Employment Secretary, Michael Portillo, he had outlined a series of changes to the benefits system.

Lilley's Labour shadow, the formidably gloomy Donald Dewar, had expressed what Dewar called (and only Dewar would) a measure of 'dubiety' on these proposals.

Mr Dewar's dubiety is extensive, some would say infinite. It seems at times to extend to the possibility that any work of man could ever produce any beneficial change, however slight, to the condition of man.

It extended yesterday to the question of the impact on women of the Government's plan. Dewar wondered how many women would be affected.

Lilley did not know. Mr Portillo, who would from time to time lean across with useful figures where helpful, appeared not to know either. Lilley muttered his apologies somewhat incoherently. Only one phrase was clearly audible, 'broken down between sex'.

Did he perhaps mean 'broken down *by* sex'? Mr Lilley did look rather tired, though even 'worn out' would be taking it too far, and few would describe him as broken down. Besides, it would be unusual for a minister to offer so personal an apology for his failure to provide figures.

The closest precedent that springs to mind was when Jerry Hayes (C, Harlow), in mid-speech to the Tory conference in 1993, stumbled on his words, threw up his hands and said to a thousand delegates: 'I'm making a hash of this, I know. I had a hard night last night.'

But surely ministers do not do that? Any minister tempted at the dispatch box to use this excuse for his lack of homework would hardly choose Donald Dewar as a sympathetic ear.

Tall, stooped and dry, Mr Dewar has a prosecuting intellect and an unforgiving tongue. He exudes a sort of bleak, gale-lashed Calvinism. To Mr Dewar, sex, far from being an excuse for ill-preparedness, would compound the error, adding to the charge of indolence the aura of sin. With Mo Mowlam, perhaps, or just possibly Clare Short, one might enter a plea of personal dissipation in mitigation for not having swotted up one's answers: but not Dewar.

Could it be, then, that Lilley meant not 'sex' but 'sexes': 'broken down between sexes'?

A mental picture of a transvestite by a conked-out car, summoning the AA, swam into our minds, but this was a long way from the Social Security Secretary's responsibilities.

We dismissed it. There was no choice but to accept his words as spoken. Your sketchwriter's guess is that what Mr Lilley wanted to say was that he could not provide the figures Mr Dewar wanted, broken down by sex.

But, as he approached this phrase, some sixth sense warned him off it. The tabloid headline: LILLEY: 'BROKEN DOWN BY SEX' loomed in his imagination. At the last minute he veered off it, clutching wildly at an alternative. Probably he meant to choose the phrase 'broken down between the sexes'.

Panic intervened and it ended up as 'broken down between sex'. Between sex and what? We may never know.

HMS Indignation   *26.10.94*

The Prime Minister appoints the Nolan Committee on standards ...

Tuesday saw the Prime Minister sleaze the initiative in the Commons's current orgy of insinuation, allegation and innuendo.

Faced with a growing clamour that he should act, John Major took what is, for a politician, always the unexpected course: he acted.

There was a feeling that this was somehow cheating.

The Commons was filled with an intangible sense of wind being taken from sails: that strange, loud silence when the breeze suddenly dies. The Chamber, fuller than it has been since the last Budget – so full that the overflow gallery upstairs began to fill with Tory latecomers – seemed to be whistling, noiselessly and collectively, for the wind.

Along the Opposition backbenches as the PM sat down, hundreds of yards of slack canvas flapped irritably in the oily swell: sails, now windless, that had been taut with indignation as he stood up.

Up in the Press gallery pencils dropped, listless, on to notebooks. Fleet Street's end of the tug-o'-war with Downing Street fell back, temporarily off-balance, as Number 10 let go of the rope.

You could almost hear the under-the-breath '*hear-hears*' from the three-piece Savile Row brigade when the PM said 'the new body will advise on general procedures ... rather than investigate individual cases'.

The British Establishment greatly prefers general procedures to individual cases. 'General procedures' has a sepulchral ring: a phrase one might intone in Trinity Chapel. 'Individual cases' has a rude sound, like dropping your aitches, or breeches: the kind of thing chaps were taught in preparatory school never to do in the street.

'General principles' are declaimed at one's constituency association annual general meeting; 'individual cases' are sniggered over in the lavatory at the Carlton Club.

As usual, the back benches on both sides failed to rise to any seriousness the rest of Britain might think the occasion demanded. Labour started shrieking 'snouts in the trough,' 'Tory placemen'; Tories squawked 'Trade-union links! Union sponsorship!'

Nobody, so far as I noticed, spotted the final irony of the afternoon. To deal with national anxieties about quangos, political appointments and party stooges, the Government has announced the formation of a quango, staffed by political appointments nominated by party bosses.

This is the ultimate quango: the super-quango: the 'Cap-that!' quango: the top-of-the-range, turbo-charged, twin-carb, GTI soft-top 320 SE automatic quango with the overhead cam and electric windows.

This is the quango of quangos: the quangissimo, quangorama or quangorooti. This is the quango of quangos, the meta-quango, the prima-quangerina. This is the quintessential quango.

Yesterday, the Mother of all Parliaments gave birth to the Mother of all Quangos.

Palace of Varieties

Sleaze – who needs it? In a mad world growing madder by the hour, your sketchwriter decided to take a stand against the media-borne rabies now infecting the pack and to declare this column a sleaze-free zone.

With the atmosphere at the Commons alive with accusation and normal politics at a virtual halt, I decided to check the alternative. I fled to the House of Lords.

Nobody pays *them* to ask questions. Few care what they ask. Perhaps the mood there would be more convivial? As MPs carped and sniggered not a hundred yards away, their lordships played host to a different cast.

Some were in scarlet and ermine, some in black silk and gold brocade, and one wore an enormous carpet. Peers were welcoming into their midst two fledgeling barons: rather bald, as fledgelings often are, and blinking in the hot television lights, Milords Sheppard of Didgemere and Hambro of – they didn't say; 'Bank?' – were being introduced into their new nest.

The man in the carpet led each in, carrying a gold stick. On each of his shoulders was a line of three of what appeared to be those red Aids-awareness ribbons. It was good to see that political correctness has reached even the most hallowed of our institutions.

There followed a great deal of bowing and scraping, backing and shunting and reading out of royal gibberish, whose details it would be tedious to relate. This sketch has already mentioned that for these bunfights the Lord Chancellor wears what appears to be a badly scorched cornish pasty on his head, but I had searched in vain for a description of the headgear that barons wear. It reminded me of something, but I had been unable to remember what.

Yesterday I realized. Their lordships were wearing giant versions of Rowntree's fruit gums: the blackcurrant ones – the most delicious in the box.

On and on the hocus-pocus went. Truly, our tradition of instant heritage is a wondrous thing. You have to keep reminding yourself that to watch the introduction of a life peer is to witness a pageant whose origins are all but lost in the mists of time (1958), cherished by a nation not many decades older than the United States and enacted in a palace constructed around the same time as St Pancras station.

At last the hoopla seemed to be over. Just when you thought it was safe to look, there was a fresh outbreak. The man in the carpet began leading the two gentlemen in scarlet nighties to a special paddock, where he made them stand side by side while he stood in the pew in front, facing them.

I was close enough to hear the commands he was hissing under his breath. 'Hats off,' he said. They removed their fruit gums. 'Bow'. They swept low. '*Sit!*' The resemblance with a dog-training session was striking. They sat. 'Rise'. They rose. 'Hats on'.

Why, I wondered, doesn't he get one of those whistles they have in sheepdog trials and try doing it from the lobby outside? 'Hats off ...' and so it went on – the whole palaver thrice repeated, in fact. Our two new barons did magnificently. In my personal *One Man and His Dog* rating, Lord Sheppard of Didgemere got 9 out of 10 and Lord Hambro full marks.

The ceremony over, the business of government resumed. A minister, Earl Howe, said Britain's contribution to EU tobacco growing subsidies was about £50 million. But, he added, 'it is surely right that we discourage smoking'.

Back in the Commons, the sleaze war raged on. There are so many madnesses to choose from at Westminster.

28.10.94   # Piddling Poodles Peddle a
                               # Passable Line

The present level of debate at Westminster was well illustrated by John Major's odd use of 'piddling' yesterday when he seemed to mean 'peddling'. The Prime Minister was concerned about people peddling – or was it piddling? – rumour. He employed the word three times in his exchanges with Tony Blair. Once he pronounced it as 'peddling', once as 'piddling' and once in a form which wounded like 'puddling'. The Tory back benches confined themselves, as usual, to poodling.

Up a creek of his own, the Chief Treasury Secretary, Jonathan Aitken, seemed to be paddling. Moments into Treasury Questions, he decided on a pre-emptive paddle and, without provocation, said that Labour's Gordon Brown deserved 'a good kick up his endogenous zone'. He was referring to an arcane speech Brown made weeks ago. Poodles behind Aitken all but wet themselves with delight at this thrust. Brown looked really – well … piddled off. Making yet another 'ho-ho' remark about his endogenous zone is rather like cracking the umpteenth back-to-basics joke to John Major: your victim may choose to respond with a weak smile, or a smack in the face. Brown chose a smack in the face. He demanded to know whether Aitken had himself paid all his hotel bill at the Ritz. It was the Labour poodles' turn to yap.

Madam Speaker protested. Surely this had nothing to do with the question, which was about unemployment? But Aitken felt that, unless answered, these allegations might well have a bearing on unemployment: his own. Asking leave of the Chair to respond, he replied by quoting a letter from the Cabinet Secretary, saying that he (Aitken) had not lied.

Ours is a strange nation. A scaffolder or a pastry-chef might think it beneath his dignity to read aloud, in the presence of his friends and for the benefit of doubters, a letter from somebody else confirming that this person did not consider him a liar: but that is what Privy Counsellors are expected to do.

Dogged Witness   *17.11.94*

If you want to know how the debate on the Queen's Speech went, ask Lucy. Lucy, a new parliamentary commentator, has a reputation for political instinct. Lucy is a dog. She found the debate boring. She wanted to go home. So did we.

Lucy has another job besides commentary. In harness, she guides Labour's health spokesman, David Blunkett. She led her master to his place yesterday afternoon in time for the set-piece debate between

Tony Blair and John Major. Blunkett settled down beside Blair, and Lucy lay on the carpet. Her jet black coat looked unusually lustrous and curly, as though permed for the occasion. She closed her eyes, perhaps to concentrate on the measures to be laid before us.

First came Sir Bob Dunn (C, Dartford) who made the opening speech, by tradition reserved (he said) for 'a genial old codger'. There was general agreement that Sir Bob was an old codger, but some question as to his geniality. He laid into Labour, calling Dennis Skinner a pipsqueak, comparing Tony Blair with a wolf and describing the Thames as designed to keep Essex out of Kent. Lucy lifted her head irritably at these attacks, thought better of her protest, yawned and shut her eyes.

She pricked up her ears to hear the next speaker – by tradition reserved for a young thruster on the Tory benches. At the last election Raymond Robertson (C, Aberdeen S) was the only Tory to reverse a Labour victory at the previous one. Lucy opened one eye in what seemed to be quizzical bemusement as to the secret of Mr Robertson's electoral appeal. As he moved to discuss the virtues of gas deregulation, Lucy closed the eye in despair.

Then came Mr Blair. Lucy sat up, stirred by the stirring of interest around her. She managed to stay alert for the first five or six pages of a speech which never quite got going but somehow never seemed to stop.

Lucy lay down again, closing her eyes.

I cannot say she opened them for Mr Major's speech. Was she listening as he spoke (convincingly) about Northern Ireland?

Did she, like me, note with amusement the PM's report of a visit to a modern British steelworks? 'One of the most efficient steelworkers in the world, at Port Talbot'. Tory industrial policy has reached its logical conclusion. 'Name him!' shouted Skinner.

The speech seemed even longer than Blair's. Mr Major turned to discuss the Criminal Justice (Scotland) Bill. Lucy fidgeted. The PM moved on to the Children (Scotland) Bill. Lucy placed one paw, pleadingly, on Mr Blunkett's leg. He stroked her muzzle.

The PM began to describe the joys of the Medical Act (Amendment) Bill. Lucy stood up and began pawing desperately at Blunkett's thighs.

Mr Blunkett rose with a light tug on Lucy's harness. All but dragging her master behind him, she was off, tail wagging wildly. The rest of us did not get off so lightly.

Dickie Pleases

Attenborough must have thought he was dreaming yesterday. It was a strange dream, taking him back to that famous film set for *Jurassic Park*, where he played the scientific mastermind.

All around him huge, extinct creatures lumbered, slumbered and stirred. Vast scaly beasts and things with wrinkled necks glared, uncomprehending, at the swamp. Re-creations from the long-lost past took living form as the banks of hot lights required for filming beamed down into the prehistoric pit in which the action was taking place. Cameras whirred. Technicians in glass-enclosed boxes peered out at the scene they were monitoring …

Yes, you guessed it. Lord Attenborough was making a speech to the House of Peers.

It was his maiden speech. Whether 'full house' signs were displayed outside the Peers' lobby we could not establish, but every seat was taken. The dress circle above was filled with critics, your sketchwriter among them.

Visibly struggling to keep a hold on his tongue and say 'my lords' whenever he would naturally have said 'my darlings', this distinguished actor-director first asked our forgiveness for not having turned up on set for a speaking role before.

Last year, he explained, he had had to cancel his appearance due to a bout of flu. Earlier this year, when he might have starred at Westminster, his lordship had been obliged to fulfil 'a lengthy professional commitment in the United States'. Then there was a charity do in South Africa in which he had a central role. All in all, it had been a busy year. Peers looked up, impressed. Nice to be in such demand! Frankly, most of their lordships are 'resting'.

Attenborough wished to speak about the Arts. He began his speech in the caves of Stone Age man, as our ancestors began to daub their walls with paint. Listening peers, to whom the historical background is most important, were even more impressed. Most of their speeches start around the time of the Norman Conquest.

We moved on from the caves. It was not long before one of England's greatest living actors was completely immersed in his role. He began to declaim, pausing dramatically for breath and emphasis as the clichés rolled.

'Rich and varied language of Art ... today as a nation we face daunting problems ... the very fabric of our society ... healing a nation divided ... supremely tragic irony ... untold damage ...' It did at one point seem that Attenborough was on the point of bursting into tears.

He recovered himself for a final soliloquy. 'The movies ...', he declared, staring round at his audience of peers as though our revels now were ended, these our peers were all spirits and, like the baseless fabric of this vision, the cloud-capped towers, the gorgeous palaces, would shortly dissolve, and leave not a rack behind ... 'The movies are the mirror we hold up to ourselves'. It was stirring stuff. Following, as it did, a speech of staggering banality from the Archbishop of Canterbury, and an opinion about war crimes from Lord Campbell of Alloway which was so hog-whimperingly tedious that a normally tolerant Chamber of fellow-dozers sat up, astonished that anyone could be quite so boring, Lord Attenborough had little competition.

As his lordship resumed his seat, there were loud cries of 'hear, hear'. Nobody, so far as we could detect, actually *said* 'darling, you were wonderful'. Sadly, the Lord Chancellor did not kiss him.

24.11.94   # The Chamber That Never Sleeps

No MP, it is well known, ever sleeps in the chamber. No Member, except Dennis Skinner, would ever accuse another of such a crime. It would be an affront to the dignity of Parliament for reporters to imply it: we have been sent to the Tower for less. MPs rest their eyes, lower their gaze, or lie back in their seats with both eyes shut to concentrate ... but they never, ever sleep.

So let us be clear that Sir Peter Emery (C, Honiton) was not asleep yesterday. Industry Questions were in full swing. The exchanges – about subsidies to shipyards – were of a complex nature and needed careful thought. Sir Peter was thinking very carefully indeed. Head back, eyes screwed up with concentration, this distinguished buffer was occupying the seat on the front bench below the gangway where Sir Edward Heath when he is there, likes to sit.

Frankly, Sir Peter was not alone in reverie. Your sketchwriter, returned from a generous lunch given by Highland Park Whisky and *The Spectator* to celebrate their annual Parliamentarian of the Year award, was himself concentrating hard on shipbuilding subsidy. Up in the Gallery, I shut my eyes to assist thought.

I was disturbed by a commotion. Skinner was shouting: 'Wake up!' Sir Edward had arrived and was standing by his usual seat, occupied by Sir Peter, who was concentrating. There were spare seats a little further along the bench, but they were not where Sir Edward likes to sit. He was determined to have his own, special place, yet too much of a gent to make a fuss. So he simply stood there.

And still Sir Peter concentrated. People began to laugh. Skinner's taunts continued. Nicholas Winterton (C, Macclesfield) leant across towards Emery to distract him from his shipyard idyll. Laughter grew. Sir Edward stood.

Sir Peter opened his eyes. He looked for a moment as though he was not quite sure where he was. Then it sank in. Honiton moved over. Old Bexley & Sidcup moved in. Sir Edward's impassive features, having betrayed no irritation while he was being disobliged, now betrayed no gratitude that he had been obliged. The proprieties had been restored, that was all.

Honest Ken's Insomnia Cure   *30.11.94*

The budget ...

For centuries Chancellors have bored MPs with Budgets, but yesterday was the first time a Chancellor has bored himself. For so fundamentally candid a man as Kenneth Clarke the effort of pretending he had anything to say was too much. It was a Budget for business, he claimed, unconvinced. It was a Budget for insomniacs.

'I'd like to say a few words about corporation tax and capital allowances,' he said, despair entering his voice. By the time he had reached proposals to tax waste disposal at landfill sites – a jewel in this Budget's crown – Mr Clarke was stifling yawns. As we moved to capital gains tax reinvestment relief on venture capital costs, a look of exhaustion tugged at the Chancellor's chubby features. One junior minister had gone to sleep.

The Commons was all dressed up. Mr Clarke had nowhere to go. It seemed a shame that Joan Lestor (Lab) had come all the way from Eccles, decked in the robes of a Mayan war-goddess, for so little. The Tories' David Ashby sported a matching handkerchief and dickie-bow in tree-frog green for an occasion which failed to rise to his costume. Ted Heath had brushed his white hair into a meringue of spun-sugar, for nothing.

Emma Nicholson (C, Devon W & Torridge), in Day-glo orange, an embraceable traffic cone, was wasted. Diane Abbott (Lab, Hackney N & Stoke Newington) in crimson silk and Simon Coombs (C, Swindon) in a decadent waistcoat which can only be called Louis XIV (we dare him to wear it in Swindon) had squandered their wardrobes on a washout. Teresa Gorman (Independent, Billericay) had found the royal blue of a Quink ink accident, while Bill Walker (C – *just* – Tayside N) had failed to find a tie to match his kilt ... and all to no purpose.

John Major, in his best sky-blue tie with white polka-dots, summed up the mismatch between outfit and occasion. The PM looked like a little fellow dressed by his mum for a birthday party, who hadn't wanted to go, and who now had no appetite for flavourless jelly.

Only once was there any stirring of interest along the Government and Opposition back benches. The Chancellor startled MPs during a passage about youth unemployment by suddenly declaring: 'There will be new pilots under the Work-start scheme'. Surprised faces betrayed all-party alarm at the damage this could do to British Airways' reputation. Perhaps we misunderstood him. Mr Clarke went on to commend Lincolnshire's pioneering 'Jobmatch' scheme: an effort better to match skill to occupation. As a Nottingham criminal barrister turned supremo of the British economy, the Chancellor approved of that.

For your sketchwriter, the occasion was saved by proximity to the MPs' overflow gallery to my left: packed on this big occasion with Tories, I could hear them better than when they are down below. Sir James Spicer entered the Chamber, one injured arm in a huge turquoise cradle. 'It's his love child,' growled a nearby Tory.

'Last time he enters the Commons frisbee competition,' growled another.

Mr Clarke unveiled plans to tax amusement arcade games. 'K Clarke the two-armed bandit,' whispered an MP neighbour. Diving at his whisky more for relief than refreshment, the two-armed bandit ground on. On the Tory benches Patrick Nicholls, a retired Party vice chairman, wore a surgical neck-support. For this Budget, that was the appropriate dress.

Nuclear Waste Question Decently Buried

1.12.94

Paul Beresford, the eminent London dentist, took time off yesterday from his professional practice to look in on his third job. His second job is being Member of Parliament for Croydon Central; but the post he was good enough to grace with his presence after lunch yesterday was yet another hobby to which Sir Paul's broad-ranging intellect has turned: being a junior minister at the Department of the Environment. Labour's John Gunnell wanted to know about new plans to bury radioactive waste and if you want to know about those things you ask a dentist.

'It is very vulgar,' wrote Wilde, 'to talk like a dentist when one isn't a dentist, it produces a false impression'. But Beresford *is* a dentist. The question required him to talk like a nuclear physicist. It is very vulgar to talk like a nuclear physicist when one isn't a nuclear physicist. It produces a serious fallout. Of that fallout the Chief Whip received an early rumbling yesterday, when Michael Brown (C, Brigg and Cleethorpes) rose.

Brown is a government loyalist, but it was not always thus, as your sketchwriter well remembers. It was he and I who in 1986 plotted a coup for which Lord Wakeham (then Chief Whip) will surely never forgive him, and for which he is still admired in Brigg and Cleethorpes. Our plot was hatched in the Tea Room.

The Government was making noises then, as it is now, about burying more low-level nuclear waste and finding new sites. Possible sites had been identified in a number of constituencies, including that of the Chief Whip himself. They also included Brigg and Cleethorpes.

Brown was furious. Local newspapers had spread the alarm, his constituents were up in arms, his Tory association was in panic, and his

Liberal opponents were sharpening their axes. He and I took tea together to discuss the crisis. 'Why don't you threaten to resign the Tory whip?' I said. He mulled it over.

'Not enough,' he said, 'insufficient damage'. He thought a little. 'I know! I'll threaten to resign not just the whip, but my seat. That would mean a by-election. I would stand as an Independent Tory. Unopposed I'd probably win, but if Central Office put in an official candidate, we'd both lose and the Liberal would win.'

'Square your association chairman,' I said. 'Make sure they'd declare themselves for you and have nothing to do with another candidate.'

'Absolutely,' he said.

We were irresponsible young men in those days. We toasted our reckless plan with a round of tea-cakes.

Within weeks, Michael Brown was a local hero, colleagues whose constituencies were similarly threatened were besieged by reporters asking to know why they had not matched Brown's commitment, the nuclear burial plan was effectively dead, and the Chief Whip was incandescent.

And is that plan being canvassed again? You can forget it. Yesterday, all Mr Brown had to say – with just a hint of menace – was this: 'Would it help my hon friend to remind him of the commitment to the electors of Brigg and Cleethorpes I gave in this House in 1986?'

You toucha my constituency, I smasha your majority. At the dispatch box, the dentist quailed. Compared to this, how much friendlier was the world of drills and syringes! How much crueller these methods than the use of pliers and wrenches! Of one thing you may be sure. There will be no new burials of nuclear waste in Tory seats this side of a general election.

7.12.94   # Santa in Hot Pursuit

A sign of the times – an unforgettable moment – occurred for your sketchwriter yesterday morning as I crossed Whitehall. Approaching the traffic island in the middle of the street a familiar figure came running in the opposite direction towards me, panting.

It was the Chancellor of the Exchequer, Kenneth Clarke. He wore a hunted look. Running after him and hot on his heels came another familiar figure. It was Father Christmas. This Father Christmas was plastered with stickers protesting against VAT on heating fuel. Running in a scattering around Santa and his quarry, like foxhounds around a hunt, scampered a handful of press photographers, snapping merrily.

As the chase receded into the distance, Santa seemed to be gaining on the Chancellor and the photographers closing in on both. Whether Clarke's persecutors ever caught him I do not know.

Whether his Commons persecutors caught him in the vote later last night you will by now know. A warning of impending battle was sounded at Prime Minister's Questions. The PM being in Budapest, his place was taken by Tony Newton, the Leader of the House. In the past, squaring up to the late John Smith, Newton has looked ill at ease. Smith had a political weightiness – a statesmanlike quality which Newton lacks.

Facing Newton yesterday was another Tony: Labour's new leader was ready. Thus far, squaring up to John Major, Tony Blair has looked tense and nervy. Major has age and experience which young Blair lacks.

It was Tony *vs* Tony: Smith's replacement *vs* Major's stand-in. Blair was at public school, Newton at an independent school, and both were at Oxford. Both are thin, spare, slightly edgy men: lightweights with classless accents. Both have boyish tenor voices. MPs crowded in for the Parliamentary equivalent of bantam cock fighting.

The two birds were perfectly matched. Newton was not overawed; Blair was not nervous. In a blur of claws each tore at the other: shrieking, jabbing their beaks and flapping their wings. The subject, of course, was VAT. Blair called the Tories unprincipled. Newton squawked 'cop-out' at him over his windfall tax. Blair, his colour rising, snapped that there were 'two types of Tory', honest ones, and Tories who would promise anything to get elected. This caused belligerent howls from supporters of the Tory cock, who strutted to the dispatch box and pecked a beakful of feathers from the Labour bantam, yelling that there was only one type of Labour MP, the cop-out variety. More cheers.

This was too much for the bantam Blair. His own supporters roaring him on, he pecked viciously back and dared to throw a third question (he almost never does) about grinding the faces of the poor. More squawks from Newton, who told his foe to stick to two questions in future. Roars and bellows from all sides ('*Order! All* of you!' – Madam Speaker) and, wings flapping, our two principal chickens were pulled back into their boxes in a flurry of flying feathers.

8.12.94   # Now for the Headache

The Government is defeated over VAT on fuel ...

Yesterday in the Commons was the morning after. You could almost hear the *plink*, *plink*, *fizz*. Did I really do that? Did we really say that? Do you think he'll remember? Is it too late to apologize? Was I totally out of order, or only a bit? Ooh my aching head.

Dennis Skinner summed it up. Squaring up to the Foreign Secretary, who was trying to persuade us to feel interested in the former Yugoslavia and squaring up to half a century of Eton and Cambridge-educated circumspection, the Labour Member for Bolsover said – or rather yelled:

'Why should any Serb or Muslim, fighting each other, believe they've got to take any notice of this broken-backed Government which has lost control over its own rebels, can't raise taxes and has lost its authority?'

With that faintly wounded chuckle at which he so excels, Douglas Hurd replied that he was more used to hearing this kind of outburst from Mr Karadzic in the Balkans than from Mr Skinner in Bolsover.

Elsewhere, the mood in the House gave little indication either of broken backs or of rebellion. It was more like the mood in a household after an exceptionally wild party the night before, a party in which things had got quite out of hand.

Some members of the parliamentary household had enjoyed themselves rather too much. Some had not enjoyed themselves at all. For others, it had all ended in tears. Those who had scored were walking on air. Those who had bombed were looking distinctly sheepish. Everybody needed a good night's sleep.

But it was not inside the Palace of Westminster, but all around it, that the importance of the hour showed. As dusk fell, an aerial view of the site would have shown the Houses of Parliament themselves in near obscurity, and all around it patches of brilliant light as television crews and journalists interviewed ministers, backbenchers, and each other, taking care to keep Big Ben in shot in the background. The Commons appeared like a dark castle, surrounded by a floodlit moat. The chamber had produced its fireworks the night before. The morning after, it was the media who were partying.

PM has a Funny Turn in the Commons

13.12.94

Has the Prime Minister been eating magic mushrooms at Essen? Has he taken up yoga? Acupuncture? Bath salts? Few have ever seen John Major so laid back.

The premier who reported his European summit adventures to MPs yesterday seemed a new man: punchy, confident and witty. Was this cheery cynicism really the demeanour of a man whom the weekend Press had said was fatally wounded, staggering at the cliff's edge? How did this relaxed belligerence fit with the image of a cornered PM, a leader at bay? Why these jests, this merry optimism, from one whom a score of editorials depicted as a broken reed? Major was upbeat, cheeky, rude to his critics, and often funny yesterday. Nobody knows why.

It is difficult, when all the other commentary points to a story of gathering darkness, to know how to report an incident which runs against the gloomy tide. All one can do, then, is report it. Major looked happier than many of us can remember him.

Paddy Ashdown, ever the spoilsport, tried to sour the mood by raising a subject which normally causes an involuntary tightening of John Major's neck muscles: referendums. Neck muscles stayed loose. Casual as you please, Major implied he really had no problems about referendums, as long as there were important questions to ask. 'If there are, we will.'

He must be very confident there will not be. His answer carried something of the hint that, if Britain were to be visited by a fleet of UFOs bearing hordes of little green men with one eye and feelers, he would be happy to have a referendum about that too.

Bill Cash urged the PM to stop a Labour government surrendering to Brussels by calling a referendum in advance. Major suggested that if his hon friend wanted to stop a future Labour government, he might do a little more to assist the present Conservative one. Winston Churchill (often bolshie) asked Major to accept his congratulations on Essen. A wry Major said he was touched.

Labour's Derek Enright accused the PM of persecuting British workers by his Euro opt-outs. Major said that was 'codswallop'. Dennis Skinner yelled something or other of limited coherence. 'Dear oh dear,' said Major. 'I do think he's ageing.'

Another Labour backbencher accused Major of self-delusion. 'If he wants to see self-delusion he should look in the mirror,' snapped our shin-kicking premier. Denis MacShane (Lab) tried another party dig. 'Dear oh dear,' said Major, adding that MacShane shouldn't have bothered. 'It's certainly not worthy of a reply.'

But it was the PM's reply to Teddy Taylor, a Tory without the whip, that astonished by its carefree aggression. Taylor said the Spanish Prime Minister was claiming victory over fishing rights. Unruffled, Major smiled that premiers – *foreign* premiers, that was – often hyped things up for their domestic audiences. González would never face the cross-questioning that British premiers had to answer. 'Some of my fellow heads of government could scarcely find their way to their national parliaments with a guide dog'.

Dear oh dear ...

14.12.94   # Is It a Bird? A Plane?

Imagine you are Foreign Secretary. The High Court has ruled that British aid to a foreign project was unlawful. Should you appeal? You ask your Permanent Secretary to study the case urgently and advise. He asks his staff. Their advice arrives.

'Permanent Secretary: First the bad news, then worse. There are no grounds for an appeal. We'd lose. Second: the project complained of is not alone. We have identified three more that also fall foul of the law. They may well come to light. Can you fix this?'

No, he can't; but he knows a man who can. A very nice man. A very, very nice man. Another memo goes up ...

'Foreign Secretary: pre-festive bother, I fear. Please see the attached – from our legal pests. Statement to the House? Good luck! See you after Christmas. I'm off to the Azores – lovely in December. Humphrey'.

Could a junior minister handle it? No. An Eton and Oxbridge Christopher Reeve is needed: a blend of Jeeves and Wooster with phenomenal powers of sliding out of difficulty. Only SuperDoug could save the day.

MPs filed into the chamber. The mood was expectant. How would the Government wriggle out? The doors behind the Chair swung open. Something tall with wavy silver hair slipped past Miss Boothroyd.

Was it a bird? Was it a plane? No, it was SuperDoug, striding confidently to the Dispatch Box. His mission? To explain.

Readers, have you ever seen those victims of fraud interviewed on television? They are at a loss to explain why they missed the small print; why they ever believed the bland assurances; indeed they are at a loss to remember what the assurances were. They realize it looks like gobbledegook now.

But it sounded so convincing … at the time. That is how it feels after you have witnessed a Hurd explanation. SuperDoug got away with it. Again.

Looking back, one realizes that logic was stood on its head. Reviewing one's notes, I read – with incredulity – this: 'I have not in any way crossed swords with the Court.' What did he mean? That he did not in fact challenge the rule of law? Sentenced, handcuffed and led to the cells, any gangster could say as much.

And what were these other projects, the mini-Pergaus we never spotted? A project to build 'a Metro in Ankara'. *What?* Taxing the British poor to build a Turkish Tube? A 'Botswana flight information' project! But Botswana is a vast, remote semi-desert. Have the bushmen noticed the flight congestion above? 'A television studio in Indonesia.' Come again? 'Helping link a wide-spread community of poor people,' explained SuperDoug.

Crikey, there are parts of Britain where the viewers are still waiting for proper television reception. And nobody except Labour's George Foulkes even bothered to ask about the projects.

Mr Hurd's illogic was staggering. Why was the aid budget not to be reimbursed for years gone by? Budgets were framed to meet commitments, he said, not the other way round. Then why was the aid budget being reimbursed for future years? New commitments, as yet unidentified, he purred, could now be afforded.

SuperDoug was asked why he had continued funding Pergau out of the aid budget after officials said it was wrong. So as not to break Mrs Thatcher's promises, he said: dearie me, one couldn't break promises. That it might be funded out of a different budget – as it will now be – cannot have occurred to him.

Nobody asked him why. SuperDoug is a very nice man, after all: a very, very nice man.

15.12.94   # The Plot and the Putdown

Disturbing news. There has been another break-in at the office of the Leader of the Opposition. Actually sitting at the Leader's desk yesterday evening, a rank Tory was spotted. A Mr Tony Blair, 41, of Islington, is wanted for questioning ...

Wednesday brought a new plot. Keen-eyed observers noticed an odd inquiry down on the Order paper for Foreign Office Questions, from Labour's Tam Dalyell. Tam has smelt more rats than we have had hot dinners. Half the rats he smells are real rats; the other half turn out to be pseudo-rats. The problem is, there is no way at first of knowing which kind of rat Tam is smelling. He does not know himself. At first he allowed only its whiskers to appear in print ...

'*Mr Tam Dalyell (Linlithgow)*: To ask the Secretary of State for Foreign and Commonwealth Affairs, if he will make an assessment of a film, a copy of which has been sent to him.' What film? What was it about? Who sent it? Dalyell was keeping us guessing. 'Question 14,' called Madam Speaker. The reply from Douglas Hogg, Minister of State, deepened the mystery. Decisions to prosecute, he said, were for the police. What could he mean?

Tam's supplementary hardly helped. It was bizarre. More a speech than a question, it started weird and got weirder. Speaking in the low, portentous tones, dark with significance, that he adopts for these occasions, Dalyell asked whether Hogg had seen 'a film by Alan Frankovitch' called '*The Maltese Double Cross*'?

So this was about Malta? Then why did Tam next raise the conduct of 'the hon Member for Southend W'? Was it about Southend? No, for now Dalyell began to talk about 'bombers who were about to be identified'. New clues tumbled out: Bengazi, Tripoli, Lockerbie, Mrs Thatcher ... it now seemed it was the Libyan bombings Dalyell was talking about, except that he claims the bombers were not Libyan at all. MPs listened with growing amazement. How would Hogg reply? He didn't. 'Truth to tell,' he grunted, 'I'm awfully fond of the hon Member, but he does sometimes behave in a dotty manner'.

The minister sat down. Eyes blazing and mouth agape, Dalyell looked like a wounded bull-elephant. MPs giggled and clucked at Hogg's put-down. That Hogg's rudeness was actually less patronizing than (for instance) Douglas Hurd's courtesy would have been, nobody seemed to spot. The Foreign Secretary would have handled Dalyell as a Harrods floor manager might handle a nutty but important customer: with kid gloves, respectfully declining to follow the line of complaint.

But he would have given it no more real consideration than Hogg did: less, in fact, for Hurd cloaks disregard in *politesse*, Hogg cloaks a rather open mind in a brutal manner. If I ever sound dotty, I hope he would tell me so ...

But not, I must warn, through the Commons Chair. Miss Boothroyd was enraged. This was not least (perhaps) because Hogg's apparently incomplete answer led her to believe he had not finished, so she took his answer to the next question (15) as a continuation of his answer to the first one, 14, from Dalyell. Her numbers got into a dreadful tangle.

Her vengeance was terrible. Later, during Points of Order, she told the House she had taken 'considerable exception' to Mr Hogg. Every hon Member, she said, had 'a right to a proper response'. I think she meant a polite response. Nobody at Westminster ever gets a proper response.

Mugwut of St Stephen's   *20.12.94*

On the pavement at the St Stephen's entrance to the Commons yesterday occurred a little scene which could signal a new era.

Not that the scene was unusual: Labour candidates regularly win by-elections, and regularly pose outside the Commons before taking the Commons plunge. Ian Pearson, victor of Dudley, was the latest in a long line of grinning newcomers. So why the excitement, crackling in the dry air of a cold December afternoon? Why the bystanders, straining to see? Why the array of cameras, microphones and technicians, jostling for position behind the crowd barriers?

Because Tony Blair was coming to pose with Mr Pearson. The Labour leader was due at 3.00.

All of a sudden, the world wants to look at him, shake his hand, get his autograph. A nation and its news media who have long known in their heads that the Tories are losing now start to feel in their guts that Labour is winning.

The second follows from the first but there can be a long delay while the reasoning sinks in. It has sunk in now. The strange half-light, in which one Government is written off but the succession is not comprehended, is ending. Leadership begins to pass before a general election sets the seal on its passage. You could tell that from the mood on the pavement.

At 3.05 Tony Blair came out. His hair was perfect.

His dark suit, double-breasted and expensively cut, set off a shirt sufficiently blue to reassure Tory doubters, with a tie red enough to satisfy 'old' Labour yet silken enough to please the City. His shoes were shiny and his fingernails clean. He grasped Pearson's hand.

Mr Blair did not speak, for this was not a speaking engagement, it was a smiling engagement. He just stood, in a frozen handclasp and a frozen smile for 45 seconds while the cameras whirred. There were small cries of joy and squeaks of excitement from the crowd. 'It's *him*,' said the woman next to me.

The 45-second freeze-frame allowed me a hard look at Blair. I realized what he reminded me of. Did you see the film *Gremlins*?

The story begins in cutesy style but turns very nasty. It features a breed of cuddly, fluffy creatures with large pointed ears and sharp teeth. The leading gremlin (at first everybody's pet) is named Gismo. Gismo appears friendly. In this phase a gremlin is called a mugwut.

But under certain conditions metamorphosis can occur. Then the mugwut changes irreversibly. Its behaviour becomes shockingly violent and peremptory, brooking no obstruction. The gremlin's fur loses its strokeable quality, and turns spikey and punk-like. The teeth and ears grow. Claws appear. The creature can be vilely destructive.

According to *Gremlins*, a mugwut goes feral if (a) it ever gets wet; or (b) it is allowed to eat after midnight. Have you noticed how Blair's minders never allow him out in the rain? Have you ever seen Tony Blair permitted anywhere near food after midnight?

After Gismo had clasped Mr Pearson's hand for a while, the whole entourage re-entered the Commons. But shouts of 'come back, Tony,' brought Gismo and Ian out again, alone this time. For stragglers among the snappers, they staged a second smile. Then they were gone, Gismo scuttling up the stairs, the lady next to me murmuring 'isn't he nice?'.

Will Gismo repeat the performance, this time on the steps of Downing Street? Yesterday looked a convincing rehearsal. But only if the rain (and the night-feeding) hold off just a little longer.

The World of Penguins   *24.1.95*

Jet-age intercontinental travel leaves us struggling to adjust. After Christmas your sketchwriter sped to Chile, then Antarctica. There he saw the whole gamut of polar life crowding the shores: teams of portly waddling mammals, full of self-importance, waving their flippers, squabbling in cliques, and guarding their territory.

But try as I might to see them as penguins, I kept seeing them as MPs. It took a week to accept them as wingless birds – and then it was time to go. Waving farewell to Antarctica your sketchwriter jetted in to London hours before the Commons sat yesterday.

And I looked down. There I saw teams of portly waddling mammals, full of self-importance, waving their arms, squabbling over territory. Try as I might to see MPs I kept seeing penguins. Must another week pass before the shriek of the chinstrap penguin and the smell of guano fade from my thoughts at Westminster?

The chinstrap is the closest parallel: a chippy and cantankerous bird, the bovver-boy of the penguin community. But there are other parallels with MPs: in Antarctica, as in politics, plankton is the elemental form of life. Krill feed off plankton. Penguins feed off krill. Seals feed off penguins. Nobody much eats seals.

At Westminster too the plankton are where it all starts. Yesterday David Congdon (C, Croydon NE), a retired computer consultant and sometime member of Croydon council, asked Social Security ministers to permit him to welcome their decision to cap housing benefit.

Geoffrey Clifton-Brown (C, Cirencester & Tewkesbury) was keen to welcome the reformed habitual residence test.

Never mock plankton, a primitive form of life but basis of the party food-chain and noble in their way. Where the current goes, there will the plankton be. Nor should we mock the krill, a prawn-like being with rudimentary powers of self-propulsion.

Yesterday Peter Pike (Lab, Burnley), admittedly a rather large prawn, was ritually outraged about Tory management of income support; while David Evennett (C, Erith & Crayford) was overjoyed that the Government's medical tests for incapacity were 'seen to be fair and consistent'.

Such expressions of opinion are habitually greeted with supporting sighs of assent or dismay from the massed plankton, wriggles of excitement from other krill ...

... And shrieks and pecks from the penguins.

Yesterday Angela Eagle (Lab, Wallasey), a feisty little chinstrap, squawked at ministers that legions were being ripped off by occupational pensions, while John Marshall (C, Hendon S), a portly penguin, flippered his fellow-birds into a show of support for rent-ceilings for housing benefit.

Alan Duncan (C, Rutland & Melton), a trim bird, his beak a-jab, led the younger Tory chinstraps in an attack on Tony Blair's pension proposals.

The seals had seen it all before. Down below the gangway, old buffers with tummies bask near-horizontal in the lights, whiskers a-twitch, emitting the occasional low bark as the debate (or dyspepsia) moves them.

Yesterday Sir Peter Emery (C, Honiton) kept a weather-eye open from his favourite rock next to Sir Edward Heath's reserved sand-patch. Labour has its ageing bull seals too (and cows) though of late Mr Hattersley has been missing from the beach.

But when those old boys want to settle a score or take a careless penguin they can move with astonishing speed and power. But mostly they daydream ...

Or do I?

Early Birds Enjoy the Cream   26.1.95

Pubs are to open on Sunday afternoons – and now a new victory for consumer choice! Parliament is open on Wednesday mornings. For us, no more queueing at 2.30 to drink at the fount of wisdom provided by MPs.

Yesterday was launch day. A waiting world (of three journalists) could move straight from our Weetabix to the assertion by an MP that 95 minus 67 is 17 and that the Foreign Secretary should resign. Both assertions were made before morning coffee. Over biscuits we could watch a shadow-minister, Labour's George Foulkes, make what Jim Lester (C) described as 'his normal, colourful, florid and inaccurate' speech, after which Mr Lester made his normal, ponderous and worthy one.

Then we were able to witness an hour and a half of a lawyer who looks like Mr Blobby lecturing a lawyer who looks like Zippy in *Rainbow*, before an audience consisting of one black lawyer and one white lawyer.

All this, and more: then Questions to the Scottish Secretary (about roadside services on the A9) at 2.30. Truly, Wednesday was a cornucopia of passion, insight and concern. It was too much for the Strangers' Gallery whose 14 occupants at the start had dwindled to seven within 20 minutes, half having no doubt left in shock.

Jim Marshall (Lab), before turning to his speech about the Pergau dam affair, welcomed the morning experiment, recalling the last one, in 1967. That was 17 years ago, he explained. As he spoke I counted (discounting officeholders) three MPs voluntarily present on the Government side. Two had come to make speeches themselves. Nobody knows why the third came; nobody understood why he stayed.

The first of our two Tory orators was Michael Jopling who made a deeply-felt speech congratulating himself. His suggested reform (morning sessions) had failed before, he said, only because debates were too controversial. This debate was uncontroversial. Marshall had called on the Foreign Secretary to resign and Labour's George Foulkes had described the Pergau affair as 'a sickening example of the culpability of this discredited Government' and insinuated that Mrs Thatcher had been trying to enrich her family. His fury at the Government had 'the total support of the Labour Party'. Bearing a lonely burden, Mike Watson, the only backbencher behind him, glared supportively into space.

A small audience? Yet numbers yesterday were swollen by the allure of two novelties: this was the first morning session: and for many the first chance to see George Foulkes exploding before lunch. It is not that Foulkes lacks energy – the volatile Scot has a bombshell quality – it is just that, as bio-rhythms go, one had always supposed that Foulkes's peaked later in the day. After a Scotch Whisky Association reception last year Mr Foulkes unfortunately collapsed in disorder on top of a policeman. If that was Foulkes by night, many had wondered what Foulkes by morning might be.

I can report that he was magnificent. This tubby whirlwind, creating his own weather system, blew himself into a localized but intense hurricane, bellowed 'systematic abuse and corruption!' at the Tories, and so impressed Mike Watson (Lab) that Watson called for morning sittings on Monday, Tuesday and Thursday as well.

What? Foulkes with your Shredded Wheat every day? *Embarras de richesses!*

1.2.95   # MV Bottomley Surges Past Dazed Penguins

Mrs Virginia Bottomley swept into the Chamber yesterday in black, cerise and a silk scarf, to offer us (as Margaret Beckett observed) 'a great many statistics, some of which are correct'.

There is something awesome about Virginia Bottomley. She ploughs, relentless, across her field like a reinforced icebreaker smashing its way at full steam through a sea of pack-ice. It is done with no great delicacy but enviable power. Commons penguins look up in wonder from their floes as the MV *Bottomley* goes crashing past, billowing statistics from her funnels while the ice field cracks before her. The sheer momentum of a Bottomley at the dispatch box astounds.

Yesterday a group of Labour backbenchers tried to block her course. As each rose and was bashed back down, her eyes began to blaze. She looked wildly around the Chamber with a 'who's next?' glance – half belligerent, half coquettish.

The Liberal Democrats' Alex Carlile was presumptuous enough to ask why spending on mental health services was so niggardly in London.

Three blasts on the ship's whistle and she was away. She hit him with specialty centres for cancer, with specialty cardiac centres, with what she called 'supervised discharge' and 'a more assertive, proactive approach' ... She hit him with hospitals, she hit him with Sir Louis Blom-Cooper, she hit him with sympathy and she hit him with concern. The one thing she did not hit him with was an answer.

Five yards away sat her husband Peter. Mr B stared at Mrs B adoringly throughout. He gritted his teeth when she gritted hers; he glared at her hecklers; he smiled in triumph when she scored. One Bottomley gazed up at another with such bottomless adoration that we felt very sure that even after all these years, power, among Bottomleys, is still an aphrodisiac.

Ghoulish Unionists Betray Their Fears

3.2.95

Rather like Banquo's ghost, your Ulster Unionist MP now moves into his favourite role: the resident spectre of the Commons. He sees himself as the betrayed, here to haunt his betrayer: come amongst us to shriek, rattle his chains, and generally float around in a phantasmagorical manner.

He visits the Chamber to remind governments of nemesis and judgment: to howl, rattle his chains, and display his wounds – a living victim sent to represent living victims, visible symbol of the treachery of England, confronting us with our perfidy, and threatening nameless retributions.

The one thing the Unionist MPs never do is cheer up or join in. Nobody has ever heard an Ulster Unionist say anything in the Chamber which raised the spirits or lifted the heart. It is times like these when we sense a weird paradox: that your Unionist fears and distrusts England, with which he protests himself to be seeking a deeper Union, more than he hates the rest of Ireland, towards which he displays a ritual but knock-about hostility.

So do not imagine that the Ulster Unionists are upset. They love times like this, times which confirm their myths and offer them their cue.

Yesterday, John D Taylor (UUP, Strangford), a heavy, powerful, iron-haired man, left his chains behind but sat in on Treasury Questions to grind his teeth audibly in public and say 'boo' to the Conservative Party.

Is it wise, he asked the Chancellor of the Exchequer, 'to continue to raise interest rates in advance of a general election?' A little, nervous giggle ran across the Government benches. Luckily for the Tories, Kenneth Clarke does not believe in ghosts and took no notice of the imprecation.

Some way behind the Chancellor sat Ann Winterton (C, Congleton), next to Ian Paisley, who had chosen a massive suit in battleship grey for the occasion. The Wintertons do talk to ghouls, and Mrs Winterton was talking to Mr Paisley, who was whispering something to her.

Other Tories pretended he wasn't there. Nobody really knows why Paisley and his flesh-creeping sidekick, the Rev William McCrea (DUP, Mid Ulster) a gospel singer known in the Province as the Singing Nun, sit among the Tories. They certainly do not support them. Your sketchwriter's view is that it is to put the wind up them.

7.2.95 # Knight of the Shires Roams Robin Hood Country

Not so long ago and perhaps a little belatedly, the Queen knighted Jerry Wiggin (C, Weston-super-Mare). This will have surprised only Jerry Wiggin, who in his own mind had been a knight for decades and must have been a trifle disappointed that Her Majesty took so long to notice. 'Mr Wiggin' had never sounded right.

There is something touching about the way self-assurance settles about the shoulders of a middle-aged backbencher. Not, of course, that Sir Jerry lacks distinction. He was Parliamentary Secretary at the Ministry of Agriculture, Fisheries and Food from 1979–81. According to the *Register of Members' Interests*, he is a consultant to British

Sugar, an adviser to the British Marine Industries Federation, an adviser to the Weighing Federation and the Security Industry Federation and a consultant to Sears plc. To crown these adornments (and this is what must have swung it with Her Majesty) he is an adviser to the British Holiday and Home Parks Association.

Stuck for small talk at the Honours Investiture ceremony, the Queen could have consulted the register and asked him about his sponsored visit in 1992 to Photokina, Cologne, as the guest of Kodak Limited. Or she might have inquired about the market research for which, apparently, he kindly undertook to visit France in 1993 as a guest of British Midland Airways. Educated at Eton (shooting colours) and Cambridge (shooting colours) and a man of many parts, Sir Jerry radiates a natural dignity and sense of self-worth, such as might befit a sultan of Somerset and nabob of Weston-super-Mare. I like to imagine him helping with the donkey rides.

And Sir Jerry is also a retired tenant farmer. It will have been knowledge gained in this field which led him into the chamber yesterday afternoon to debate the Agricultural Tenancies Bill (Lords) (Second Reading). Sir Jerry told the Agriculture Minister, William Waldegrave, that his new Bill was more or less on the right lines.

It is one of the delights of parliamentary life to watch a knight of the shires sharing the special knowledge he has gained with a wider public. Peering over his half-moon glasses at Mr Waldegrave, he expressed his pleasure that 'the various interested parties have managed to agree'.

Sir Jerry began to bristle a little as he described the iniquities of the former system for agricultural tenancies. It was based on 'the Robin Hood principle' he said, his colour rising. The rich had been robbed to pay the poor. Tenants had had a good deal. Now, some would 'scream their heads off'. And 'what right' had anyone to be a farmer? Sir Jerry was quivering with outrage.

He moved, briefly ('the fact of the matter is'), to attack county council smallholdings and to touch on the Less Favoured Areas Ewe Premium. Not for nothing had the 93 members of the public now staring down in bafflement from the Strangers' Gallery travelled to Westminster to witness our Mother of Parliaments in action. Around him, the five other backbenchers in the Chamber fidgeted. Upstairs, the two journalists in the Press Gallery rested their pencils.

And I asked myself whether in the history of the world any square yard has ever been occupied by anyone more confident of his opinion, secure in his authority, or disregarded by everybody else, than a Tory backbencher of a certain age and status, debating a specialized subject of which he has personal experience, at half past five on a Monday afternoon?

8.2.95   # Antonio and Giovanni

It is unusual to see Norma Major at the Commons, let alone Joan Sutherland. But yesterday both Sutherland and her biographer, Mrs Major, watched in horror from the Special Gallery as Norma's husband slugged it out on the floor of the House with Tony Blair.

Shrieks of 'dimwit' from Major, and 'disabled' from Blair filled the air, while backbenchers roared. Might Betty raise her baton and Dame Joan lead Norma and friends in Verdi's *Anvil Chorus*? It only needed an anvil and Allan Stewart's pick. Both women looked stunned.

As opera, however, the first problem Sutherland will have diagnosed in PM's Questions was that yesterday's soprano (the SNP's Margaret Ewing) was scratchy and shrill. Her unstructured aria about the rape of industry lacked generosity. Her gestures were wooden, there was no light and shade, and her voice cracked on 'manufacturing base'.

Then came Giovanni Maggiore, playing 'Prime Minister'. Dame Joan will immediately have spotted a difficulty this actor is having with the part. Maggiore is a soft baritone of limited vocal range, attempting what is essentially a tenor role in the heroic mould. Thus, in his quieter and more thoughtful passages he sings pleasingly, but where pitch and volume need to be raised Maggiore suffers a painful constricting of the throat which produces a sound not unlike that of a chainsaw in a distant forest. Yesterday was a case in point. The libretto of this scene, after Antonio Blair challenges Maggiore to say where he stands on a single currency (in the celebrated passage: '*Dammi una riposta: si o no?*'), calls for a thundering denunciation of Labour's Leader; but as Maggiore's recitative listing dates, criteria and agenda for the IGC gathering in 1996 swelled to its climax (with growling background *continuo* from the Tory chorus) there was a knotting of the vocal cords.

The climax itself – Maggiore's famous shout of '*cretino*!' (subtitled 'dimwit!' at the Commons yesterday) – emerged more a strangled yelp than the full-throated denunciation for which the script calls. Shouts of Bravo from elements in the audience owed more to sympathy than admiration. Upstairs in the Gods a hissed chant of 'Giovanni was my toyboy' from the tabloid scribblers was suppressed by the ushers.

Then came the second leading man, Antonio Blair, current heart-throb in Covent Garden and La Scala. Joan Sutherland may have sensed that for all his boyish good looks, this light and engaging tenor displays serious limitations in a leading role.

A deeper, richer timbre is called for: Blair has no reach into the bass register at all. Wherever an *appassionato* passage is reached young Antonio flips up an octave, his eyes rolling and his voice taking on an unpleasing metallic edge. The suspicion grows that we are listening not so much to an historic declaration as an irate telephone call. The '*Si o no?*' aria should have been majestic. The role calls for stature. Antonio Blair had none.

Having observed Antonio's recent performances, your critic has formed an impression which may have struck Dame Joan, too. This tenor is not born to be an operatic hero: he is a natural stage villain. No Othello, Blair is an ideal Iago, Scarpia or dwarf Alberich. He could play the poisoner in *Lucia di Lammermoor*. Listening to Mr Blair on *Today*, I sense that his is a voice (like Clive Jenkins in the 70s) which the nation could come to detest. The third miscast tenor to sing yesterday was Petruccio Ashdown. For him, surely, Puccini created Lieutenant Pinkerton?

Loneliness of the Long-Distance Liberal

14.2.95

'Un homme avec Dieu est toujours dans la majorité.' Numbers don't count as long as God's on your side, said John Knox – but why in French? For Paddy Ashdown any language would have served, yesterday. There must be Mondays when the loneliness of the long-distance Liberal Democrat gnaws at the stoutest heart, but Mr Ashdown always manages to convey the impression that God is a Liberal Democrat too.

There he stood, backed by a little cheering claque of fellow Liberals, itself backed by a big green leather sea of empty Opposition benches, making a brave speech about our common European destiny, while Tories giggled, a couple of Labour backbenchers chatted among themselves, and Dennis Skinner (Lab, Bolsover) kept up a machine-gun stutter of toxic expletives.

Poor Mr Ashdown: it was actually quite a good speech. Each Liberal Democrat leader fancies himself on guard duty over the Liberal conscience during the long watches of the night. He keeps his hopes alive by whistling in the dark and scanning the horizon for the glimmer of dawn. Will it be him who leads his troops into the sunrise of a Liberal revival? The dawn never comes. Whistle on.

Ashdown was whistling bravely. He has the advantage of believing what he says about Europe. He has the disadvantage of being the chap Dennis Skinner has devoted the second half of his life to tormenting. Skinner has positioned himself permanently right in front of Ashdown and sits directly beneath the same microphone. It is almost impossible to get a television shot of Ashdown without the leering image of Skinner directly in front. It is totally impossible to hear an Ashdown speech unpeppered with ridicule. Skinner has turned himself into an audio-visual limpet.

Like one of those creepy late-night films in which the toys come alive and an innocent nursery tale flips into a gothic horror-movie, this is the story of a Liberal organ grinder dogged by a loony-Left monkey gone feral, refusing to depart, clawing his shoulder, shrieking and spitting, and spoiling his music with demon cackles and a lunatic grin.

When Ashdown finally passes on to the great Liberal Democrat pasture in the sky and they place a modest headstone, eulogizing his virtue, by his grave, Skinner's smaller memorial will be found just in front, blocking it and poisoning the flowers. It will be inscribed with lapidary grafitti: a spoilsport footnote to a Liberal life.

16.2.95   # Saint Gumgum

Wearing a cream tie decorated with enormous pink pigs, John Gummer yesterday went ape, about Streatham High Road. Nobody knows why the Environment Secretary so spectacularly lost his rag. Questions were as hog-whimperingly boring as ever: Labour spokesman Keith Vaz no oilier than usual: and Streatham High Road has until now hardly drawn a tut-tut, let alone provoked a Cabinet minister to a fit of blind rage.

But there it was. Gummer lashed himself into a storm on Streatham High Road. The storm did not break at the beginning. The question came from Keith Hill (Lab, Streatham), who said out-of-town shopping was taking trade from Streatham High Road, and asked the minister to refuse appeals for planning approval.

Gummer said he couldn't comment as an appeal was pending, but indicated sympathy with Mr Hill's concerns. John Marshall (C, Hendon S) protested that out-of-town shopping drew custom only because customers preferred it.

Marshall was wasting his breath. In this Cabinet Gummer represents an inglenook ungraced by Adam Smith's bust. Fogeys in flight from vulgar Thatcherism may rest there, the small talk being of how dreadful it is to have women priests, how sad that cobblers' shops are dying out, how maddening that you can't get nut packets open, nobody sells sherbet any more, the new version of the Lord's Prayer does not mention God, and BR serves UHT milk. I know these people. You met them at Cambridge: they wore gowns to Hall although you didn't have to, and wanted the Grace to be in Latin. They had usually been to grammar school. It was of such that Lady Chetwode (after meeting Betjeman) said 'We invite people like that to tea, but we don't marry them.'

Gummer answered Marshall with mounting impatience. 'I'm not going to be drawn on Streatham High Street,' he declared in heroic tones, for all the world as though taken by Satan on to a mountain and tempted with every pleasure to which flesh is prone. St Gumgum was piously resisting the last and greatest enticement of all: the temptation to be drawn on Streatham High Street.

Then Labour's Keith Vaz chipped in. A genial young man of whom the worst that can be said is that he sounds occasionally oleaginous and occasionally scheming, Mr Vaz delivered a harmless homily on the need to resist what he called the 'monstrous sheds' of out-of-town shopping, and welcomed Gummer as a late convert to the Vaz point of view.

And Gummer completely flipped. This, he squealed, was pretty rich, coming from Vaz. The whole of Britain was littered with Labour's planning disasters. Nothing since the War had done more damage.

How dare Vaz lecture him? 'The hon gentleman really ought to retain himself [*sic*].' Labour didn't *have* a planning policy. Gummer's party did. Gummer's party didn't rat on promises, as Labour did. On and on he yelled at the startled Vaz.

His little eyes popping out with fury, his head jerking like a thing possessed, his tie swinging and pink pigs flapping all over the place, the Secretary of State's rage blew over only when he literally ran out of air in his lungs to shout with, and subsided back on to the bench, eyeballs swivelling as he gasped for breath.

If this is what Streatham High Road can do to Mr Gummer, think what Tooting Bec Common, Streatham Hill, or Streatham ice rink might do, and quake.

24.2.95   # Catch-22 Quango

Lord Nolan concludes his investigation ...

Sadly, there were no hymns. The Methodist Central Hall, however, was a quaintly appropriate venue. Yesterday morning Lord Nolan and his committee on 'standards in public life' assembled there to wind up six weeks of evidence-gathering. I went along to watch.

Lord Nolan has one of those round, amiable, glowing faces that speak of Wright's Coal Tar soap and a vigorous towel-dry. With his hair parted in the middle and his sympathetic smile he reminds us of the chap on the front of Quaker Oats packets.

He was flanked yesterday by about three and a half pages' worth of *Who's Who*. As the Great Ones discussed the need to scoop public appointments from a more democratic pool, I cast my eye across their names. Not a single Mr. Two lords (both Rt Hon), two MPs (both Rt Hon and one of them a CH), three more knights, a dame, a professor and a lady styled 'Diana Warwick'.

To watch the committee yesterday was to sense how, once a body like this has been set up, every pressure is upon it to conclude that something needs to be done. Otherwise, why would they have been set up? And the more they recommend should be done, the more valuable they will be judged to have been. Only Tom King yesterday questioned the need for action with any vigour.

I watched the committee cross-questioning a Labour MP, Tony Wright, who had written a pamphlet. Within seven minutes of his arrival he had proposed the establishment of a massive new body: the Public Service Appointments Commission.

This would be a quango. The Nolan committee was being asked to recommend it. One quango creating another quango to supervise more quangos. Perhaps the closing hymn should have been *Wider Still and Wider*.

Rogue Chancellor   28.2.95

MPs respond to the collapse of Barings Bank ...

Rogue was the catchword yesterday. 'One rogue trader,' we heard, had caused a spectacular City collapse. MPs listened to a Statement describing a rogue operator who was 'a single trader'. And who might this rogue operator be?

Ken Clarke's chubby, ruddy countenance and cheeky grin, his eternal optimism in the face of apparent ruin, misled some of us into supposing that this Statement was *about* the Chancellor, rather than by him. A beaming Clarke described how a single chap, operating at arm's length from the organization of which he was supposed to be part, could spread mayhem where there had been order. A resumé, surely, of the Chancellor's own career?

With only a desk, a computer and a telephone, explained our jovial Chancellor, a fellow can now mislead the markets worldwide. Not half, eh Ken!

Maybe Clarke had a certain fellow-feeling with Barings' own rogue operator. Alone at his desk at Number 11, after all, the Chancellor has wrecked the Prime Minister's careful new line on a single European currency. With only a word-processor and a City lectern he has rocked sterling. 'Unauthorized dealings,' said Mr Clarke yesterday, 'undetected until too late.' One could almost hear the sigh from Number 10. Our rogue operator, Clarke, continued, had 'inevitably' caused 'some turbulence'. We thought of his recent remark that monetary union had no constitutional implications. Unauthorized?

Should Government crack down on such operators?

Ah well, pleaded the Chancellor, it was important that we refrain from heavy-handed interference.

'He has now left his desk,' said Mr Clarke of Barings' man. We thought of Clarke's desk at the Department of Education, where teachers are still angry. We thought of his desk at the Department of Health: nurses still recoil at his name. We thought of his desk at the Home Office, left with only the Sheehy report ticking gently upon it. This Barings fellow is just a novice: he has left only one desk so far!

'I suppose he finds it embarrassing,' chortled the Chancellor, 'to describe his responsibility' for wrecking 'an entire 250-year-old banking group'. The Conservative Party, we mused, is older yet. 'His explanation will indeed be interesting.'

Why doesn't Kenneth Clarke wear a bow tie? To observe this Chancellor's irrepressible insouciance as a great bank goes down is to wonder whether there is any event at all which could dent his jollity. The South Sea bubble? 'A necessary correction to over-ambitious trading.' The Great Depression? 'These things are cyclical.' The Black Death? 'A helpful reminder about standards of public sanitation.' The San Francisco earthquake? 'A slight rearrangement of the Earth's crust. To have left it any longer could have caused greater damage.'

MPs who had arrived under some misapprehension that the financial world was reeling under a massive blow were cheered as much by Mr Clarke's jaunty air as by his words. He took particular pains to thank the Governor of the Bank of England for working 'over the weekend' to find a solution. The Governor immediately abandoned his skiing holiday in Avoriaz without even unpacking his bobble-hat. Was there no limit to Eddie's commitment?

But Clarke saved his best reassurance until last. To troubled back-benchers he explained that all this had happened 'on the far side of the world'.

One could feel the sense of collective relief. Thank heavens it wasn't in Cleethorpes.

Electric Debate Illuminates a Static Policy

2.3.95

The Government shakes off an Opposition ambush on Europe ...

Set-piece debates often fall flat. Unusually yesterday, a big Commons occasion provided static electricity in megawatts, and two fine and memorable Commons performances. They could hardly have been more different from each other.

The Labour leader was crisp, sharp and super-articulate. He moved with a light touch through scrawled notes, departing easily from them to meet the moment. Interrupted by a Tory, Blair spat back: such interruptions were 'all set out in the Conservative Research Department brief'. Labour cackled. Tories hid their briefing packs – and Blair moved swiftly off the question.

But the core of Blair's performance yesterday was a passage which MPs will remember as 'the five questions'. He read out four statements from Cabinet ministers expressing wildly different views on the single currency. After each he challenged the Prime Minister – unable to respond – to say if he agreed.

Then Blair read out a fifth remark. It was a direct quote from Major himself – as you could see from the Prime Minister's grin and nod.

But Blair had shrewdly calculated that Major was unlikely to leap up and say: '*I* said that.' Labour's leader then presented his opposite number's silence as an unwillingness to agree even with himself. Everyone roared with laughter.

It was clever and it was funny. That it was *slightly* cheating is an observation which weighs little at the time, sinking quietly into the memory, to wait as subliminal evidence in case other such evidence should join it. Likewise, Blair's refusal to allow or respond to a second interruption from Norman Lamont sent a little flurry of unease down into the subconscious. One would normally give way to the previous Chancellor of the Exchequer. What was the Leader of the Opposition worried about?

The more you hear Mr Blair, the more you hear the courtroom lawyer. Deft, sharp-toothed and persuasive, he picks the policeman's evidence to pieces. You nearly forget that another character is also on

trial: his client's. Here the advocate's evasions almost escape notice …
but not quite. You are left with a nameless doubt.

He sat down – and John Major stood up – to a huge cheer. The Prime
Minister so often fails to rise to these occasions, but yesterday he did.
His voice lost its flatness: it rose and fell; he varied his pace; and he
injected light and shade into his delivery.

As ever, Mr Major was not seriously troubled by questions or
interruptions from the other side: it was his friends who caused him
difficulty.

Sitting with his arms folded, Norman Lamont was perhaps
pondering whether to break with tradition and ask a helpful question.
Tradition won. Mr Lamont put in the knife with a quote from Mr
Major's other friend, Kenneth Clarke. Mr Major winced. Many good
speeches, like so many good novels, contain a passage about which the
meaning of the whole construction turns. Sometimes this is a matter of
tone, sometimes of logic. Yesterday, both logic, Mr Major's own tone,
and the cheer which followed, pointed to this sentence: 'I make no
apology for deciding, as a matter of national policy, that we should not
make such a decision without the facts at our disposal.'

He had decided not to decide. That this might be more rational than
it appears was not lost on the government benches.

'Wait and see' is a fine English phrase. Perhaps Mr Major has
decided to make a virtue of it.

3.3.95　　　　　# Mr Lamont Asks a Question

This sketch is becoming worried about Norman Lamont. He is starting
to behave rationally. This, as everyone at Westminster knows, is political
suicide. It defies a superior rationality known as the survival instinct. In
politicians a sudden craving to be rational represents what seeing your
whole life flash before you represents in drowning men: a kind of
hallucination triggered by despair. Woolly minded outlooks are to MPs
what wet noses are to dogs: a sign of health. Every MP knows the horror
of the insistently logical constituent whom you wish would go away.

Mr Lamont asks the Prime Minister questions about Northern
Ireland – such as whether and when the terrorists will be made to lay

down their arms. These questions are fair and logical. They go to the heart of the issue. They should, therefore, never be asked. Colleagues shake their heads: 'Poor Norman. Worrying about the Union when he should be worrying about his peerage.'

On Wednesday, to Tony Blair's chagrin, Lamont asked the Labour leader how he reconciled what he says now with what he said in 1983: that membership of the EEC removed Britain's economic freedom. It was not offside to ask such a question: what was offside was to expect an answer, and sulk when he did not get one. Rightly, Mr Blair took no notice of Lamont's inquiry. When Lamont tried to ask a second question, Blair refused to let him – presumably in the belief that it would be the same as his first. A wise precaution, but Lamont began fidgeting like a man with piles.

He was soon on his feet again, asking the Prime Minister whether he agreed with Lord Lawson (his predecessor as Chancellor) that a single currency meant political union; or with Kenneth Clarke (his successor) that it did not. A very reasonable, apt and lucid question, so it was crazy to expect a reply.

As the PM is a gentleman and Lamont is one of his own side, Major was not so rude as to refuse an answer: he promised one later. This is a version of the Queen Mother's response to unwanted invitations: 'Perhaps another time.' Meant as a courtesy, it was taken as an affront. Lamont's piles began to play up again. By the time I left the Chamber, his face was ashen.

And when he rose yet again, this time to interrupt the Foreign Secretary and ask the same question, you could almost hear the flap of the vultures' wings. A chap, if he's a *chap*, in the Tory party, does not ask the same question twice of his own front bench. He takes a hint. Lamont's old colleagues muttered angrily, reminding themselves of all the questions they could have asked him once, let alone twice, but did not, when he was Chancellor.

Yesterday, Mr Lamont stalked into the chamber: in George Eliot's phrase, 'like a malign prophecy'. Time was when his arrival caused a hush in the Commons. Yesterday it caused a giggle. Labour MPs made a space for him on their side, pretending to wave him over. Tories looked away.

In the Conservative Party you can be taken seriously and regarded with affection; or taken seriously and regarded without affection; or regarded as nuts but with affection; or regarded, without affection, as nuts. As one who occupied mostly the third category and saw this or either of the first two categories as tolerable places to be, but looked with horror upon the fourth, your sketchwriter wishes to advise Mr Lamont that the danger is imminent. Rationality beckons, Norman – and that way lies destruction.

7.3.95 # Virtual Minister Proves There Can't Be Anything to the Job

Bad dreams recur, and some are familiar to many. One of the commonest is of being thrust into an unaccustomed role: on a stage but unacquainted with the script; in the pilot's seat but unable to fly; or in an exam room, but ignorant of the syllabus.

A variation on this might be to find yourself at the dispatch box on a Monday in the Commons, facing the Opposition as a junior minister for the Civil Service, but knowing nothing about the Civil Service. Indeed, so far as you can remember, you were not even a minister on Sunday. Dennis Skinner is shouting: 'You dirty, double-rat!'

Mr John Horam, MP, found himself in the middle of exactly this nightmare yesterday afternoon. He was the Prime Minister's last-minute replacement for the minister Robert Hughes who resigned over the weekend. Horam had had literally hours to bone himself up on his new job, and prepare for the questions on the Order Paper. It would have been upsetting if he had come unstuck. It was somehow even more upsetting that he did not. There really cannot be anything to the job.

Had we not known of the circumstances, we would never have guessed, apart from Labour's jeers. Horam looked and sounded as though he had been a Civil Service minister all his life. Had Mr Major wandered down the Strand, picked someone at random from a bus queue, and offered him or her a morning's Civil Service coaching in not answering questions, would we have noticed anything untoward? It's profoundly unsettling. If you don't know anything about flying, you cannot be a pilot. From this we conclude that pilots are useful. But if you don't know anything about the Civil Service, you can still be a Tory minister. From this we conclude that Tory ministers are not useful. Horam was once a Labour minister – but it made no difference. He was once an SDP spokesman – but it made no difference. In calling him a dirty double-rat, Skinner omitted one of Horam's rat-incarnations. 'Triple-rat' would have been more accurate. The point is: any rat will do.

The day cannot be far off when they will install one of those hot-chocolate vending machines at the dispatch box, with an internal tape-recording programmed to say 'my Honourable Friend is absolutely right' (to Tory questioners) or 'that's pretty rich, coming from the party which had to go to the IMF with a begging bowl in 1976' (to Labour questioners) or 'what *would* be interesting would be to discover the Hon Member's own policy on this issue, as his party has several' (to Liberal Democrat questioners).

No, the really disturbing nightmare is not that John Horam couldn't handle it, but that he could. A question on quangos? What could be easier? Governments, all governments, are concerned about quangos in general, but attached to them in particular.

A question about the hiving off of public services? As a Tory, Horam could make the case for hiving off public services just as easily as he could make the case against, when a Labour MP.

And there was a question on the importance of science. No minister – Labour, SDP or Conservative – doubts the importance of science. Mr Horam was sure, yesterday, that science was important.

And I reviewed his performance on video. Alone in a darkened room it was virtual reality. A virtual minister in a virtual vacuum; a virtual U-turn in political allegiance – and virtually indistinguishable from all the rest.

Vehement Veggie   9.3.95

'There's an old joke in the East End,' Tony Banks began. 'Yes. And you're it!' shouted several Tories, suffused already with that old East End spirit.

Mr Banks (Lab, Newham NW) was recommending his Bill promoting vegetarianism. There's an old East End attitude towards vegetarian leftwingers, too, but he did not mention this.

As Chris Patten used to say, we can see a Banks joke coming from the other end of Victoria Street.

His old East End joke yesterday was the one about how, if you think the bottom has fallen out of your world, you should eat one of Bill Bloggs's sandwiches. Then the world will fall out of your bottom.

Most of Mr Banks's jokes seem to be about bottoms, and the rest are about bladders, breasts and the excretory functions. No debate about EU clean beach directives is complete without a Banks quip concerning floating voters and voting floaters, etc.

Psychoanalysts studying his speeches may one day be able to diagnose the problem, which probably has more to do with early weaning than Karl Marx. In the meantime, Mr Banks is the closest the Commons has to a walking *Viz* comic.

Psychoanalysis may also be able to discover why Mr Banks, crusading in the cause of tolerance and peace, becomes so intolerant and aggressive. He has told us more than once how he would like to see hunters torn limb from limb. Sometimes as he preaches his message of love, his face becomes quite twisted with hate.

Yesterday, praising the eating habits of vegetarians ('I'm no food fascist,' he barked, in tones suggesting he would frog-march to the guillotine anybody who suggested otherwise) he warned meat-eaters that they would grow a third breast, go bald, contract cancer, suffer a series of massive heart-attacks and, condemned to obesity, halitosis and acne, die a lingering death. And serve them right. Mr Banks has come to vegetarianism relatively late, without pressure, in his own time and through argument. He would not extend the same courtesy to his countrymen.

Still, it was a clever and entertaining speech. Banks at his best is one of the Commons's best speakers. So it was a pity he launched his attack on fat people while standing right next to Labour's largest lady backbencher. 'A glance around the Chamber,' Banks declared to suppressed mirth, would show us that British men and women were too fat and getting fatter.

Mildred Gordon (Bow & Poplar), beside him, gave a pained smile. The admirable Ms Gordon has actually been looking rather good of late and looked smashing yesterday. She could eat alive a blow-dried, lemon-faced stick insect with a shrivelled bottom like Banks.

A problem for vegetarianism, he explained, was that some vegetarians adopted an unlikeable style. 'So sit down!' shouted someone. However, our born-again veggie persisted: 'Vegetarians look better, too.' An assortment of noises from colleagues suggested doubt on this score.

As he resumed his seat it became apparent that a Tory, Peter Bottomley (Eltham) was minded to oppose him. 'Speak for England!' shouted one old buffer, as Bottomley rose. But the MP, a vegetarian himself, spoke instead for tolerance and against hysterical food-faddism, slightly spoiling the effect by declaring: 'Hysteria comes from cheese!'

All good fun. The House laughed, voted, and nothing will come of it. Some MPs eat meat, some eat cheese and some do not. All are hysterical. It must be something in the water.

An Antidote to the Mogadon Factor

10.3.95

It's amazing how often MPs unwittingly provide the answers to their own questions. Or how often MPs *are* the answers to their own questions.

Or in Teresa Gorman's case, both. Mrs Gorman (C – whipless – Billericay) told Home Office ministers yesterday of her worries about drug abuse in prisons. Warders, she suggested, actually condoned this because when prisoners were spaced out on illegal substances, they caused less trouble. Gorman called it the 'Mogadon factor'.

She conjured up for MPs a vision of prison screws operating as a nationwide uniformed corps of high-pressure drug dealers. 'Cop a toke of this, prisoner number MB1605. Skin up and chill out.'

In the face of a prison population completely monged (as I believe the jargon has it) on soothing substances, Mrs Gorman seemed to think it desirable to gee them all up a bit. We needed to put a bit of a shock through their systems: something to get the adrenalin pumping.

Well how about the lady herself? In the language of stimulant v sedative, upper v downer, La Gorman is a stimulant, an upper. In the language of electro-magnetism, Gorman is a massive high-voltage shock. In drugs terminology, this woman is crack, smack, speed, whizz.

Put Mrs Gorman on your board of prison visitors and before long the boys will be on the ceiling and breaking rocks.

Her great crusade, of course, is to publicize the benefits for women of hormone replacement therapy. Should this electrifying woman ever decide (at the age of 109, perhaps) not to stand again for Billericay, Essex would lose its zing. Heaven defend us from the Conservative Whips' Office's evil strategy: GRT, or Gorman Replacement Therapy.

But Mrs G was not the only self-prescribing therapy yesterday. John Greenway (C, Ryedale) was anxious to reinforce police numbers. Mr Greenway is an ex-policeman. We don't want to lose you, Mr Greenway, but ...

Also in his place to torment the Home Secretary was David Evans (C, Welwyn and Hatfield). He rose at Question 9, demanding that Mr Howard 'make the prison regime more rigorous'.

That was the written part of his question. The spoken part followed. Here, the difficulty for sketchwriters is to render Mr Evans's prose in any recognizable form of notation. Teams of top transcribers in the offices of *Hansard* have yet to crack the problem. I shall now try ...

'Wotwiv nine-cole horses – ahem – gole olf courses – an Sky TV an thy send aht warders fersteaknchips, *my* seenyaci'izens wanna now when criminoohs willwannaget *in*-na prison not *ah*-tavit ...?' Evans glanced down at his papers.

'Reading!' shouted Labour MPs, under some misapprehension. Evans can't.

Here too, though, if Mr Evans's question is how we could make prisons less bearable for prisoners, Mr Evans's answer is, surely ... Mr Evans.

Prisons already arrange to have 'writers in residence' and 'artists in residence'. How about an 'Evans in residence'? That would turn the tide of senior citizens trying to break in and begin a wave of desperate attempts to get out again.

If we could get Mr Evans out of the Commons and into some of the excessively pleasant penal establishments of which he complains, we should have solved two problems at once.

Whether Messrs Major, Blair and Ashdown could provide, on their own, the answers to their questions, we may doubt. That as a trio they deserve each other equally and cancel each other out completely, is certain. Answering the Labour Leader yesterday, the Prime Minister began caustically: 'The right hon gentleman is a distinguished lawyer.' There were giggles.

Next, up popped Paddy Ashdown, coughing and spluttering and in no mood for a joke. 'The right hon gentleman is *not* a distinguished lawyer,' said Major.

Major accused Blair of idiocy, Blair accused Major of double dealing, Ashdown accused Major of hoodwinking waffle and Major accused Ashdown of feeble-mindedness.

Another Thursday, another Prime Minister's Questions.

Prescott's New Clothes   *15.3.95*

R.I.P. John Prescott. The Hull bruiser is no more. In his place yesterday was a scrubbed, shiny-faced, hair-combed, shoe-shined, silk-tied, charcoal-suited New Labour clone. The Islington Reich had tamed Mr Prescott and sent him along to deputize for Tony Blair at Prime Minister's Questions, John Major being away in the desert avoiding Mr Clinton.

Labour's deputy leader arrived clutching his question, typed in such big, block script that I could read the first sentence from my perch 20ft above him. I knew before Tony Newton (Leader of the House, standing in for the PM) what question he was about to be asked.

Up got Mr Prescott with the dutiful eagerness of a boy Reading Aloud in Class. He delivered his script word for word, not a syllable, hair or cuff out of place. It was about the Greenbury committee on executives' pay.

Mr Newton replied that the PM would be studying the committee's conclusions with Clare. There were wrinkled brows. With Clare? With Norma, surely? '... Er, with *care*' Mr Newton stammered.

Prescott's next question commenced with the phrase, also written, 'Whatever the Right Honourable gentleman may say ...' This was probably meant as an instruction from Blair's office to Prescott, to use the second question regardless of Newton's first reply – but he read it out, anyway. There being no instructions for a third question, and having survived his script without a fluff, Prescott sat down. Phew! No rapped knuckles in the leader's office, then.

Any resemblance between this Mr John L. Prescott and the John L. Prescott who once delighted us with his mangled syntax but plain meaning is purely coincidental. The New Prescott's syntax was plain. It was the meaning that had got mangled.

The taming of the Old Prescott was as significant in its way as the birth of a new Clause Four. It was – in the Hamlet cigar ad-speak beloved of Labour's new leader – a 'defining moment'.

23.3.95   # Doing It By the Book

On a shelf in *The Times*'s room in the Commons sits a slim blue volume: the *Register of Members' Interests*: its purpose 'to provide information of any pecuniary interest or other material benefit which a Member receives which might reasonably be thought by others to influence his or her actions, speeches or votes in Parliament, or actions taken in his or her capacity as an MP'. In general, the theory works. Scandals involving MPs' interests are unusual. When they occur the register is there as our lodestar.

But of course financial scandals are hardly the flavour of the era. It is sexual scandals that now dominate the media. Could the thinking behind the register have a wider application?

Wild horses would not drag her name into this column, but a respected lady Labour MP has put to me an intriguing idea. What Ms Short – *oops* – suggests is ingenious. To take the wind from Peter Tatchell's sails, she suggests, why not set up a *Register of Members' Sexual Interests*?

It might need to go into many volumes. This column proposes that, as with the financial register that includes separate sections for 'visits', 'shareholdings', etc, each MP's chapter in this register would include sections. The first would be 'Orientation'. This would contain simple guidance: 'straight', 'gay', 'lesbian', 'bisexual' – or 'celibate' (for Sir Edward Heath).

There would need to be a section entitled 'Status'. Here, we suggest, the MP should say whether he or she had a permanent partner, whether married, whether keeping a mistress (or a toyboy). It is suggested, too, that in this section the MP might enter any claim they wished to make to sexual fidelity. An absence of such a claim would be taken to indicate that no promises were to be implied.

I think there might also be a 'Special Interests' section. This would take a similar form to the 'Hobbies' question in *Who's Who*. It is suggested that 'research assistants' would not be a suitable entry under this section. For Mrs Currie the thrill of swinging handcuffs at party conferences is probably political; I could name other MPs, however, whose interest in police weaponry borders on the obsessive. This would also be the place to mention Chelsea strips, and, in the case of one former MP, 'rumpy-pumpy in the showers'. Just as the financial register contains a section for foreign visits, so should this one. It would not be necessary to recite what happened. We can assume it.

Still for decision is whether actual occasions as well as general predilections should be declared. In order to confine our register to one bookshelf, I suggest not.

Why, you ask, should MPs volunteer to the press the means for further ridiculous stories? You misunderstand. The purpose is to kill the hysteria, not to feed it: to take the excitement from the hunt, by open disclosure. The register would be published on December 31, on the morning the New Year Honours list is declared. The effect of deluging the media with so many stories all at once would be to diffuse the focus on any individual one: an editor's nightmare.

What MPs don't realize (and for a moment I am serious) is that nothing more spoils a reporter's day than the response 'so what else is new?' *Fear* is oxygen to an investigative journalist. Like bullocks in a field, reporters follow anything that runs. Like bullocks in a field, they have no horns but once momentum has built up they will trample. Those too craven to stop running invite their fate.

Flabby and Feckless 28.3.95

Behavioural psychologists studying animals' conception of the world have argued that only humans are aware of what they are. The consciousness which dawns in the human infant that he or she is one example of a class of similar beings, never dawns (for example) in hamsters. Hamsters lack the conceptual apparatus to make sense of mirrors.

So, far from knowing that it is an exceptionally fat hamster, a hamster does not even acknowledge hamsterhood – let alone obesity – as a condition. Having failed to clear the 'hamster, know thyself,' hurdle, it cannot grasp the 'hamster, improve thyself' imperative. This is one of the reasons for stunted moral growth in hamsters. Watching Questions to the Heritage Secretary yesterday, I realized that MPs may be more like hamsters than they are like human beings. Let me explain …

Mr John Marshall (C, Hendon S) had put down a question about the importance of competitive sport. Fair enough. No athlete himself, the portly Marshall is still entitled to an opinion on how we might all be improved. You would expect him, though, to cover his own back. A self-deprecatory acknowledgement of his own failings would have done the trick. Imagine our hilarity, then, when Mr Marshall rose and, quivering with what we shall call indignation, barked at minister Iain Sproat: 'Have you read the editorial in today's *Daily Telegraph* which says we are raising a generation of overweight kids because of their diet?' Sproat shared his dismay.

Sitting right behind Marshall (the backdrop in any TV frame) was Robert Key, once a minister with responsibility for sport. Mr Key, a capable, jolly man, must weigh all of 17 stone. His large, pink face was illuminated by a genial grin. Answering Marshall, Mr Sproat probably weighs in as the lightest of the trio: no more than a couple of stone overweight.

Get the picture? One plump Tory MP in the foreground, one massive Tory MP in the background, addressing one chubby Tory MP at the dispatch box, on what a disgrace it is that children are fat. There were shouts of 'look behind you!'

But my purpose is not to mock, still less to allege hypocrisy. The hypocrite fears scrutiny but these men seemed oblivious to the fact that anything jarred. They stood there in all their fatness, condemning the fat. Such behaviour invites only one explanation: MPs, like hamsters, are intellectually unable to grasp that *they are themselves members of the species they judge.* In this they resemble journalists. I believe that an MP, so far as he conceives of himself as a metaphysical entity at all, supposes himself a pure, disembodied intelligence, shorn of those impedimenta like a body, a past, a present, a mistress, financial interests, etc, which encumber his constituents. He can pronounce on such things with no sense of shame, having recourse only to pure reason. As a theory, it would explain 'back to basics'. Those who find the scene unbelievable will hardly credit what happened next.

Another chubby former Sports Minister, Richard Tracey, rose to commend to all citizens the qualities of 'discipline, commitment, courage, winning modestly and losing gracefully'.

From backbench Tories all around him – men and women who as a body today exemplify to an almost unparalleled degree a want of discipline, a failure of commitment, a lack of courage, an immodesty in victory, and a gracelessness in defeat – came a merry and unabashed 'hear, hear'.

Rolls-Royces, Hats and Other Ominous Signs

30.3.95

Occasions, like institutions, are given away by the smallest of outward signs. The presence of marble, plate-glass, Mercedes Benzes, Royalty, Men with Walkie-Talkies and Women in Hats, is an unerring tell-tale. Don't even think about going. The occasion will be fatuous.

Nearing yesterday's Royal Institute of International Affairs Conference on Britain in the World at the Queen Elizabeth II Conference Centre, I saw a line of seven Mercedes, a Daimler, two Rolls-Royces, one stretch Cadillac, three Jags and a vastly increased incidence of women in hats.

The plate-glass doors of the marbled Conference Centre loomed. The walkie-talkies crackled. The heart sank.

Having failed to arrange accreditation I just walked in, carrying my LT two-zone Travelcard. The walkie-talkies were too busy walky-talkying to each other to notice. The Hats only ever notice other Hats. The key to establishing one's place in the sun on these occasions is to remember that *nobody* has any business to be there. Nobody has any business. Everybody is there.

Prince Charles was there. The PM was there. The Foreign Secretary was there. Henry Kissinger, Sir David Puttnam, Lord Weidenfeld and Mr Russell Twisk of the *Reader's Digest* were there; 706 grandees, diplomats, politicos, aidniks, peaceniks, warniks, apparatchiks and spooks were there; 200 journalists were there, watching them watch each other.

The bunfight divided into two sections: grand and not-so-grand, each graced by nomenclature which appears to be English but has no real English meaning. The grand bunfight was called 'Plenary Session'. 'Plenary' is Eurospeak and means the real McCoy. Other sessions were called 'Break-Out Sessions'. 'Break-Out' is PR-speak and means nothing. I headed for a Break-Out Session, on 'Democracy and Development', which means foreign aid. The panel was chaired by Diana Warwick (recycled from the Nolan committee; within a radius of one mile of Westminster and Whitehall everyone chairs each other's committees). It comprised a 'rapporteur' (Eurospeak for God knows what. He seemed to be writing) and four speakers.

The 'rapporteur' was a professor. The speakers were one Tory baroness and Privy Counsellor, one Labour baroness, one baron professor, and a Nigerian general. The general did not turn up as he was under house arrest.

The first speaker from the floor was an Anglican cleric with a beard. It struck me that if you wanted a mental checklist of what to avoid if democracy and development are to thrive, you could do worse than start your list with beards, generals, peers, Privy Counsellors, professors and priests. The ideal speaker for this conference would be titled The Reverend the Right Hon General Professor Lord Beard, and would arrive in a stretch-Cadillac, his wife in a hat.

Nothing of consequence was said. In the absent general's place a stand-in (with a beard) said that the last person he had substituted for was the late Diana Dors. He seemed to think this was incongruous. But Diana Dors could have substituted for any of us. Dionne Warwick could replace Diana Warwick and the Nolan Sisters staff the Nolan committee, for all the difference it would make.

It was time for lunch. The hour of the Hats was nigh. An address by the Prince of Wales would be followed by a meal of quails in a chutney sauce. The conference was said to mark a turning-point. Only for the quails.

Turning the Tables

4.4.95

Four hundred and eighty-nine journalists now have parliamentary press passes. We know this because it was revealed in a written answer from the chairman of the administration committee last week.

Peter Bottomley (C, Eltham) had inquired. Bottomley is on the warpath after newspapers suggested that MPs were enjoying an effective three-day week.

'Will he arrange to monitor for a week the number of journalists in the gallery during each hour the House sits?' Bottomley added.

'Yes,' was the reply, 'I have asked the Serjeant at Arms to make arrangements for the first full sitting week after the House returns from the Easter adjournment.'

I regret to say that Bottomley's warning has yet to sink in. Choosing a particularly riveting moment of yesterday afternoon's proceedings when, at 5.43pm, MPs were considering new clause 1 at the report stage of the Finance Bill, I peered in to check. David Winnick (Lab, Walsall N) was on his feet. Besides Winnick there were 17 MPs in the chamber.

There was one journalist in the Press Gallery. He was not taking notes. Where were the other 488? We must pull up our socks fast if we are to survive the head counts.

Mr Bottomley's spies will either have to keep a continuous tally, or make random swoops. For if the count takes place at the same time each hour we will soon learn when that is, and file in like prisoners to the prison yard for the taking of the register – then escape back behind bars. Many journalists consider the Bottomley plan outrageous.

But this column is concerned not that it is too bold – but that it is too timid. The mere fact of a reporter's physical presence is no guarantee that he or she is listening, understanding, or, indeed, awake. Ten seconds of Winnick yesterday had my eyes glazing over.

There are two ways Mr B might check that we were doing our job. The first (and less ambitious) is that Madam Speaker be empowered to interrupt MPs' speeches at any point, crane her neck up at the Press Gallery, select any journalist at random, and call: 'You – yes, *you*, young lady – Alice Thomson! What was Mr Winnick just saying?' And (assuming she had a note) Alice would have to try to read her shorthand back as MPs giggled and jeered.

For expert political editors, this spot-check could go further. As (for instance) Mr Major droned 'I refer my Rt Hon friend to the answer I gave on 20 March 1991', Miss Boothroyd could bark up at us: 'Now let's see who really knows their stuff. To what is the Prime Minister referring here? Hands up! Yes, Peter Riddell ...'

But my more ambitious plan is, I think, the best. Apart from questions to departmental ministers, each Wednesday would feature a quarter of an hour for questions to newspaper editors. On the first Wednesday after Easter, we might have questions to the Editor of *The Independent* newspaper.

Mr Ian Hargreaves, sitting among us upstairs, would be flanked (as secretaries of state are flanked by junior ministers) by his lobby correspondents. Hargreaves would quail as he saw that question 1 was from Jonathan Aitken: 'When did the Editor last meet Mr Tim Laxton, on his staff, and will he make a statement?'

Tories would cheer and Labour boo as Aitken tried to trip Hargreaves up. Tory poodles would chip in with planted questions designed to assist the Chief Secretary.

After all, if the media do now wield the power that everyone says we do, perhaps we should be held to account.

5.4.95   # New Man Comes of Age

As the Commons tottered towards its Easter break, John Prescott, one-time ship's steward and activist in the National Union of Seamen, halted tantalizingly before pressing on to pass yet another sad milestone in his rake's progress from real to plastic politics. The sad milestone was Mr Prescott's very first soundbite. The tantalizing pause beforehand was when Labour's deputy leader blew a kiss at Employment Minister Ann Widdecombe.

It was a breath of fresh air: the old, working-class, devil-may-care Prescott that we all remember, taunting a bossy Tory lady. Prescott had just entered the Chamber to deputize for Tony Blair at Prime Minister's Questions. When Major is away, the House Leader, Tony Newton, answers for him; so Blair sends his own stand-in and the occasion becomes a duel between seconds. In magnificent form yesterday, the terrifying Miss Widdecombe had been ranting statistics all afternoon.

Catching sight of Prescott, she tossed in a slighting reference to the admission he once made that Labour's minimum wage would cause a 'shake-out' in the Labour market.

If a water bed (queen-size) were to rise up and walk, it would look, and move, like Miss Widdecombe. A woman of her build should never attempt a derisive toss of the upper-torso while shouting 'shake-out!' Adjacent MPs flinched in horror as, for a moment, Miss Widdecombe's shake-out appeared an all too real possibility. Mercifully, all stayed safely gathered in.

The minister went on: it was British workers who would be 'shaken' by Prescott's minimum wage, she yelled; and it was their jobs they would be 'out' of.

Taking his seat, John Prescott looked up at her, leered, and blew her a cheeky little kiss. It was painful to be reminded what fun the Hull MP they used to call the Mouth of the Humber, once was. No longer. His tailors have now made him a jacket with Tory vents, and trousers with turn-ups. This we could bear if New Labour's teenage spin-doctors had not been to work on the speech as well as the deportment of this magnificent relic of the class war.

The last time Prescott appeared at Prime Minister's Questions in his leader's place, the PR pixies had made him read his questions out – so there was no danger that a piece of unscripted Prescottian prose might invade prime-time TV.

This time it was worse. They had actually fashioned a soundbite for him.

Mr Prescott's double-barrelled question, about the Government's increases in personal taxation, was designed as a setting within which this pearl was to be displayed. As he neared the end of the second stage of his inquiry, he drew himself up, paused, and, *ever*-so slightly self-consciously, bellowed 'People now know' (the cameras swivelled) 'that when it comes to tax' (wait for it!) 'YOU CAN NEVER TRUST A TORY'.

Boom-boom! His first soundbite! The man who has given us sound-chews, sound-gobbles and sound-munches galore, but never anything so compact as a bite, had finally done it. It was like junior's first shave. John Prescott's political testicles have dropped. Farewell to the politics of boyhood. Farewell to dockside rallies and rainy streets of Hull. Farewell the seafaring trades unions. Farewell workers' rights and the class struggle.

Hello to the world of AutoCue and camera angle; of powder puffs and media poofs; of buzz-words, boo-words, key phrases and – yes – soundbites. Welcome to New Labour, John!

Natural De-selection

To every cloud there is a silver lining: even global warming and rising sea-levels. 'I have the honour,' declared John Gummer, the Environment Secretary, yesterday, 'to represent a constituency almost all of which would disappear beneath the waves'.

MPs looked up. For many the thought was occurring, perhaps for the first time, that global warming might not be all bad. Naturally there was sorrow that so many innocent electors would also have to sink beneath the waves alongside their MP: but no great prize comes without a price.

Labour's Paul Flynn (Newport W) had just reminded MPs that large swaths of South Wales (for instance Newport) would disappear too, if the sea rises. English Tories cheered up. Sadly, the Chief Whip was not there. Has it struck Mr Ryder that if carbon dioxide levels continue to increase, some of the first constituencies to go submarine will be Billericay, Southend E, Great Yarmouth, and Holland-with-Boston? All will join the North Sea.

Submerged, or cast adrift in small boats, will be Sir Teddy Taylor, Michael Carttiss and Sir Richard Body. That takes care of one third of the Tory Euro-rebels. A fourth, Teresa Gorman (whipless, Billericay), who does not believe in global warming, will presumably refuse all offers of help and sink beneath the waves still protesting her scepticism; until the brine engulfs even Mrs Gorman's song, rising finally in rebellious bubbles to the surface. That moment the Chief Whip will especially savour.

Relatively small further increases in the sea level will swamp the West Midlands, seeing off Aldridge Brownhills and Wolverhampton SW, and dispatching Richard Shepherd and Nicholas Budgen. Northampton N (Tony Marlow) and Ruislip, Northwood (John Wilkinson) will also go. That will leave only one Tory Euro-rebel, Christopher Gill, marooned on a hill in Ludlow, where he can do no harm.

Such a development will also consign Westminster itself to the sea-bed; but the look on Mr Ryder's face in recent months has suggested that no upheaval could be called a catastrophe if certain individuals were among its victims. As for those individuals, it would not take John Wilkinson long to convince his pals that global warming is actually a Brussels-organized conspiracy to drown English patriots.

Missing from the Chamber as MPs discussed rising sea-levels was Andrew Robathan (C, Blaby). A pity, as when his question was reached, it had to be missed. Robathan, who was once in the SAS and for all we know may have killed for Britain, wanted to ask Mr Gummer 'what assessment his department has made of the damage being done to British wildlife by feral mink?' Those mink, of course, are Canadian. Tory Eurosceptics will hear no ill of Canada just at present, as they are supporting our Commonwealth cousins against the evil Spaniards.

How, then, do Bruge-ists see the Feral Mink Question? Apart from insisting on keeping border controls (to stop further mink arriving *via* the Continent) it is intriguing to know how the furry menace can be traced to Brussels, blamed on Jacques Delors, or linked to the evils of a single currency.

Now we never will know. I blame Robathan. How can an ex-SAS officer fail to make it back, when our own Betty Boothroyd, trained only with the Tiller Girls, crawls through landslides in the Atlas Mountains to be here on time?

Can the epithet 'Supermadam' be long delayed?

Metaphorical Menagerie   *25.4.95*

In 1976 the Speaker (Selwyn Lloyd) was clear: 'I always object to the use of animal terminology when applied to Members of this House.' He was banning the description by an MP of the Members opposite as 'laughing hyenas'. Withdrawing the words, the MP substituted 'laughing Ken Dodds opposite', which the Chair found satisfactory. How Lloyd would have viewed Michael Foot's description of Norman Tebbit as 'a semi-house-trained polecat' we shall never know.

The hyena issue was settled, but this sketch has always been unhappy with the ruling. Comparing MPs to animals is a staple of the sketchwriter's trade and we hate to do to them what they may not do to each other. So, on a dull Monday in the chamber, I took refuge in a trawl through abusive language conducted for me by Phil Mason, guru of Commons arcana. Mason has scoured *Hansard* since 1861.

Mr Mason and I can offer candidates for coming by-elections a list: Speakers' rulings on animal metaphors since 1861. Which animals may, and which may not, be likened by MPs to other MPs?

The first animalistic references consisted only of noises. 1872: *'amid the general confusion were heard imitations of the crowing of cocks, whereat the Speaker declared the scenes unparliamentary, and gross violations of order'*. So no cock-a-doodle-dos.

In 1884, when a Member used the words 'bigoted, malevolent young puppy', Mr Speaker must have been in a forbearant mood. He allowed it. 'But if I was mediating taste, I would decide differently.'

1885: 'Jackal.' *Banned.*

1886: 'Tory skunks.' *Speaker*: 'Highly improper.'

1923: 'Chameleon politician.' *Out of order.*

1930: 'Insolent young cub.' *Banned.*

1931: 'Lie down, dog!' *Banned.*

1931: 'Noble and learned camels' [of the Lords]. *Banned.*

1936: 'Swine.' *Banned.*

1946: 'Silly ass.' *Banned.*

1948: 'Dirty dog.' *Banned.*

1949: 'Stool pigeons.' *Sp*: 'Most unworthy.'

1952: 'You rat.' *Banned.*

1953: 'Cheeky young pup.' *Out of order.*

1955: 'Rat.' *Out of order.*

1955: 'Ratted on a friend.' *Out of order.*

1956: First use of 'twerp', during Questions to the Air Minister. *Ruled in order.* (*Sp*: 'I think it was a sort of technical term of the aviation industry.')

1955: 'Twerps.' *Allowed.* (*Sp*: 'It appeared to be directed to a multiple object.')

1972: 'This young Twerp' [of Prince Charles, by Willie Hamilton]. *Out of order.*

1977: 'Snake.' *Banned.*

1978: 'Bitchy' [of Mrs Thatcher]. *Out of order.*

1985: 'Baboons.' *Banned.*

1985: 'His shadow spokesman's monkey.' *Banned.*

1986: 'Political weasel and guttersnipe.' *Allowed.*

1987: 'The morals of tom cats' [description of other Members' ethics]. *Banned.*

1988: 'Rat.' *Allowed, this time!*

1989: 'Political skunk.' *Out of order.*

1989: 'The attention span of a gerbil.' *Allowed. But Sp*: 'It does not help us here.'

1989: 'The wolf of Dagenham.' *Allowed. Sp*: 'I've heard worse.'

1992: 'The hamster from Bolsover' [of Dennis Skinner]. *Allowed.*

1992: 'Cruel swine' [of Kenneth Baker]. *Allowed.*

But perhaps the oddest ruling was when Mr Speaker inexplicably allowed a backbencher to say of Mrs Thatcher that she was 'behaving with all the sensitivity of a sex-starved boa-constrictor'. The Speaker added: 'It does not add to the dignity of the House.'

It is a tribute, I think, to Lady Thatcher's strength that it occurred to nobody, least of all the Chair, that she could need protection.

Sir Edward's Piano Tour *28.4.95*

At Sir Edward Heath's home in the Close, by Salisbury Cathedral, the great man is said to keep a grand piano, on whose shiny top stands a forest of photographs. There is (perhaps) Sir Edward with the French President; Sir Edward with Otto Klemperer; with Khrushchev, Brezhnev, Nixon and de Gaulle.

Jostling with Sir Edward and Moira Shearer, the Emperor of Ethiopia and Margot Fonteyn, is (no doubt) Sir Edward with the last surviving Hottentot. Adjacent stands Sir Edward with Sir Winston, the photograph as yet unclaimed by the National Lottery.

This piano is (visitors report) a wondrous sight. Yet, generous host though he is, in a populous country like ours it is sad but true that many millions will never be able to visit Sir Edward's piano themselves. Whole swaths of our nation will never marvel at this witness to his past statesmanship.

Yesterday at the Commons, kindly Sir Edward did his best to put that right. The House and the listening public were taken on a guided tour of the ex-premier's piano-top. Time being short, and the debate being on China and Hong Kong, this tour was restricted to the Far Eastern section of its polished surface.

We did not proceed straight to Hong Kong. Sir Edward had also been to Vietnam. 'In Vietnam they said to me, "why have you come so late?" ' We understood it was Britain which was late, not Sir Edward.

From Hanoi we flew to China, Sir Edward arriving in humorous mood. 'I said: "Chairman Mao gave me two pandas. They have died. Can I have two more?" ... They said Yes, for a million dollars a year. "We have a market economy now." '

More seriously, Sir Edward had heard talk of the Chinese leadership being in trouble. This was rubbish. 'Having met them all ten days ago, I've never known them so relaxed.'

China's stability assured, we moved to human rights. 'I was once asked by Deng Xiaoping ...' asked, it seemed, what *he* would do about human rights.

Sir Edward had been unable to advise. That disposed of that.

How about Tibet? 'I went to Tibet several years ago and saw it all then.' Ah, Sir Edward did not exactly say *what* he had seen. And the Dalai Lama? 'I talk to the Dalai Lama frequently.' Some MPs, however, though glad about this for the Dalai Lama, remained concerned about his future. Not Sir Edward. 'I put it to Deng Xiaoping ten years ago: "Can the Dalai Lama go back to Tibet?" He said: "Yes ... if he goes as a spiritual not a political leader. So he can't complain." '

And then back to Hong Kong. 'I found the utmost admiration for the police chief there.' This officer will be relieved to hear of Sir Edward's researches, and their result: 'He will be allowed to stay on.'

Aware that we had only explored a small corner of Sir Edward's piano, time nevertheless pressed, and, sadly, the tour had to end.

It had been a rambling affair, punctuated with a few lazily delivered kicks to the present Governor's shin (just to help him in his task), and interspersed with a couple of half-pats on the back for the Foreign Secretary, Douglas Hurd, delivered with weary condescension.

Sir Edward was pleased to acknowledge that Mr Hurd seemed to be making progress in his intellectual journey, judging his speech to have hit a 'quiet and conciliatory' note of which Sir Edward approved.

'I hope the Foreign Secretary will be able to carry on this reconciliation.'

Having made Mr Hurd's task just that little bit harder, Sir Edward sat down.

Drone of Victory Deafens Bleating Goat

In extremis, the Opposition Leader has a tendency to bleat. *In extremis*, the Prime Minister has a tendency to drone. Together, they often sound like a goat being dive-bombed by a model aeroplane. Sometimes the model aeroplane crashes, and sometimes the goat gets tangled in the washing.

At PM's Questions yesterday, the model aeroplane escaped, leaving the goat with horns impaled on a couple of bloomers, bleating.

'Quit while you're winning' is good advice. We usually ignore it. Tony Blair persisted with what had proved a winning theme on Tuesday, pushed it just a little too hard, and stumbled.

On Tuesday the Labour leader had been crisp and scathing in his condemnation of the Government's unseemly scramble to remove a new tax threat to mortgage protection payouts. Mr Blair made skilful fun of the confused messages coming from dithering official sources at differing times that morning.

Even John Major had to grin, and came as close to saying 'fair cop' as any Prime Minister dare. Blair sat down to roars of approval from his own side, and sheepish faces on the government benches.

Alas, the temptation to scamper on to the stage for one last encore proved too great. Yesterday Blair seized upon a new Treasury review of a new tax threat. He tried to link this with Tuesday's panic, demanding to know why we had not been told about the latest twist. Major dismissed this with the flourish of apparent authority: and it did sound as though the 'New Tory Shock' story was bogus. The House sensed it.

Unfortunately Mr Blair still had an unused soundbite to offer us. Just as a feature of 90s Islington is the *Prêt à Manger* croissant, so a feature of 90s new Labour is the *Prêt à Manger* soundbite. These savoury croissants come hot, do not come cheap, and do not keep. Like the ones you buy, a Blair soundbite is prepared a little beforehand: made *for* the moment, but not quite *at* the moment. In his heart, Mr Blair knew that this one was not right for the moment. But why waste it?

Alas, the temptation to scamper on to the stage yet again and proffer the soundbite proved irresistible. Blair rose. Picture his problem. It was the precise opposite of those games in which one person supplies the opening sentence of a story, and the next supplies the following one. Here, the final phrase was supplied.

The soundbite waiting, even as he rose, to ping from Mr Blair's cranial microwave, was: '… all the hallmarks of his Government: it begins in incompetence, falls into confusion and ends in chaos.' His challenge was to supply the sentences preceding this.

And here, we fear, the bleating started in earnest. As the model aeroplane had just demonstrated, the evidence the goat had laid before us did not merit the charge of incompetence, the front bench facing the goat was not (on this occasion) in confusion, and the model aeroplane's flight had not, this afternoon, ended in chaos. 'All the hallmarks,' therefore, though a tasty filling for any croissant, were simply not there.

All Mr Blair could do was pretend that they were. And – you know – an encouraging thing about both this Leader of the Opposition and this Prime Minister is that neither of them is very good at pretending.

On Tuesday, Major failed to convince us that Downing Street was not in a tangle. On Thursday, Blair failed to convince us it was. One-all, then, for the goat, the croissant, and the model aeroplane.

11.5.95   # Corpses From Under a Shroud

The debate on London's hospitals was conducted in the time-honoured style of MPs. Behind flimsy arguments and haphazard logic were wheeled in an army of corpses and a platoon of mangled accident victims. Opposition troops advanced waving shrouds; the Government returned fire with a salvo of statistics. There was blood, and numbers, everywhere. Nobody won.

Margaret Beckett, Labour's health spokesman, brought the first corpse to the chamber. Mrs Beckett rose and within a minute a London husband had found his wife dead in bed. Beckett blamed the Government. That was at 4.28. At 4.29 there was a dreadful motorbike accident, but the nearby hospital was full. She blamed the Government.

Some minutes later there were multiple car crashes in her speech. Before long, Mrs Edith Berry's kidneys were not functioning, and as we approached the end of Mrs Beckett's text a man was found with a badly broken arm, in hospital for 24 hours, the arm unset. She blamed the Government.

She sat down. Virginia Bottomley stood up. But still the carnage continued. Hampstead's Glenda Jackson (Lab) interrupted to bring us a constituent who had suffered third-degree burns to 40 per cent of his body. There being no ambulance, he went to hospital in a fire engine. Ms Jackson blamed the Government.

Now Harry Greenway (C, Ealing N) decided to join in. To Labour cries of 'he needs care in the community!' the quirky ex-headmaster introduced us to 'a lady who collapsed before my eyes' (he was probably making one of his dreadful speeches). Labour backbenchers looked up, interested. Would Greenway blame the Government?

'An ambulance arrived within seven minutes.' Bad news. Labour groaned. Greenway was not getting into the spirit of things.

But nor, in a sense, had Mrs Beckett. This poised, bird-like woman is never less than crisp, and attacking Bottomley she was as tart as ever. But did we sense that her heart (or, perhaps, her head?) was not in it? To Alan Howarth (C, Stratford-on-Avon) who had asked whether as an ex-minister she did not recognize that hard choices had to be made, her off-the-cuff answer struck an odd note. People do bring ministers hard choices, she said, but sometimes you had to reply: 'Yes, there is an admirable case in logic for what you say, but it is not the right way to proceed.' If that is the banner Labour's NHS crusade is asked to march under, one can see why they prefer to wave shrouds.

Bottomley faltered too. She seemed exhausted. Her script was bellicose but, stumbling frequently on her words, she seemed to miss her old, mad momentum. Mrs B seems to go full tilt or not at all. Her husband Peter watched her anxiously, wringing his hands and knotting his fingers. A claque of Tory loyalists supported with kindly interventions, but there was no other Cabinet member with her on the bench.

Still, she had her ammunition and she used it. She deployed £2 million extra for primary healthcare in Barnet (which contains two backbench Tory waverers). She also deployed Edmund Burke, a sign of desperation. Mysteriously she at one point deployed '200,000 one-year waiters'.

But the marvel was her plan for St Bartholomew's Hospital. The Health Secretary confirmed it would close, but would consider a plea that 'the name live on'.

Where? On a telephone box? Peter Brooke's face registered something as close to disgust as a gentleman ever gets.

15.6.95   **'It's Mine and I'm Keeping It'**

They are scraping the raised eyebrows from the ceiling of the members' smoking room. According to weekend gossip, Edward Garnier (C, Harborough) is angling for another East Midlands constituency. He has his eye, say the wagging tongues, on a neighbouring seat: Rutland and Melton. Even after forthcoming boundary changes, this patch remains rock-solid Conservative. The seat based on what is now called Harborough becomes a little less safe.

Splendid plan. One drawback. Rutland & Melton already has an MP: Alan Duncan. Mr Duncan is reported to be incensed. At 38, he had not planned to retire.

Maybe there has been a misunderstanding? In theory, a rejigged boundary between neighbours gives each MP the right to try for either seat. In practice, moving in on what is seen as another fellow's seat can be the single worst sin you can commit in the Tory club, less forgiveable than murdering your mother, voting to ban fox-hunting, being found *in flagrante delicto* with a brigadier's daughter, or running over your constituency lady chairman's Cairn terrier.

Or, indeed, and less controversially, running over the brigadier's daughter and being found *in flagrante delicto* with the terrier.

It was therefore unlucky for Mr Garnier that his question (put down weeks ago) appeared on the order paper yesterday. 'Question 3: Mr Edward Garnier (Harborough): *To ask the President of the Board of Trade what his department is doing to promote exports from the East Midlands.*' Since tabling that question, Garnier has begun an export drive all on his own, starting with plans to export himself. This is an export too far. A wall of import barriers is being hastily erected around Rutland & Melton. Free trade has its limits.

Ten yards up from him sat Mr Duncan. It was probably the first occasion on which the grinding of an MP's teeth has become audible up in the press gallery. The question was quickly reached. A ripple of giggles ran around the chamber as MPs read it, and the penny dropped. Garnier called 'number three, Madam'. The junior minister, Richard

Needham, got up and burbled a little awkwardly about regional export promotion.

Garnier rose. So did the giggles. So did Dennis Skinner. Miss Boothroyd ignored the last two. Embarrassed – and gabbling – Mr Garnier galloped through a prepared paeon of praise to 'the Business Link office in Market Harborough' and the 'co-operation of the Foreign Office' in promoting exports ... 'not only from my own constituency ...' Duncan's patience snapped. 'But from mine as well!'

The front bench winced.

How painful it is to have to report these family rows.

Mid-life High Noon   *23.6.95*

John Major calls an unexpected election for the Conservative Party leadership ...

If John Major should ever contemplate a new career, he might consider professional poker. Not a twitch, not a frown, not a shake of the hand or tremor of the voice betrayed at 3.15 what he planned for 4.30. Maybe he knew he had won already? You've certainly got to hand it to the guy: if he was under any stress, he didn't let it show. Prime Minister's Questions yesterday saw Major at his most relaxed.

Jokey, in fact. Mr Major achieved his best joke of the parliamentary session, describing nepotism among Labour councillors in Monklands as so rife that their personnel department had turned into something like a family planning centre.

The PM ambled in just two minutes before his Questions were to begin, and sat back grinning. Behind him the backbenchers from Hell bayed their support in that bloodcurdling Tory way that only Tories do. Hear those hounds, and any leader with his wits about him knows the clamour carries less comfort than silence. Major didn't seem to care.

Perhaps in the derisory way he tossed aside both hostile and friendly questions we might have recognized a hint of impatience for the real fixture of the afternoon, but we thought it was the heat.

Labour's Janet Anderson tried running up the flagpole her party's new plan for neighbours to report each other to the police. The Prime Minister failed to salute it. Sir Don Thompson (C, Calder Valley) bowled him an easy if fatuous ball about terrorism. The PM batted it aimlessly to one side.

Tony Blair then tried one of those sneering questions that so rarely work. It didn't. The Labour leader suffered a relapse into the problem which has troubled him before: the premature soundbite. '… no longer trusted to govern the country' would have been a limp offering at the best of times. Blair chose the moment when Major had just said how important was Sir Patrick Mayhew's part in the Ulster peace process. Blair was left sounding sour. Major hardly bothered to drive home this small advantage. Onlookers might, at this point, have guessed that he was preoccupied – but the Prime Minister then engaged in an offbeat diversionary tactic: launching into a passionate denunciation of the barbarities of the Burmese Government, at the invitation of the Liberal Democrats' Sir David Steel.

Does a man with a mid-life High Noon on his mind choose his eleventh hour to debate Burma? And when Labour's Dr Norman Godman (Greenock & Port Glasgow) found the PM ready to wax menacingly expert on the future of the Brent Spar, any suspicion that the future of J. Major was what preoccupied him vanished.

Denis MacShane (Lab, Rotherham) tried to be clever. He called Jacques Chirac 'the Prime Minister's new friend' and invited Major to wriggle over Chirac's decision to raise the minimum wage in France. Major declined to wriggle. This was, of course, 'a mistake,' he said, in his matter-of-fact, 'so what else is new' voice. And that was just about it. Showdown ahead? Big gamble in prospect? No. It was a sunny afternoon and Downing Street has a rose garden.

This man might have been planning to dig the rose garden; or water the rose garden; or read in the rose garden; or sunbathe in the rose garden. Even snooze in the rose garden. But gamble the premiership of the United Kingdom? In the rose garden? Before tea? Never.

27.6.95 # Vulcan Launches from Slopes of Gorman

Television viewers yesterday watched the first Tory leadership campaign in history to be launched from the bosom of Teresa Gorman.

Viewers were startled by the strange green-clad torso behind John Redwood as he spoke at his press conference yesterday. No head was visible in the frame.

I can reveal that it belonged to Mrs Gorman. We would recognize that bust anywhere. Once, as Redwood parried, a hand could be seen tugging at her lapels, drawing them together like green curtains across the cleavage. We trust the hand belonged to Mrs Gorman.

With such a launching pad, how can a campaign fail? Mrs Gorman was joined in a little claque of MPs in what television producers call a 'doughnut' around their hero: surely the whackiest doughnut in history.

Behind her, bullet-headed blond rightwinger Tony Marlow (his mates call him 'Von Marloff') wore a ludicrous striped blazer. Beside him, Bill 'Biggles' Walker had not opted for the kilt he often sports in the chamber. Norman Lamont (every day more like Badger in *Wind in the Willows*) joined Christopher Gill, a suitable extra for *Dad's Army*; and ex-minister Edward Leigh, to whom *Some Mothers Do 'Ave 'Em* could offer a role.

From time to time this bizarre claque would interrupt their master's flow with a raucous little chorus of 'hya, hya', 'hearrr, hearr' (from the Scot) and 'yeah! yeah!' from Mrs Gorman. It sounded like *The Goon Show*, but which of us can choose his claque?

And John Redwood did himself no harm. He achieved a tactical masterstroke by excluding from the room the observer who first recognized he was not human. It is five years since I uncovered Redwood's Vulcan origins, and the revelation has damaged him.

Reaching the conference 20 minutes early, I was told the room was full. Journalists with me were similarly barred. Watching the Vulcan's performance on Sky (where else but on satellite?) I saw no journalist I recognized. The room was 'full'. But not with humans. Redwood had packed it with alien clones. Reading aloud his letter to Mr Major, Redwood's voice-teachers had told him to inject 'passion'. Vulcans cannot feel this emotion but know that Earthlings often shout when passionate. So he shouted every eighth word ('... to regain the TRUST of the British people!') It produced a weird effect.

How did he view Wales? 'It-is-a-beautiful-country,' said the Vulcan, because that is what Earthlings say about Wales. Instructed by his minders to display humour, Redwood told us he was a 'jobseeker'. He followed this with the smile he has now learnt to do very nicely: a triumph of muscular control.

Most sinister of all was a Vulcan triple-bluff. Mr Redwood made a joke about a Vulcan being unable to see the joke about Vulcan jokes. There was a danger that his microchips might fuse at the fiendish internal logic of this inferential sequence, but, though his eyes bulged for a moment, all was well.

Few, however, will have failed to notice that, asked point-blank whether he was a Vulcan, Redwood replied that many people had seen his parents. *He did not answer the question.*

All in all, it was a successful performance. His claque of Earthling riff-raff cheering, he wound up the meeting. What, we wondered, would be his final word?

'No extra charge!' he declared. Mr Redwood must have seen this in a supermarket, recorded it as a useful idiomatic phrase, and inputted it onto the wrong disk-drive in his logic system.

29.6.95   # The Real PM

Two green worlds were separated yesterday at Westminster by the walls of the parliamentary palace, a busy road and a hundred yards. Two more different worlds can hardly be imagined.

On College Green, just over the way from the House, there now exists a kind of permanent media funfair. Bystanders gawp and Japanese tourists shake their heads in bewilderment as a dozen groups of men and women, with cameras and fluffy sausage-microphones charge around, sweating in the sun and setting up interviews.

In the air-conditioned Commons chamber, little more than a hundred yards away, all was cool, green leather at 3.30pm. John Major had arrived to make a statement on the Cannes summit. MPs on both sides listened intently as difficult questions, difficult answers on complex matters were exchanged across the floor. Outside there was no time for complexities. Rival television crews vied to attract the attention of passing political entities and nonentities. 'A quick interview for us, Mr Cash?' 'Over here, Mr Hayes, over here!' 'Which candidate best reflects your opinion of the single currency, Mr Leigh?'

The sun shone and the interviews were unremittingly banal: the same questions, the same clichés, the same tired metaphors, over and again. 'Stalking horse ... Redwood gaining ... Portillo hiding ... Major steadying ... How many? 80 ... 100 ...?' The vocabulary, absurdly overheated, was of blood, knives, killer punches, knockout blows.

From time to time, when the flow of interviewees failed to meet demand, interviewers took to interviewing each other. A shrewd lady from a small radio station hovered with a tape-recorder, recording other people's interviews. Such is the feeding frenzy: media people have begun feeding off each other's offal.

Inside the chamber, the House heard a calm and measured statement from the Prime Minister. Listening, I reflected on how much he has gained in poise and authority. Tony Blair, too, struck just the right note: light but insistent, sceptical. In reply, John Major was genuinely dignified, firm, yet relaxed; informal, with no hint of pomposity. Beside him, Douglas Hurd looked tense, tired and sad.

Outside, on College Green, there had occurred what was for me a moment I will always remember. A man called Tim Muffett had been interviewing a man called Peter Friel, who was a John Major lookalike. It was a spoof interview for an entertainment programme, *Paint It Red*. The lookalike was quite convincing.

So convincing, in fact, that a member of the public assumed this was indeed the PM. He barged in on the interview and began berating the surprised actor. He accused him of wrecking the economy and lying over Northern Ireland. 'Go back to the lunatic asylum you came from!' he yelled. The cameras whirred. Inside the chamber, the real Mr Major faced an unreal Iain Duncan Smith (C, Chingford), who declared: '1997 isn't going to happen!' 'The end is nigh,' shouted Dennis Skinner. To a polite but sharp question from Labour's Tony Wright, the real Major then gave the quietest and most convincing explanation of why he would not prejudge monetary union that I have ever heard.

In the midst of heat, a little cool: in the midst of a spreading unreality, a real Prime Minister answering a real question with a real argument about real politics. Two calm voices amidst the Babel.

4.7.95

Bottomley in a Cloud
of Banality

What an exit! Virginia Bottomley made what everyone expects to be her final bow as Health Secretary yesterday in a riot of mixed metaphor. As an oratorical sunset it was psychedelic. Statistic upon statistic streaked across the sky in a magnificent valedictory display.

Her vocabulary scaled new heights of gobbledegook, her prose plumbed new depths of banality, her cliché was fabulous. We can all be trite, but who but Mrs Bottomley can be so exuberantly trite?

The jargon was awesome. One-year waiters, two-year waiters and evidence-based responses jostled with demand-led facilities and innovative service as Mrs Bottomley levered up – or down – her league-tables and outpatient waits.

The Health Secretary was dressed in an elegant cream suit with sky-blue blouse and chiffon scarf in delicate turquoise print. Her outfit hardly matched her vocabulary, which was all 'levers', 'spatchcocks' and 'gut-reactions'.

Dates, figures and surgical operations flew through the air: 82 per cent over 13 weeks, 95 per cent over 26 weeks; 1948, 1979, 1985. Intensive care, intrusive surgery … we were spared hip operations. Unreality swelled to a defining fatuity when Dale Campbell-Savours (Lab, Workington) told us that due to a dispute about speech therapists, '20 per cent of children in my constituency are unable to speak properly'.

Mrs B has no trouble speaking properly but seemed to be having difficulty speaking sense. Then, all at once, the river of stale imagery which winds its reliable way through every dispatch box speech, regardless of speaker, burst its banks. One of Labour's health plans, she said, 'was waved about as the last bullet in their threadbare locker'.

Was the locker hand-knitted? Big enough to wave a bullet in? Was the bullet big enough to wave inside or outside a locker, threadbare or otherwise? These and many other questions Mrs Bottomley never answered. Opposition proposals were 'a spatchcock … plundering that newly found popularity while genuflecting to the old vested interests'.

Meanwhile (and simultaneously) Labour were 'not only turning the clock back, but taking it down off the wall and jumping on it up and down'. Why not just hit the clock with the spatchcock?

'We have levered up standards!' she cried. Her kingdom was 'an evidence-based service based on research strategy, day-surgery, bio-pharmaceuticals, lasers, genetics, information technology ...' creating 'an innovative service, evidence-based at every level, a public service with strong ethical foundations'. Golly. Ethical foundations, too. This was worthy of Tony Blair.

'It's for tomorrow's patients!' she declared.

'No tomorrow for you,' called a Labour heckler.

But on she went. Three years as Health Secretary, three years of management-consultant gibberish, three years of inexhaustible energy, exhausted metaphor, leaping ambition and plonking expression, blew themselves out in a glorious tropical storm of political unlikelihood and verbal infelicity.

There were seven backbenchers behind her to witness it. What a woman! What a way to go!

Leader of the Pack   *7.7.95*

To those who have travelled in the African bush, the sketchwriter's view down on to the Tory benches in the Commons chamber triggers a memory. Prime Minister's Questions is like an East African waterhole at sundown.

The noises, the jostling and grunting and trumpeting, are the same. The squabbling is the same. The tension is the same.

The waters are murky but the animals must drink.

This is a place of danger and excitement, of refreshment and death.

All the animals were there yesterday. As African dusks go, this was an unusual one. For a fortnight there had been turmoil among the animals. Their leader had been challenged.

John Major is not really one of the Great Beasts of Westminster, but an agile cat for all that: a quiet lion in his middle years, a cat with talents but lacking what they call 'serious mane'. Shockingly, a cool young cheetah had bid for the lion's patch. The bush had been agog.

In the cheetah's shadow had waited an old lion with mane so serious he is all mane. He hoped to inherit. Behind the old lion had crouched a young lion with ambitions of his own but unsure when to show his teeth and his telephone lines.

The big fight had been on Tuesday. Most of the wild dogs and all the hyenas had lined up with the cheetah. The crocodiles had refused to declare themselves while the jackals and baboons declared themselves for both sides. The mature antelope quietly supported the status quo.

The wildebeest stampeded this way and that; the snakes bit anything that passed (as is their nature); the springbok were scared; and the vultures waited. Tony Blair was seen watching through binoculars from the Lodge bar, amused.

As everybody knows, the incumbent won. Yesterday he reshuffled his pride, and led them down to the waterhole with him for Prime Minister's Questions. At his entrance, the animals squawked, shrieked, grunted or roared – each in his own peculiar way. The old lion – who has become his deputy and had been roaring all morning (on every channel) – settled down and yawned.

Among the other animals there was a sort of twittering anticipation. It has been some time since it was possible to come down to drink, and the banks of the waterhole filled fast. Squeaking and growling filled the air. Crocs cruised. The old buck on the front bench below the gangway watched, amused. From a tree came an angry gibbering sound: Mrs Gorman. Then, to everybody's surprise, in slipped the cheetah. It was rather brave. John Redwood seemed uncertain where to sit, hoping at first to take a seat that had already been booked, then being forced to move off it, not for the first time.

To even greater surprise, the cheetah tried an exploratory snarl. Redwood suggested Major take heed of Redwood's ideas in the years ahead.

Rather unusually (for this lion) Major resisted the temptation to be too generous in victory. He effectively suggested the cheetah hunt his own patch in future.

There was one bizarre moment at the Tory waterhole yesterday, when a tourist tried to intervene. It was Tony Blair. He had a question for the lion. Betty Boothroyd, the Park Warden, completely failed to notice him and had to be reminded of his existence.

So must we be. However absorbing this savage documentary has been, British politics can present, and now reverts to, a wider frame.

Hair-Raising Sexism   *12.7.95*

By happy coincidence, Michael Heseltine entered the chamber just after a new young minister, questioned about age discrimination, had announced the title of an official pamphlet: *Too old? Who says?*

Who indeed? The Deputy Prime Minister and First Secretary of State has had a sleek new hairdo for the job, a sort of ash-blond supertrim, and was plainly having a good hair day. So was Cheryl Gillan, the new junior Education and Employment minister. As a backbencher, with her ritual offerings of joyful tidings at Prime Minister's Questions, she was called by this column a little ray of sunshine. However bleak the outlook, Mrs Gillan could always find a fresh posy of optimistic news to lay at the PM's feet. Now our little ray of sunshine has been given a candle of her own to hold, and bade to shine.

She, too, had visited the hairdresser before her first ministerial outing, and was having a very good hair day indeed. Michael Fabricant (C, Mid Staffs) was having a bad hair day. Sketchwriters had declared a voluntary ceasefire on Mr Fabricant's wig until Christmas, but yesterday he tore up the accord with a gratuitous and sexist reference to another MP's hair.

'How lovely it is,' he breathed, 'to see such a good head of blond hair on the front bench.' Heseltine had not arrived, so Cheryl Gillan knew the remark was meant for her. She was not sure how to take it.

The House took it with hilarity: Mr Fabricant's own hairdo is blond, and summer is a bad time for wigs. In this heat the perspiration must be vile and the temptation to whip the thing off powerful; but rumour has it that Mr Fabricant's hair is a complicated marriage between art and nature, where divorce would take time.

And now Mrs Gillan's boss, Education and Employment Secretary Gillian Shephard, enters our story. Beneath Mrs Shephard's mumsy good humour lurks a secret feminism, and she was irked by Fabricant's remark. But she had to wait for her revenge until one of the questions she was to answer came up. When it did the Tory on his feet was no longer Fabricant but the stooped and schoolmasterly Bob Dunn (Dartford), congratulating her on her new Cabinet role.

No matter. For the passing moment Mrs Shephard was cross – on Cheryl's behalf. She was cross with men, any men. Dunn was a man.

'And *I* congratulate my hon friend,' she snapped, 'on *his* lovely blond hairstyle'.

Mr Dunn's hair isn't blond, it doesn't amount to a style, and frankly it isn't lovely. Bemused, he took it on the chin. Fabricant escaped the chamber, probably in terror. If this was what Mrs Shephard could do to someone who had not offended her, how might she deal with someone who had?

Shortly afterwards John Major arrived in a new orange tie and his old grey hair. Shephard found herself wedged, a brunette buffer-zone, between the Prime Minister (bad hair) and his Deputy (good hair).

Still, Mr Major had some excuse for looking dishevelled. On the day after it was reported someone had fired a gun at him, it was crass of Jim Dowd (Lab, Lewisham W) to inquire why he needed a deputy. Major had no trouble with the answer. But when Denis McShane (Lab, Rotherham) asked him to protest at French nuclear tests in the Pacific, the PM seemed to fumble for notes.

Unable to find them and forced to his feet, Major hesitated. He knew what he *thought*; and he would have to say something. 'No,' he said. MacShane look stunned.

How seldom ministers realize that brevity can be the nuclear option.

4.10.95   # A Picture of Dorian Blair

The Labour Party Conference ...

Before Tony Blair's speech, a chap near me growled: ''E thinks 'e's the dog's bollocks.' Well he's entitled to. It was a commanding speech: a real dog's bollocks of an oration.

Echoing John F. Kennedy, Newt Gingrich and Jesus Christ, and interrupted by 13 minutes (in total) of mid-speech applause, the Labour leader came as close as a politician can to offering a glimpse of the Promised Land. We can identify six key elements to this: new Britain, new Labour, new technology, New Testament, new audience – and old Tony.

Before this week new Britain was a sun-drenched dependency in the Pacific. But as Blair himself said, picturing the future: 'Virtual reality tourism allows you anywhere in the world.' Thrilling to his picture of a classless, crime-free, brotherly, sisterly nation, delegates filed out into a grey sky and spitting wind. It spoilt a Britain where we half-thought (though he never quite promised) there would be no more rain.

What, then, is new Labour? Tony Blair has discovered what other socialists have missed. That a Tory speech goes down well in Britain. He therefore gave one. There were even cries – non-ironic – of 'hyah! hyah!' during his passage on law and order. But the British enjoy a *frisson* of modernism too. So with Mary Wilson sitting proudly behind him, Blair treated us to a 1990s rerun of Harold Wilson's Sixties dream about the technological revolution.

Few understood much of this but we knew it was terrifically important – probably for the young. But there was something for older voters too. Blair offered the New Testament. Within moments he was quoting Christ. Near the end he declared (twice): 'Be strong and of good courage.' The tone was positively messianic. Mr Blair has yet to declare: 'As God said and rightly ...' but he will. 'Discipline! Courage! Determination! Honesty!' Caught on a cusp somewhere between Florence Nightingale and Ché Guevara, Mr Blair's peroration approached the phrasing they embroider on school caps. We loved it.

Commentators will say he is winning his audience round, but I think he is winning a new audience. There are missing faces this year and many unfamiliar ones. Politicians used to think that if the audience didn't like the message, you changed the message. Mr Blair has changed the audience.

So was it new Britain? Or the old Britain that Labour never noticed? New Labour? Or old Harold repolished? New Testament? Or old-time religion? Perhaps Professor Hawking is right: Blair has fused the funnels between black holes and is taking us time travelling. Old Tony stays as fresh as each succeeding dawn.

On Tuesday this sketch suggested that, like Dorian Gray, Tony Blair keeps a likeness somewhere, absorbing his sins and ageing for him. A friend has sent the quote from Wilde:

'Now wherever you go you charm the world. Will it always be so? ... You have a wonderfully beautiful face Mr Gray. Don't frown. You have. And Beauty is a form of genius – is higher, indeed, than Genius because it needs no explanation ... it cannot be questioned. It has its

divine right of sovereignty. It makes princes of those who have it. You smile? Ah! When you have lost you won't smile.'

Yesterday Tony Blair made a beautiful speech and made it beautifully. It will not stand question but does not need to. As Wilde says: 'Beauty is the wonder of wonders. It is only shallow people who do not judge by appearances.'

Yesterday Dorian Blair was the dog's bollocks.

7.10.95   Achtung Neues Britannien …

Disziplin. Mut. Entschlossenheit. Eherlichkeit … That was Tony Blair at the climax of his Tuesday speech – translated into German. We know this because his office has issued a special German version with his photograph on the cover.

Neues Labour. Neues Britannien. Eine Erneuerte Partei.

Somehow, it strikes a chill. The chill, no more than a passing shiver, resurfaced during John Prescott's rallying performance yesterday. In pride of place was a passage about smashing the fat cats. It carried a measure of menace and glee, and met a level of cheering, which may propel a tiny cloud of anxiety, no bigger than a man's hand, into our otherwise sunny recollection of this conference.

Still, Prescott's was a fine, thumping, funny speech. Even after a triumphant week it isn't over until the fat man hollers. Very much the Les Dawson of the Labour Party, John Prescott dares, and wins. A moment to savour was watching the signer for the deaf trying to convey a passage in which Humphrey the cat is dragged back through the Downing Street cat flap, 'screeching and scratching and spitting every inch of the way'. On reaching the cat flap, the signer nearly did himself an injury. Prescott's wife Pauline watched doe-eyed. She had arrived a little late. We had heard earlier that uniformed officers had been briefly called into the foyer. It may have been the fashion police going in to break up Mrs Prescott's hair.

'We're on our way!' bellowed her husband. The leader sat not yards away with that papery skin and thin, strained, brittle smile. The fat man leads the shouting; the control-freak watches. 'Anständige Menschen, gute Menschen. Patrioten … Das ist unser Volk,' says

Blair's text. Prescott launched into a bullying attack on a journalist. It was meant to amuse. It went too far. Again, that chill.

Then they sang the slaves' chorus from *Nabucco*. Disziplin. The next song, a pop number, went: 'Movin' on up!' Blair's spin-doctors may not realize that in full the lyrics continue: 'Who d'you think you are? This time you've gone too far.'

And, after *The Red Flag*, everybody sashayed out. Leaving, I pushed past the hungry-faced demonstrators who used to be found inside Labour conferences but these days press noses to the glass. Within you meet Norman Tebbit and the tribunes of industry, come to deal.

Und in der Fusion von Wirtschaft und Technologie, da liegt die Zukunft.

Do you remember the last pages of Orwell's *Animal Farm*? The pigs have taken control of the humbler animals, occupy the farmhouse – renamed New Animal Farm? – and invite the humans, former foes, for drinks. Napoleon, the pigs' leader, makes a speech ... '*He, too, he said, was happy that the period of misunderstanding was at an end. There had been rumours ... that there was something subversive and even revolutionary in the outlook of himself and his colleagues. Nothing could be further from the truth!*'

The humbler animals press noses to the glass:

'*No question what had happened to the faces of the pigs. The creatures outside looked from pig to man and from man to pig again. But already it was impossible to say which was which.*'

Ihr Nachbar ist mein Nachbar. Das ist der echte Patriotismus eines Landes.

Permed Pretender   *11.10.95*

The Conservative Party Conference ...

'Who dares wins!' cried Michael Portillo in what can only be seen as a coded message of support for John Redwood's bid for leadership of the Tory Right. In a vulgar speech, largely devoid of content, Mr Portillo wowed Tory representatives here in Blackpool by declaring in his gruffest voice that a Conservative government would never do a number of things nobody had ever suggested a Conservative government would ever dream of doing anyway.

The conference loved it, cheering and stamping. If there is a section of the party unimpressed by the spectacle of a politician with permed hair strutting his way into their affections on the reflected glory of real soldiers who take real risks, it was silent yesterday.

Mr Portillo took no risks. The more blood a Tory speaker brings into his speech, the less of his own he risks. I remember the Michael Portillo I used to know and ask myself whether this new Portillo has honestly come to believe all this guff, or whether he knows it's guff, but says it anyway. It is debatable which would be more chilling.

The Tories' new logo this year seemed to glow behind Mr Portillo. Conference-goers are calling it 'the whoosh!', and it seems to be based on those Union Jack arrows marching over the Continent in *Dad's Army*. The Tory arrow curls and swoops upwards in a gravity-defying whoosh! like Mr Portillo's hair. The Portillo lip is also beginning to do this. Even the Portillo gaze keeps lifting as he hears the trumpets. It is as if the whole Portillo persona teeters on the point of lift-off, ready for whoosh! The Defence Secretary must find the persistence of gravity in his political career immensely tiresome.

Watching Tony Blair last week, and Michael Portillo yesterday, it struck me that a modern political audience expects to be masturbated by its speakers. Portillo knows this. It is rather unsavoury.

Equally sinister is the new party chairman, Dr Brian Mawhinney. Dr Mawhinney comes over as a 1990s version of the child-grabber in *Chitty Chitty Bang Bang*. Someone has told him to smile more often and the effect freezes the blood. Mawhinney is a powerful speaker, a wonderful sneerer, and so deadly a communicator of unarticulated menace that, should he tire of politics, he could walk straight into any of a dozen Pinter roles or get a top job as a police interrogator. This man can say, 'from the bottom of my heart' (he did yesterday) in a way that has every male in his audience moving instinctively to protect our groins.

The speech chilled rather than rallied. Outside the hall a kiosk is selling 'Ice Cold Slush'. Inside it, so was Mawhinney. 'I will skip quickly over the Liberals,' he sneered, 'like the rest of the country.' And like Alan Howarth.

Breathless Birdman Flies to Freedom

17.10.95

Michael Howard sacks the head of the Prison Service …

Especially in the House, it can make an enormous difference where you pause. Hecklers crouch ready to leap into the tiniest gap. Offer a chink of silence and gigglers stand poised to giggle. Guffaws are lobbed like grenades on to so much as a handkerchief of unprotected space in a minister's text.

Take, for instance, the key passage in Michael Howard's statement yesterday on prison security.

Journalists knew the script before him (we had the advance text) but MPs, who did not, could not anticipate his words. How he read them was critical. The Home Secretary could have said:

'*I have come to the conclusion, with some sadness …*' and paused. Tories would have shot up in their seats. Was Howard about to resign? The Official Report this morning might have read: 'Hon Members gasp'.

Or he could have said '*I have come to the conclusion, with some sadness, that this requires a change …*' and paused. 'Of Government!' a dozen Labour members would have chorused. 'Bye-bye', others would have cooed.

Or he could have said '*I have come to the conclusion, with some sadness, that this requires a change of leadership …*' and paused. Dennis Skinner would have cut the air with 'you're sacked, then' within a microsecond. The Official Report would have noted: 'Hon Members: "… of Home Secretary!" '

Or he could have said '*I have come to the conclusion, with some sadness, that this requires a change of leadership at the top …*' and paused. 'Hooray!', 'good riddance!' and 'pack yer bags', the Opposition would have shouted.

But Michael Howard is a canny chap who, though he never commands the House, knows very well how to dodge it. So he took a deep breath and sprinted straight through the sentence, allowing so little space between words that not so much as the blade of an assassin's knife could be inserted. '*IhavecometotheconclusionwithsomesadnessthatthisrequiresachangeofleadershipatthetopofthePrisonService.*'

25.10.95   # Lords of the Jungle

It was billed as the battle of the titans. This was to be Michael Heseltine's debut at the dispatch box as Deputy Prime Minister. John Major was away in America so the Lion King would roar on his behalf. Tony Blair would field his own deputy, John Prescott, in his place.

Nice as they are and sharp as they sometimes can be, Mr Blair and Mr Major are hardly Rambos of the Commons chamber. Though their spats grow daily more vicious, the hatpin is wielded as often as the cudgel. Both can seem close to crossing the floor and pulling each other's hair. Prescott and Heseltine, however, are different: more of the old-school stampers and roarers, Big Cats.

Heseltine, the man who for two decades has fused hearing aids and rattled pearls, dentures and teacups at Bournemouth, Brighton and Blackpool; Prescott, the trade unionist whom Tory mums use to frighten naughty children ('eat your runner beans, George, or Mr Prescott will come and get you'), the former ship's steward who has massacred the English language, curdled the mushy peas and warmed hearts in working men's clubs from Hull to Doncaster ... Now, at last, these two bruisers were to meet in combat. Two great beasts of the political jungle, in the same clearing, at the same time!

Lesser political animals – the Tory and Labour herds – peered nervously through the bamboo. The monkeys of the press gibbered in the trees. What could we expect? An anti-climax, naturally. From one side of the clearing entered the Lion King, to roars from his supporters. From the other, Buffalo Prescott stomped in, snorting. The buffalo's supporters roared even louder. 'Questions to the Prime Minister,' called Betty Boothroyd from the canopied safety of Madam Speaker's tent. And the lion and the buffalo lunged forward at each other.

And missed each other. And lunged past each other. And bellowed and postured, and made a lot of noise and no sense at all – and crashed uselessly into the undergrowth. And that was it. Part of the problem was that both were visibly nervous. Michael Heseltine's hand was shaking when he picked up his notes. John Prescott shouted out his questions like a schoolboy at reading practice. Determined to make an impact, Heseltine went even further over the top than his opponent, succeeding (where none has before) in making Mr Prescott sound positively statesmanlike.

Each achieved one half-strike. Welcoming Heseltine to his post, Prescott noted his presence at the dispatch box for Prime Minister's Questions, and congratulated him on achieving his dream. This rattled Heseltine, but he retaliated with spirited mockery of Prescott's 'minder', the shadowy Peter Mandelson, Mr Blair's spin-doctor *extraordinaire*. As Mandelson was at that moment skulking just behind the Speaker's Chair and some of the Tories could see him, this cheered the government side. But what would it have meant to the electorate beyond?

Thereafter, Prescott's question (about the cost of something or other) and Heseltine's answers (pre-packaged; nothing to do with the question) generated noise, but little else. A number of small trees and shrubs were trampled in the fracas. Prescott left unharmed.

Heseltine left reflecting, perhaps a little ruefully, that being Prime Minister was a little bit harder than he had thought. Some of the rest of us left appreciating, rather more than before, John Major's steady bat.

A Session of Mists and Numbing Dullness

9.11.95

On a misty London autumn day, Parliament was prorogued yesterday amid the customary flummery performed in a near-empty chamber to a smattering of baffled tourists. Few know why the session ends now. Few care to inquire. I cannot remember when the place had a scratchier, more distracted feel. MPs know they are sinking to new depths in public esteem and are not confident that their decision to disclose fees will bring the decline to a halt.

It has been plain from frontbench questions and backbench heckles that the Opposition sees Monday's resolution as the beginning, not the end, of a long war of attrition on Tory Members' interests. Careless how they risk bringing their whole House, rather than just the Tories, into disrepute, they relish the discomfiture of the Conservative Party: a great hot-air balloon, leaking in all directions and dipping ever closer to the waves as its panicking passengers jettison directorships, consultancies, mistresses, Cup Final tickets ... anything, to delay the approaching dunking.

Tory depression this week is easy to explain. More mysterious is the continuing benightedness of the principal Opposition. Tony Blair, who has led them to a record lead in the opinion polls and fresh from a great speech to his party conference, is greeted twice weekly, as he strides in for Prime Minister's Questions, with a cheer so low as to be almost sullen. Attendance has been thin for a party riding a wave of public support and heading for victory. Questions to ministers from Labour sound, too often, ill-coached and unconvinced. One bad speech from Jack Straw on the prison crisis left his party dismayed and reeling.

Why so downhearted? Your sketchwriter remembers the cruellest days for Labour in the early 1980s when, with Michael Foot as their leader, it was impossible to believe they could win and possible to doubt whether they would survive as a mainstream political party. Yet they were in better heart then than now.

I used to sit opposite them, on the Tory benches. Margaret Thatcher looked unstoppable, yet the Opposition would roar their outrage at her Government with a moral confidence and sincerity that – though miles higher in the polls – they cannot match today.

They knew she could beat them but they were damned if they were going to join her: as with some doomed prophet, fatalism and self-belief marched hand in hand. Echoing the Gospels they might have cried: 'It needs must be that offences come, but woe unto those men through whom they come!' Now they *are* those men, or expect to be.

The Commons just risen had developed the air of a long-stay, low-security mental asylum. Here, someone would be shouting at a tree; there, another would be weeping quietly alone on a bench; a third would be stumbling through the marigolds mumbling to herself; while a handful more would be jabbing fingers at each other in inane dispute. Sitting in my seat above the chamber last week, just after a ministerial statement, a man's voice was suddenly raised in a string of shouted obscenities, 'you f****** hypocrites, you're all ...'

'Routine stuff,' I thought, 'but they're warming up. I wonder if the Chair heard.'

Then I saw a terrific struggle in the Strangers' Gallery, as a mad interrupter was dragged by attendants from his seat. Down in the chamber MPs stared up in shock. Had it been one of their own number they wouldn't have paused from their Christmas card lists.

New Black Rod, Same Old Story   *16.11.95*

The Queen opens Parliament …

Yesterday paint was thrown over Dr Brian Mawhinney, the Tory chairman. It can only improve him. Afterwards he looked happier than we have ever seen him. He had been recognized at last!

Your sketchwriter watched the Queen's Speech on television. The grey plastic set seemed a bland frame for such visual richness, so I adorned mine with a piece of tinsel and a strip of synthetic fur from the detached collar of an old anorak. Readers may like to try this. Her Majesty looked more comfortable. The ceremonials might be improved, henceforth, by the ritual daubing of the party chairman in paint before the Queen arrives.

Waiting in the Commons had been Dennis Skinner. Before the Queen's Speech begins, Black Rod, a chap in tights carrying a billiard cue, marches in to summon MPs. Last year, Sir Richard Thomas retired as Black Rod. Yesterday General Sir Edward Jones took his place.

'New Labour,' growled Dennis, 'new Black Rod.'

After lunch, debate commenced. By tradition one senior and one junior government backbencher propose and second the motion. Douglas Hurd and Gyles Brandreth (Chester) were given the honour. At first Douglas Hurd looked and sounded awkward. For so long the statesman defending sticky wickets abroad, the requirement simply to offer a charming description of his own constituency (Witney) seemed to discomfit him.

He tried a poetic line or two: 'On a spring evening,' burbled the white-haired luminary, 'when daffodils are bright against the grey stone.' Alarmed, one began to miss Mr Hurd's more familiar style – on Bosnia, for instance. Fortunately he quit the daffodils pretty fast.

And this newest backbencher soon found his old stride. Who can better his depiction of the Commons' loss of touch with voters? Members of Parliament were 'playing out the old play'. But 'beyond the footlights, half the audience had walked away, and the other half are watching with mounting irritation'.

'Political success,' said Hurd, 'may well go to those who sound least like politicians.' Everone murmured 'Hear, hear'. He made a dignified plea for less juvenile debate – what he called 'empty noise and phoney warfare'. Again, everyone murmured 'Hear, hear'.

And within twenty minutes they were all at it.

But first a pleasant distraction. After a stilted start, Gyles Brandreth gave one of the best junior supporting speeches made in recent years. His wife, he told MPs, had heard him described on local radio as 'an expert on the marriage Act'. This had surprised her. 'She nearly fell out of her bunk.'

A sparkling speech deserved sparkling heckling – and Brandreth got it. 'Quite simply,' began this near-miss winner of one of Britain's most marginal seats, 'Chester is the best place in the world. Two thousand years of matchless history ...'

'And a one thousand majority,' shouted Joe Ashton (Lab, Bassetlaw). 'Actually it's 1,101,' said Brandreth.

But good humour evaporated when the big boys got up. Tony Blair made an undignified, nose-thumbing speech. John Major responded with a plea for 'an end to this silly name-calling'. He then called Blair's speech 'copper-plated nonsense' and his opinions 'total baloney'. And sucks to you too.

New Labour, a relaunched Prime Minister, a new Black Rod, a new session ...

... and there they go again. Douglas Hurd watched sadly, thinking perhaps of the Witney daffodils.

22.11.95

The Only House Where No One Talked of You-Know-Who

The Princess of Wales told all in a Panorama interview but a day later MPs stay silent ...

Never let it be said that MPs miss the public mood. One topic preoccupied the nation yesterday. One affair, on television interview, one Royal Personage, dominated everybody's thoughts. No bar, bus or taxi was free from its discussion. Nobody could overlook the drama.

Except the *Inverness Courier* and the House of Commons. The *Courier* must answer for itself. At the Commons, despite all expectations, nobody thought to raise the royal controversy. Nobody mentioned it at Prime Minister's Questions, and the House moved to debate social affairs, MPs defining that term differently from Their Royal Highnesses.

Doubtless John Major was briefed to answer any royal question which might arise. Madam Speaker will have been forearmed to nip in the bud any improper references to the Palace. Tony Blair will have prepared his own response. But the subject never came up. Thus does our Mother of Parliaments keep her finger to the national pulse. Tourists and visitors in the Strangers' Gallery must have been baffled.

Annie Coleman surely was. Miss Coleman, dressed in red, was sitting in the Special Gallery where her MP, Nigel Jones (Lib Dem, Cheltenham), had arranged a ringside seat. Miss Coleman is 105.

She looked as sharp as a pin, paying careful attention throughout Prime Minister's Questions, smiling when John Major regretted (to the Tories' Sir Donald Thompson, MP) that his powers did not extend to causing the rain to fall in Yorkshire. She listened as MPs discussed attitudes to the Nigerian regime, and inclined her head, covering her face for a moment, as Major and Blair capered through their usual forgettable ding-dong.

Miss Coleman heard Mr Major exchange views on Ireland with the Ulster Unionist leader, David Trimble; and answer a question from John Wittingdale (C, Colchester South & Maldon) about the drug Ecstasy.

I wonder what she made of it? Returning, I found the *Hansard* for Tuesday November 25, 1890, the sitting day in the year of Miss Coleman's birth closest to yesterday's date. James Tynte Agg-Gardner was the MP for Cheltenham. Victoria was Queen and Edward, later the Seventh, Prince of Wales. Alexandra was his Princess.

November 25 was the opening of the new session, but Victoria did not come. The Gracious Speech mentioned trouble in Ireland. A potato famine was rife there. There was no drought in Yorkshire, however, and Ecstasy was not a problem. Opium was.

Nigeria was not called Nigeria, but the *Annual Register* records that in Lagos 'the natives were opposing the Government proposal to light the town by electricity'. Inland, there had been a small uprising among the Yoruba tribe, whose Chief the British Resident had killed.

The Leader of the Opposition, W. E. Gladstone (Edinburgh, Mid Lothian) replied to the Gracious Speech in galumphing prose ('I intimate no misgiving on the subject ...') and interminable sentences utterly unredeemed by wit, irony or polish. Thuddingly prosaic, the speech boasted a Blairite high-mindedness, but no soundbites. Most of his speech was about Ireland. Replying for Lord Salisbury, the Prime Minister, was the First Lord of the Treasury, a certain Mr W. H. Smith. Yes, the same one.

Annie Coleman was not even a year old. She will not recall. So let us hope she remembers yesterday, the day the Commons didn't discuss the *Panorama* interview, with pleasure.

29.11.95
Proposals I Do Not Intend to Make

As so often, the heckle said all. 'Is that it?' shouted Dennis Skinner, as the Chancellor moved listlessly to what passed for a peroration. Kenneth Clarke, who succeeded yesterday in boring first the Opposition, then his own side and then the press, had succeeded finally in boring even himself.

Budget-makers love natty titles to dub their creations: 'a Budget for Enterprise', 'a Budget for Growth', a 'Steady As She Goes' Budget. This, however, was an 'Is That It?' Budget.

Dame Jill Knight (C, Edgbaston), in Quink-blue with buttons, who has watched the Budget game long enough to acquire some sixth sense, started yawning even before Mr Clarke began.

Up in the overflow gallery, two senior Tory backbenchers went to sleep. One of them, a corpulent chap who represents a Midlands seat, managed to stay awake for an early section, which he could understand: 'the PSBR is the difference between two enormous numbers,' said the Chancellor, possibly in an attempt to explain his Budget to himself. Our Midlands Tory nodded wisely. But, as Clarke undertook to 'embrace change in a flexible way', our friend's nods turned to a slumping motion.

He struggled to keep his grip on consciousness through the passage on challenge funding and the Private Finance Initiative, but began to slip again as the Chancellor turned to projected public spending for 1998–99.

The landfill tax proved too much for him. As Mr Clarke detailed a £2 per tonne tax on inactive waste, inactivity – or the Commons central heating – overcame the somnolent Midlander. His head fell back against the oak panelling.

Even the excise reprieve for rolling tobacco ('A Budget for Marijuana Topers?') failed to arouse him. When Clarke announced his plans for very strong cider, our friend's head lolled heavily to the left. For the next hour he never moved again.

His colleague, a fellow-sleeper, loses his south London constituency to boundary changes at the next election and is looking for another seat. Important interviews lie ahead so we dare not name him. But our south Londoner gave up the struggle as Clarke, stifling a yawn, said: 'Let me turn to some other proposals I do not intend to make.'

Just before pegging out, our friend had managed to prop his head in a corner of the gallery, against some railings. As the Chancellor turned to savings and long-term retirement bonds for the elderly, the backbencher's eyes shut.

As Clarke outlined new incentives for employee shareholding schemes, the south Londoner's lips drew back from his teeth in a rictus grin which I once saw on a dog which had drowned in a flash flood.

He was out cold.

It is held to be disrespectful to allege that a Member of Parliament is ever asleep in the Chamber, but sleep is the most respectful explanation possible for this MP's expression. When the Chancellor mentioned 'the backbone of our modern, dynamic economy', his head came loose from the moorings of the rail, and slumped forward. This woke him.

Dazed for a few minutes, he began to absorb Mr Clarke's words on the new tax regime for savings income. Turning round, he observed his Midlander colleague, still asleep. Looking across to your sketchwriter, opposite him in the press gallery, he gestured to me, pointing out his sleeping colleague.

'The enterprise centre of Europe! That's where we're going!' cried the Chancellor, trying to rally himself as much as the rest of us. The Tory who had just woken up continued to try to point me to his sleeping colleague.

As the Chancellor sat down, and the Conservative MPs filed out, he had the good grace to waken him. Both left, one of them still uncertain where he was or what he had just sat through.

He had missed nothing.

Straight Man Steals the Pantomime Show

President Clinton addresses Parliament ...

Nearly all the Williams were there. Waiting for President Bill in the Royal Gallery of the House of Peers were four other famous Williams. William I, a gilded statue, stood at the door. In oils, the portraits of the Williams II, III and IV peered dispassionately down from the walls at this presidential Willie-come-lately to the hall of fame. The boy who will one day (God willing) be King William V, being at Eton, was unable to attend.

Presidents and Kings have their paths smoothed before them. Mr Clinton breezed in to the sound of trumpets, found a crowd assembled for his address, gave it, and breezed out again. Sketchwriters, however, had been waiting an hour.

Before the President came the dignified part of the British constitution, Black Rod, in silk and lace, with billiard cue. Then came the even more dignified part of the constitution, the Baroness Thatcher. In hot pursuit came the undignified part of the constitution, George Foulkes (Lab, Carrick, Cumnock & Doon Valley); and, moments later, the efficient part of the constitution, House Leader Tony Newton.

Also present was the invented part of the constitution, Deputy Prime Minister Michael Heseltine. Tony Blair, looking tense, arrived early, and waited.

Even the photographers wore ties. One straightened his as the pantomime part of the constitution, the Lord Chancellor and Madam Speaker, processed forward in funereal tights and gilded brocade, knocking 'em cold in black and gold.

And we were ready. A fanfare of what sounded like antique cornets rent the air, the noise being similar to that of a New York traffic jam. Maybe this was to help Mr Clinton feel at home. He rose to speak.

The President spoke well. Surrounded by all the ridiculous flim-flam of invented British antiquity, Lord Chancellor in ludicrous fancy dress, the backdrop of unspeakable Victoriana, Mr Clinton appeared as one from a quieter and deeper-rooted tradition.

In plain grey suit, single-breasted, he spoke calmly, in tones more thoughtful and less showy than our British appetite for political theatre expects. It was a beautifully crafted speech: relaxed, considered, delivered with poise. I felt ashamed to reflect that the US President was the least vulgar thing in the room. America was restrained, understated; Britain, as ever, pantomime.

Madam Speaker thanked him. The three ships, she said, which had taken the early settlers to America, had summed up, in their names, every settler's hopes: '*Godspeed, Discovery* and the *Susan Constant.*' Susan must have been quite a girl.

Madam Speaker also quoted Thomas Jefferson, revealing that he was her hero. She did not mention that he insisted on sleeping with his slaves. As Miss Boothroyd and her retinue departed, her train-bearer looked distinctly nervous.

Tony Banks is for Life, Not Just for Christmas

8.12.95

Who would be Prime Minister? One afternoon you are jetting around the world, talking to foreign leaders. The next you are telling the Commons that a puppy is for life, not just for Christmas.

Yes, really. Yesterday, Tony Banks (Lab, Newham NW) asked John Major to remind Santa that a pet was not a festive gift, but an all-year-round commitment.

Mr Major looked bemused. Michael Heseltine stared at his shoes. Major had sold him a pup only last June – the office of Deputy Prime Minister. He was still feeling sore.

Banks looked smug. His majority is in almost five figures and this MP is not just for Christmas. He yaps at the Tories, nips his own leader's calves, and embarrasses the Chair with his language. Banks leaves little messes all of his own on the Commons carpet. Tony Blair must often have been tempted to bundle Banks into the boot and abandon him on the hard shoulder of the M1. Perhaps at the next election the voters of Newham North West should have handed to them with their voting slips a leaflet warning, '*Remember, Tony Banks is for life, not just for Christmas*'.

But how was the PM to respond? All he could do was repeat, po-faced, RSPCA advice to would-be pet-owners.

It is a novel way of using the premier: as a mouthpiece for important public service announcements. We wondered what other festive advice Mr Major might be asked to offer. 'Clunk-click, every trip,' perhaps, or 'If you're on your bike, wear white!' Now the nights have closed in, should not the Prime Minister be primed to warn grannies not to open the door to men claiming to be from the gas board?

Nor do the possibilities stop there. During the thoughtful bits in his speeches, Major often adopts an engaging Mystic Meg tone; so he might consider ending each PM's Questions with a multi-secular thought for the day: 'Remember, tomorrow is the first day of the rest of your life!'

After his pronouncements on responsible pet-ownership, John Major sat down, looking philosophical. His reverie on animal rights was disturbed by a query about mere human rights and the European Court. But David Atkinson (C), hot-foot from his constituency of Bournemouth E, brought the Prime Minister hard up against the Big Issues with the grim news that as the millennium approaches, legions of the nation's computers 'will fail because they are not programmed to recognize the double zero in 2,000'.

Apparently they are panicking in the palm courts. Mr Major, switching from his Mystic Meg voice to his computer-hacker's voice, and switching in his mind from abandoned puppies to crashing laptops, found this 'a very helpful intervention'.

To whom? It is, we suppose, conceivable that an intending puppy-purchaser might reconsider his gift in light of the PM's advice on dog-ownership. But does hysteria grip the nation's IT technicians today as they ponder that missing 00 to which Mr Major yesterday alerted them? And it got worse. Within minutes, responding to Hugh Bayley (Lab, York), poor Mr Major found himself obliged to declare, like some demented nutritionist, 'Beef is a safe and wholesome product!' He forgot to remind us to floss our teeth. There was no evidence, he added, that 'mad cow' disease infected humans.

'Look among your own Cabinet!' yelled Tony Banks. It was a cold day but Madam Speaker's expression suggested it might be time to put this puppy out.

If It's Stationery – Privatize It   *14.12.95*

Betty Boothroyd had a twitchy look yesterday as ministers announced the privatization of Her Majesty's Stationery Office. HMSO print *Hansard* and all the official parliamentary papers. With each passing month Madam Speaker hears the shells landing closer to her own trench.

There's a festive game in which you start with a phrase, then lop off the last word, then the last two ... successively increasing the size of the amputation until a surprising result is reached. Tory privatization policy seems to resemble this. The statement yesterday suggested that, for the moment, it is the *office* which is to be shunted off into the private sector: that is to say the staff, the administration and the printing works are to go.

As Roger Freeman, the Minister, pointed out, this will enable the company to use the machinery for other publications too. *Titbits*, perhaps, *Boyz*, or *Just Seventeen*? Heaven help the foreman in charge when parts of *Hello!* get interspersed with pages of *The Official Report*. Readers of *Hello!* – decent, family-minded people – would blanch at the smears, the tittle-tattle, the sheer vulgarity which passes for parliamentary debate.

But though the O in HMSO is to be privatized, the HMS (said the Minister) will stay. Staff responsible for HM Stationery remain in public employ, to give the privatized O work.

And next? The S: Her Majesty's *stationery*. The Queen's notepaper could easily attract commercial interest. British businesses have already been asked to sponsor flagpoles outside Buckingham Palace.

Next to be privatized could be the *Majesty*. When, years ago, Tony Benn made the suggestion that the Tories might get the private sector to pay for royal pomp ('The State Opening, sponsored by Benson & Hedges,' chuckled Benn), he meant it as a joke. But under the Tories the jokes of the Eighties are the White Papers of the Nineties.

Majesty cries out for flotation. The Government already seeks private sponsorship for the Royal Yacht. Thus do we remove the O, the S and the M from HMSO. We begin to understand Miss Boothroyd's anxiety. For what is left? *Her*.

And why not? The Speakership could be a real money-spinner. The Speaker's procession into the chamber, followed by the chap with the golden mace and the chaplain in antique costume, needs to be handled with reverence. It could be franchised to Classic FM: '*Miss Boothroyd's shoes by Anello & Davide*'.

The Speaker's Chair itself, in green leather, comes with a canopy fringed in brocade and tassels. Harrods could handle this with aplomb. A tasteful logo could be worked in gold thread into the frieze. The store might sell replicas.

Which brings us to the Speaker's House. Barratt Homes are seeking to reposition their corporate identity upmarket, but such an association risks re-positioning Miss Boothroyd downmarket. My own view is that the better sort of estate agency – Savills, perhaps? – should be encouraged to bid for the freehold. A small Savills banner might be flown from the tower above Miss Boothroyd's bedroom.

You laugh, reader? Wait.

19.12.95   # Freak Show

Six hybrid creatures limped, lolloped or flapped into the Commons circus ring yesterday afternoon to perform in an exotic freak show called *The Prime Minister's Statement on the Madrid European Council.*

First into the ring was something called the Partial Emu. This sadly disabled bird, seemingly wingless, was partnered by something more remarkable yet: the Push-me-pull-you Prime Minister, a creature apparently unable to say 'yes' without adding 'or no' and incapable of saying 'whether' without the suffix 'or not'.

Not to be outdone in the mutant stakes, we were next introduced (by the Tories' Sir Terence Higgins MP) to a bird called the Caw Currency – or was it the Cor! Currency? It was believed that this might fly in 1999, and would be christened 'the euro'. It was important to understand that the euro (also known as the Caw Currency) was *not* the same thing as the Single Currency, which did not exist. Sir Terence was afraid that if the euro did fly, the Non-Caw Currencies might try to raid its nest.

Just when you thought nature had displayed its strangest, in bowled the Hard Ecu, an animal which could proceed only by 'circulating in parallel' with the franc, the pound and the mark, but separately from them. Hard on the heels of the Hard Ecu came the Possible Referendum, a fabled beast of uncertain attributes, which the Push-me-pull-you Prime Minister sometimes claimed to see, and sometimes not.

It was believed that the Possible Referendum was designed to proceed ahead of the Partial Emu and possibly in tandem with the Hard Ecu (which itself, you remember, circulates in parallel with the franc, pound and mark). Such gymnastics were by way of cheerleading for the arrival of the Partial Emu, the Caw Currency and the euro, which, you remember, are probably the same thing (but not the same as the Single Currency which, you remember, is not in prospect).

It promises to be quite a floorshow.

Weirdest of all, and the last to make its entrance yesterday, was the Rubber-spined Labour Leader. With apparent ease this bird had managed to get its head right through the gap between its legs, from which unlikely position it hopped impertinently around, making sure its own position was never very far from the Push-me-pull-you Prime Minister's, and issuing a series of mocking calls to the Push-me-pull-you, demanding that it state where it stood and where it was going. The Push-me-pull-you's attempts to answer these squawks were cruelly hampered by its inability to say anything at all without adding 'or not'.

The circus baffled all spectators. Prize for the most arcane commentary from the stalls yesterday goes to Labour's Andrew Faulds (Warley E), who diagnosed 'plasticity of European purpose' on the Continent, but failed to note the plasticity of purpose on his own front bench, eight feet away.

The prize for opaque prose goes to the Push-me-pull-you Prime Minister, who, having pronounced the word 'whether' felt impelled to add 'or not' then, continuing 'we recognize our right to opt in', felt impelled to append 'or opt out'. The final 'whether or not we recognize our right to opt in or opt out' will challenge political science for decades to come. Or not.

The prize for being comprehensible goes, as usual, to Dennis Skinner, who said: 'It's a barmy name, "euro".' This was the only contribution anyone understood.

A Tory Defects

10.1.96

Barbaric regimes sometimes parade prisoners of war publicly, to prove they have not been eaten. Yesterday, as MPs resumed for 1996, the

Liberal Democratic Party took an early opportunity to show Miss Emma Nicholson to the world's media.

She had not been eaten. Flourishing, she sat arrayed in Day-Glo peach contrast to slim, ambitious Liz Lynne (Lib Dem, Rochdale) in green. Beaming from a grey backdrop of males, the pair resembled a large magnolia blossom plus one leaf. Let us hope that, in this small party, leaf never comes to resent blossom.

More than once the blossom seemed about to speak, but never did. Miss Nicholson sat silently through defence questions, smiling faintly as her new defence spokesman (Menzies Campbell) described her former defence chief (Michael Portillo) as a little creep.

Did she feel sympathy for the old firm? The Tories' ragged fortunes were illustrated by their frontbench defence team yesterday. The alleged creep being absent, two defence ministers were left to answer questions, and one could hardly speak. A throat infection has left James Arbuthnot whispering HMG's military might. It hardly inspires confidence. 'I'm extremely confident,' Mr Arbuthnot croaked. 'Unfortunately I'm also speechless.' 'You should be put down!' called Labour's Tony Banks (Newham NW), in a fit of seasonal goodwill.

Beside the thin and anxious Arbuthnot, vast brother-minister Nicholas Soames chuckled fatly: a Laurel and Hardy team, ready to break into a comedy routine. The thought of being led in war by this duo chills the blood.

At Prime Minister's Questions Miss Nicholson remained peachily impassive as John Major told the House she would soon regret her decision. Even Peter Brooke's astonishing attack failed to ruffle her. Once a rather bumbling character with a reputation for being a gent, Brooke has gone feral, morphing from Sergeant Wilson in *Dad's Army* to Victor Meldrew in *One Foot in the Grave*.

With Miss Nicholson in his sights, Brooke quoted *The Times*'s series on ageing. Among middle-aged women, he reminded us, one of 'those seven irritating little signs of the spiral towards death' was 'having voted Liberal Democrat at the last election'.

MPs guffawed. It was a below-the-belt day. Next came Ann Widdecombe, whose post of Prisons Minister was made for the clever, feisty and rather brutal Widdecombe: she appears to have stepped from *Prisoner Cell Block H*.

Her task yesterday was to defend the treatment of pregnant prisoners. In unspeakable gynaecological detail, married women from the Opposition accused Miss Widdecombe of not understanding childbirth.

The unspoken barb was that of course she wouldn't. Male journalists will long remember the horror of hearing Audrey Wise (Lab, Preston) on contractions or Diane Abbott (Lab, Hackney N & Stoke Newington) describe the moment when the cervix expands and the waters break.

Undaunted, Widdecombe barged on. To palpable disappointment among Tory men she insisted that women were not manacled ('secured') in labour.

Or in Labour. But maybe women should be manacled in the Tories? Staring glumly across the floor at the escaped magnolia, Tories pondered this. Too bad nobody secured Miss Nicholson.

Basildon Man   *16.1.96*

Poor David Amess (C, Basildon). For many years nicknamed Basildon Man, he has become famous for the frequency of his references to the town. No sparrow falls in Basildon but Amess mourns its fate. Whether the reference is to global warming or hip replacements, 'in Basildon', like some verbal tic, is inserted as others might insert "you know', 'er' or 'um'.

The result for Basildon having been the first key marginal to be declared at the last election, Amess's relieved face on a million TV screens symbolized the narrow Tory win. And there's the rub. A 1,480 majority is no guarantee of a job the other side of an election. Devoted as he is to Basildon, Mr Amess has been looking for somewhere else to be devoted to. In Southend West, where Paul Channon (majority 11,902) is retiring, he has found it. Adopted as prospective parliamentary candidate there, Amess, Mrs Amess and all the little Amesses are to move.

But not yet. One eye on Southend, the MP must still champion Basildon. *Torn between two lovers*, as the song goes. *Feeling like a fool / Loving both of you / Is breaking all the rules.* How is a chap to serve one mistress without ignoring the other? Yesterday at Transport questions, David Amess found a way. He asked the Transport Secretary about plans to privatize the Fenchurch Street line.

This line links Basildon with Southend. Is my Hon Friend aware, he inquired, that my constituents couldn't care less who owned the line, as long as the rail service improved?

The MP did not say *which* constituents. And, shrewdly, he spoke both for those who supported and those who doubted privatization. Thus he summed together both ideological camps in both constituencies.

Other issues Amess might like to pursue are traffic jams on the A13, water quality in the Thames and the prospects for Stansted Airport. Other constituencies he may care to consider, should Southend fall through, are united by the London to Shoeburyness rail timetable. They include Southend E, Dagenham, Thurrock, Upminster, Newham NW, NE and S, Barking, Romford, and Bow and Poplar. May we especially recommend Upminster? The Conservative majority there is 13,821. It already has an MP, Sir Nicholas Bonsor, but accidents can happen.

Indeed it would be possible to devise for Amess, who starts with the advantage of an 'estuary English' accent, an all-purpose speech suitable for use at constituency selection meetings, anywhere along the Thames corridor and right up to the North Sea.

The speech could begin by mentioning Amess's love of the Thames, and how he used to play, as a boy, in the mud, etc. The middle section would contain an impassioned plea for railcommuters into Fenchurch Street and a scathing condemnation of official neglect of the resurfacing of the A13. A favourable reference to taxi drivers would please about half of all potential voters.

'I could have looked elsewhere, ladies and gentlemen,' Mr Amess could conclude. 'To the English shires, the meadows of the Midlands, or to the hills of the North.

'But time and again, I am drawn back by duty and by long association to the mists of the Thames estuary. Fellow-Conservatives, the tides of time may alter; political fortune may ebb and flow. But my heart belongs to the Fenchurch Street line.'

Education Nightmare is Reality   *23.1.96*

Labour hits trouble over selective schools ...

Everyone has nightmares. We may be filing into the school examination room, knowing nothing of the subject; we may be trembling in the stage footlights, ignorant of our lines; or facing a lion, our legs refusing to move. Terrors such as these can grip and shake us until, bolt upright in a cold sweat and screaming 'Help!', we see the grey dawn outside and the tangled bedclothes around us, and, with that sweet, creeping sense of relief, realize it was only a dream.

For David Blunkett yesterday, there was no grey dawn, no tangled bedclothes, no relief. Unfortunately, it was not a dream.

He really was Labour's chief education spokesman. He really was on his feet at the dispatch box in the Commons chamber. All those jeers came from real Tories. Up in the press gallery (could he hear our pencils scratching?) sat row upon row of real reporters, smirking.

And this really was a debate on education. Yes, the nightmare was true. He, David Blunkett, was the man who had said: 'Read my lips: *no selection.*' He was the man who had written: 'I'm having no truck with left-wing, middle class parents who preach one thing, then take their children outside the area.'

He was the man at whom Michael Brown (Conservative, Brigg & Cleethorpes) was now screaming, like a demented raccoon: '*How* does he *square that*, with what *she's* doing *today*?'

'She,' of course, was Harriet Harman. Mr Brown, who told MPs he had failed his 11 plus and been educated at a secondary modern school, was reverting to playground thuggery such as young Euan Blair is unlikely to learn at the Oratory, and master Joe Dromey may miss at St Olave's.

It seems a pity that MPs seek to airlift their own children out of the worst types of school as these institutions would be excellent preparation for the House of Commons. If the political classes went to urban jungle schools and the voters went to county grammar schools, it might work well.

Mr Blunkett is blind. He has tried for years to remain consistent in what he says. Undermined last year by Tony Blair, back-stabbed over the weekend by Ms Harman, pecked at for an hour by the sparrow-like

Education Secretary Gillian Shephard in yesterday's debate, jostled by his own backbenchers and snarled and torn at now by the demented raccoon from Cleethorpes, what was he feeling? The rug had been well and truly pulled from under him.

I asked myself (the question is meant seriously) if, being blind and missing one of the senses by which your fellow men seem to communicate with each other, there are moments – whole weeks, even – when you wonder whether you might be the object of some monstrous cosmic conspiracy?

It is a conspiracy in which diverse voices from sources which you alone cannot see taunt you with false friendship, cheating promises and duff information; a pantomime of deceiving noises in the dark. You await the hour when some kind Prospero halts the play and explains to you where all the voices have been coming from.

In fact, Mr Blunkett put in a plucky and controlled performance, little helped by front and back benches around him scowling, tittering, guffawing and gesturing neurotically.

Only a powerful left hook which Roy Hattersley landed square on the government front bench's chin (it was about Tory indecision on Church schools) offered the Opposition any relief. Watching the Labour Party, seasick and squabbling, falling apart in the chamber after one political reverse, was unnerving.

It was a sight David Blunkett, at least, was spared.

24.1.96   # The House Relishes a Major Miracle

St Olave is the patron saint of Norway, and the sun is said to have eclipsed when they slaughtered him in 1030 near Trondheim: 966 years later, an even greater miracle occurred. John Major slaughtered Tony Blair at Westminster.

Whatever horrors may lie in store for this Prime Minister they will never obliterate the memory. Fifteen short minutes supplied Mr Major with joy of a more concentrated kind than he has relished in a decade. Compared with this, years of misery and frustration seemed as nothing. As he paused to acknowledge roars of support from the government benches, an expression lit his face such as can hardly be seen anywhere but on babies at the breast.

Whatever triumphs may lie in store for Tony Blair, none will quite erase the horror of that same quarter-hour. How, after 18 months of cruising in open water at full steam, could he have hit as cruel a rock, as hard, as suddenly, as this? With John Prescott's face beside him black as thunder and, from the back benches behind, the silence that claws into a man's back, the Opposition Leader's countenance, pale, jaw working, was a study in cold rage.

People will write that Mr Major put in a champion performance but, such was the mood, he could have recited *Three Blind Mice* and sounded deadly. As for Mr Blair, there was nothing he could say. Kenneth Baker almost gargled his welcome (for Harriet Harman) to 'stakeholding' in education. Major almost trilled his reply. It was Blair's bad luck that by custom he must be next to rise.

He rose. The government benches began laughing before he spoke. Adopting the expression of St Joan as they torched the pyre, the Labour leader cried: 'We see the baying mob!'

We did. We heard them, too. Unlike Mr Blair, St Joan never had to face David Evans (C, Welwyn Hatfield) bawling: '*Wot abaht St Olave's? Wot abaht the Oratory*?'. Unlike St Joan, Mr Blair then asked about the CBI. It was not a question which met the need of the hour. The mob were beginning to enjoy themselves. Major asked Blair to accept his sympathy.

Blair said thanks for the sympathy, then snapped: 'The difference between me and you is that I will not buckle under pressure' – confirming a number of MPs' doubts about his suitability for No 10. You could see the smirking Tory front bench tucking that remark into their mental files, for future use. John Prescott's face turned a darker shade of ebony.

'*Smile, John!*' shouted the Tories. Prescott's lip twitched very slightly, as though a spider were trying to get out. 'Wot abaht the grammar schools?' bellowed Evans, the first recorded occasion when grammar and Mr Evans have shared a sentence.

Douglas French (C, Gloucester) pitched in with a faintly unsavoury question about black Lego-men. Frightful in victory and frightful in defeat, the Tory party at least concentrates in defeat on being frightful to each other. In victory it starts being frightful to everyone else. Major accepted Mr French's offering rather as one accepts a disembowelled mouse on the doorstep from the cat.

But then Mr Major is not a Tory. This represents his one hope of winning the next election. Tony Blair is, and won't 'buckle under pressure'. This represents Labour's greatest peril.

25.1.96   # Harriet of Fire

After a nasty wobble, the Parliamentary Labour Party has recovered its nerve. Prime Minister's Questions on Tuesday had given it a huge fright. Labour MPs may not like Harriet Harman but, by golly, they like the sight of a Tory renaissance even less.

So they turned out in force for Ms Harman's speech on the health service. Row upon row of Labour backbenchers sat behind her, arms folded, grimly determined to approve of her performance. Up in the Strangers' Gallery her husband Jack Dromey, the trade unionist, leant forward, beard trimmed and fingers crossed. Over on the Tory back benches, MPs waited on the edge of their seats, ready with their killer interventions. This must be the performance of her career – or else.

And some performance it was. Ms Harman threw corpses at the Tories. She threw intensive care at the Tories. She threw patients dying on trolleys at the Tories. She threw infected teeth, brittle bones and tragic victims being ambulanced over the Pennines in search of hospitals at the Tories.

The appalling David Shaw (C, Dover) tried to trip her before she started. She took no notice. The ever-eager Robert Atkins (C, South Ribble) tested her with a real question. She ignored it. The redoubtable Dame Elaine Kellett-Bowman (Lancaster) complained at her. She knocked the old lady aside.

Every time there was a lull, every time there was the hint of an opportunity for any Tory to giggle at her personally, in came the trolleys again – rank upon rank of them, as patients queued while wicked Conservatives 'tore the National Health Service limb from limb'.

How can you giggle when, eyes ablaze, Ms Harman is picturing a 20-hour wait for a tragic victim, anaesthetized in a corridor, on a trolley? Between the trolleys, dental caries in Hertfordshire, osteoporosis in Dorset, the statistics and the corpses, Ms Harman scarcely paused for breath. When she did, her backbenchers filled the unforgiving second with a cheer.

It was a dreadful speech of course: one in the long line of dreadful speeches that characterize Ms Harman's parliamentary career. But it was delivered with guts, with energy and at speed, and it served the hour. Resuming her seat, the huge Opposition cheers that greeted her were a mixture of panic and relief. Harman had won the day.

Much Bickering in the Marsh   *31.1.96*

James Clappison, a junior minister, yesterday identified yet another group of satisfied customers under Tory rule. Butterflies. 'They will benefit,' he said, 'from our action plan.' The butterflies in question were the marsh fritillary, whose special needs had been raised at environment questions by Paul Flynn, the Labour MP for Newport W. The action plan in question was the 'biodiversity plan', which Clappison commended.

Co-existence in the Westminster biosphere of the eager, puppy-faced Clappison and the bitingly lugubrious Flynn is in itself evidence of biodiversity. There was something heart-warming in the sight of both taking a break from the ideological struggle to rally to the cause of the marsh fritillary: 'that delicate and most beautiful living jewel of nature,' breathed Flynn. We could extract the Tory and Labour MP from the sour Westminster air and picture both chasing across Welsh grasslands, jewelled butterflies fluttering at their knees.

Then Flynn spoilt it. He suggested that it was after 17 years of Tory misrule that the ranks of the marsh fritillary had been depleted to 60 per cent of its numbers under Labour. There are caterpillars, we reflected, which have only ever known Tory rule, moths which cannot remember the winter of discontent. Thatcher's pupae. Clappison retaliated by implying a likeness between Mr Flynn and the dingy moocha moth ... and the magic departed.

Such a shame. The only other available topic of debate this week seems to be hypocrisy. A chap isn't a chap in the Parliamentary

Conservative Party these days unless he's found yet another way of calling Labour 'hypocrites'. This presents difficulties as, like 'liar' but unlike the term 'dingy moocha moth', the term 'hypocrite' is out of order in the chamber, *if used by one Member of another*. You can brand a party, an argument, or even (possibly) a speech as hypocritical; you can probably accuse the Government as a whole, or the Labour Party, of hypocrisy; but you must stop short of actually calling another MP a hypocrite.

Members strive ingeniously to get round this prohibition. Yesterday produced two rather cunning routes. Environment Secretary John Gummer told Labour's Nick Raynsford (Greenwich) what he would need to do in order 'that you are not seen as hypocritical'. Miss Boothroyd flinched, but let it pass. Later, bearded Paddy Tipping (Lab, Sherwood) evened the score for Labour. How, he asked at Prime Minister's Questions, would John Major describe a man who promised not to raise VAT, then did: 'as a hypocrite, or a liar?'

'Or "skint", maybe?' muttered a colleague.

At the dread concurrence of both the 'L' and the 'H' words, Miss Boothroyd flinched again. Major paused a moment, in case she could intervene. But teacher was not sticking up for Johnny, so he had to plough on.

In fact the Prime Minister had another good day. His best moment was when he quoted (without attribution) the phrase 'governments cannot run companies', waited for the shrieks of Labour outrage, then revealed that the quote was from Tony Blair. The Labour leader has been knocked off his stride, and did not recover it yesterday. It lifted Tory spirits.

But hardly the human spirit. Near the end, Mr Major's throat all but gave out and he began to croak, miserably. We prescribe a break from all this, and a weekend's walk where there are butterflies.

7.2.96   # Truth Under the Covers

'I've slept with over 100 boys!' declared Peter Luff (C, Worcester) to the House yesterday. A lady tourist, ushered by chance into the Strangers' Gallery as Mr Luff spoke, dropped her jaw in amazement.

So all those stories about Tory MPs were true! It really was as bad as the tabloid newspapers said! She struggled to her seat and sat down. Composing herself, she looked up, resuming her attention to the debate.

Luff warmed to his theme. 'I was gagging,' he cried, renewed horror clouding the tourist's gaze, 'to see how we'd compare to a bunch of lechy lads out looking for a bit of skirt action!'

Our spectator was now thoroughly confused. Was it skirt action the MP for Worcester sought, or another kind of action? Or both? Was he one of these – what was the word? – bi-axial (or was it bi-focal?) politicians? Only last Wednesday, a press release from the BBC had promoted the corporation's coverage of 'the Doncaster bi-election': maybe MPs like this were elected at bi-elections?

Sadly, the truth was duller. Our tourist had missed the early part of Peter Luff's speech in support of his Bill on 'Periodicals (Protection of Children)'. Luff was not offering shock personal testimony; he was quoting from the magazines his Bill sought to improve. Madam Speaker braced herself as Luff announced: 'Men unzipped: an intimate guide to men's minds (and bodies!)'. She flinched at his declaration 'Boys in the Buff – shots so hot we sealed the pages.' She gripped the arms of her chair at the promise 'Red hot! Sizzling male model posters inside.'

In fact, young Mr Luff, fresh-faced and earnest, made his case well. His aim was to oblige teenage girls' magazines to declare what age range they were written for. This, he believed, would be a discipline for editors and a guide to parents. He accepted the strength of the argument for freedom of publication, and answered it.

Speaking without preachiness, and allowing that modern teenagers did need more open discussion of sex (and at an earlier age) than had been thought proper when their parents were young, Luff's success proved what so many MPs seem to miss: that a case made carefully and without theatricality, an argument which acknowledges objections instead of ducking them, a theme expressed without pandering to the extremism of some supporters, can be the more powerful for its modesty. Luff's case was essentially for honest packaging rather than for censorship, and very hard to oppose.

This did not stop the Liberal Democrats' dynamic and likeable Simon Hughes (Southwark & Bermondsey) from opposing it. Opposing a ten minute rule Bill is the only way any MP other than its proposer can get in on the act. Luff's theme will provide a number of radio and television opportunities in the weeks ahead. Broadcasters will be looking for an interested MP to put another view. Now they know where to look.

Mr Hughes was one of the few (among many anxious to speak) called in the much-broadcast 1994 debate on the homosexual age of consent. Opinion divided between proponents of 21, 18 and 16 as the right age. Hughes won his platform by moving an amendment proposing 17.

Yesterday, it is possible he was driven by a deeply felt objection to Mr Luff's proposals. It is possible that pigs will fly. It is possible that a day will come when Mr Hughes says something interesting. Yesterday was not the day.

8.2.96   # What the Butler Saw

Sending in the Head of the Home Civil Service to be interrogated by a committee of backbench MPs is rather like inviting an SAS captain to face assault from a team of morris dancers. Sir Robin Butler, Cabinet Secretary, was yesterday questioned by the Commons Select Committee on the Civil Service. They might better have spent the day knitting.

This was the first time I had seen the tall and athletic Sir Robin with his clothes on. Along with most of Britain, your sketchwriter first encountered him some weeks ago, appearing in a Channel 4 documentary about a lido in Brixton. Its regular habitués were interviewed, including two lesbian ladies and the Head of the Home Civil Service. He was seen executing a graceful breast-stroke. He was also filmed clad in a pink towel, which at one point seemed close to slipping.

Yesterday at Westminster, Sir Robin's breast-stroke was effortless. Far from making a splash he hardly ruffled the water. Towel never slipped.

The MPs, chaired by Giles Radice (Lab, Durham N), had hoped to probe a little beneath the surface of change in the Civil Service. Butler was not playing their game. But with such skill was he not playing that we were not even conscious of the refusal. Afterwards, one could not remember a word he had said.

MPs took turns at trying to pin him down. I studied each reply, seeking a pattern we might commend to any ambitious young civil servant. In fact, Sir Robin's approach is almost formulaic.

Here are the elements of what I call A Talent to Diffuse:

☐ Be relentlessly pleasant.

☐ Sound bluff. 'Grapple' with the question. Avoid the weaselly *Yes, Minister* style.

☐ Use self-deprecation.

☐ Don't deny: play down.

☐ Never admit an 'either/or' situation.

☐ Insist that whatever has been cited is not new, and has been around since Adam.

☐ Never contradict ministers. Explain what they really meant to say.

☐ Describe the unworkable as 'an *aim*'.

☐ When asked for a solution, repeat the problem.

☐ If pushed, cite a need for security in public buildings.

Was privatization 'political or managerial'? David Hanson (Lab, Delyn) asked. 'I hope the two are the same,' Sir Robin said, earnestly. Had Mr Heseltine made a difference? asked Tony Wright (Lab, Cannock and Burntwood). 'His activities impinge on me,' Sir Robin said. What about Heseltine's idea to recruit from the professions? 'I do agree with the *aim*.' Giles Radice then suggested that Heseltine had trouble reading. Sir Robin was afflicted by a sudden deafness.

Was it advisable to combine his jobs as Cabinet Secretary and Civil Service head? 'Yes, in the absence of a better solution.' Problems were not problems, but *seen by some* as problems.

Performance-related pay? We've had it for years, Butler said. A huge cut in Civil Service costs? 'A great challenge.' Did it cause tension? 'There is *always* tension.' Were civil servants policy-makers or (as Stephen Dorrell had claimed) purchasers? 'Both.'

Ambassadors on boards? 'We've done it for 20 years.' Why couldn't the *Civil Service Handbook* be placed in the Commons library? Ah, 'nothing sinister': secrecy was needed 'for the security of public buildings'.

Only once did the towel seem close to slipping. Asked about a scheme to let private-sector workers try their hand at Whitehall, Sir Robin assured MPs they would be placed 'where they can't do much damage; drafting answers to MPs' letters, and Parliamentary Questions'. The committee bristled. 'Their drafts have to be checked,' Sir Robin added, securing the towel. But the *frisson* was intended.

16.2.96   # Scott-free

The Scott report on arms sales to Iraq is published ...

The Government got off, but Scott-free has taken on a different meaning.

Mayhem ruled the Commons press lobby for ten minutes from 3.30. '*Please* behave like adults,' wailed a lady supervisor, as we fought for copies of the Scott report before the statement at 3.40. In came boxes the size and weight of five bricks.

Sweating attendants struggled with these as hacks clawed their way to the counter then staggered off to rip them open. Journalists bore aloft copies of the big green documents, like an army of leaf-cutter ants carrying away their booty, each to his electronic nest.

Down in the Chamber the hush was broken by grunts of concentration and the sound of MPs pawing the index for their own names. The Chamber was packed. Then, at 3.40, Miss Boothroyd fired her starting gun. The race was on: a race to grab the advantage fast and hold it against all-comers.

It was a race Labour's foreign affairs spokesman, Robin Cook, relished. He knew there was nobody in the Opposition who could do this as well as he – indeed, few who could do it at all. Speed of comprehension; choice of ammunition; confidence of manner; command of the House; these qualities make Cook one of the best parliamentarians of his day. He struts, he frets, he thrusts and parries like a thing possessed.

As Ian Lang, the President of the Board of Trade, commenced his statement, Cook became a demonic little ball of energy. His ginger hair all but stood on end, his brain in overdrive as he shuffled pieces of paper madly across his lap, reaching for the index, underlining here, scribbling there and pacing furiously forward and back.

But Mr Lang got off to a strong start. This cool and understated character has never been seen in such storming form. Friends call it assurance, critics audacity; let us say *chutzpah*.

It galvanized the government benches which, by the end of Lang's speech, were bawling not for their own ministers' survival – they assumed it – but for Robin Cook's resignation.

Listening to Lang one might have thought Sir Richard had been appointed to inquire into the probity of Mr Cook, and reported unfavourably. Lang sat down with the Opposition subdued, the argument moving the Government's way.

Cook rose to a chorus of 'Resign', and wrestled it to a halt. To Labour cries of 'Ooh!' and 'Aha!', he flung down quotations from a report he could only have skimmed. It was done in the impressive sub-Churchillian style Mr Cook has made his own: a symphony of dark pauses, gravelly outrage and vocal dips and dives. By the time he resumed his seat, it was Labour MPs who were howling for more, the Tories quiet.

In the questioned that followed, Lang fought back hard, rallying his own benches to an attack which soon lifted Tory spirits again, but it never quite regained the force it had before Cook rose.

The Liberal Democrats' Menzies Campbell questioned shrewdly. Labour's Gerald Kaufman, who had found himself in the index, intervened to good effect. The former Chief Whip, Sir Timothy Renton, found so many references to himself that he had to summarize.

The action settled down to the familiar ding-dong, tension having passed its high-water mark.

Ministers survive. But if Lang had stumbled during his first, critical quarter-hour, or if Cook's counter-attack had failed (as Neil Kinnock, after Westland, once failed) things would be different. They are now set, and no broadcasting studio will change them.

The chamber does matter.

Oil Poured on Welsh Slick   20.2.96

The Commons Statement on the *Sea Empress* oil tanker was a let-down. Given the swagger with which ministers faced criticism in the

Scott report, we had been looking forward to their reaction to the foundering of the *Sea Empress*.

She had not foundered at all, surely! Just a slight brush with a few offshore rocks: perhaps a couple of *teeny weeny* 'holes', more like perforations really. Which ship is without them, the occasional bump being so much part of nautical life?

Afloat? Of course she was. Well, *mostly* afloat, anyway. The tugs were there just as a sort of insurance policy. And those reports that the crew had been winched off? Greatly exaggerated. This was a purely precautionary measure: the sea had been a touch rough and the crew had needed a break, enjoyed it hugely, and were full of praise for Welsh hospitality.

The oil slicks, then? Ah yes, the oil slicks. Too much had been made of the oil slicks. You will always get a certain amount of oil floating around near any port. *Some* of this *might* have been associated with the alleged 'holes' in the *Sea Empress* but it was far too early to say, or to bandy about words like 'leakage'.

Nor were ornithologists by any means agreed on the threat from oil. A little extra oiling from an external source can usefully supplement grease produced by a bird's sebaceous glands. Dead birds washed up on the shore, you say? Ah, but dead from what? It might be a sudden chill.

Lessons to be learnt? A few, perhaps. Starting from the recognition that *no individual had made a mistake*, rules which were already splendidly tight would be improved yet further. In fact it was fair to say that what happened off Pembrokeshire was a triumph: a successful example of Toryism in action … Or that is what we expected. Disappointingly, Sir George Young, the Transport Secretary, actually conceded that there might be a problem. Naive fellow. He just doesn't get it, does he?

The Opposition called for an inquiry, and it is to be hoped one is instituted. Starting an inquiry is like laying down a good young wine in the cellars against a rainy day. If inquiries are begun often enough they will each be popping up when least expected, one by one, nicely matured, years hence, providing refreshment for the political and journalistic classes of the day.

The problem at Westminster now is that inquiries seem to be fizzing away and popping their corks all over the place, occupying so much attention that there is hardly time to cultivate new controversies into which to begin new inquiries. Retelling the past is actually taking more time than the past took to occur the first time round. That means there is no time left for the present to happen, and we could get into deficit.

The price of feasting so long with Scott may be that we neglect to lay down inquiries for the next generation, depriving our children of subjects for intelligent conversation.

Evans Above!   22.2.96

'Get stuffed' may not be the sort of expression you expect to hear MPs bandying about in the Chamber, but then David Evans is not the sort of man you expect to see as an MP. The language occurred, of course, during Education Questions. Mr Evans was speaking for himself yesterday, though he often claims to voice his wife Janice's thoughts. He was concerned about standards of teaching in schools.

Opinions are divided about David J. Evans (C, Welwyn, Hatfield). Some think him a ludicrous bundle of noisy Cockney buffoonery. Others disagree, defending him as a refreshing change from the manicured mediocrity of his parliamentary colleagues. Your sketch-writer's view is that Mr Evans is a ludicrous bundle of noisy Cockney buffoonery *and* a refreshing change. His daughter, a singer, has just brought out a CD, *Amanda Evans Alone*, which is by all accounts excellent, showing a thoughtful, soulful talent. Inherited from Janice.

David Evans Alone was different. His Question yesterday to Education ministers was listed 14th: MPs barely reached it before time was up. Evans had the first 55 minutes preparing himself for the moment, bouncing gently, then with increasing violence, on his seat, his face turning slowly from his usual pale pink, through mid-pink to hot pink. As Question 13 closed and his moment neared, Evans' features reached the shade you might expect to see on an exceptionally ardent baboon's bottom.

'David Evans!' called Madam Speaker. To say that Mr Evans 'stood up' would be to mislead. He rises as though from an unseen bouncy castle beneath. He defies gravity: a defiance the more audacious when you note his size. Mr Evans wanted to know what plans the Secretary of State had to sack bad schoolteachers.

'Most teachers,' he declared, 'are absolutely excellent.' From Evans this was shockingly conciliatory, and we waited for the punch. 'BUT,' yelled the MP, 'A recent sur-vye ...'

This pronunciation of survey reminds us of the (apparently true) story about another Cockney, the late Lord Bottomley, who as a Labour MP was sent to Southern Rhodesia by the Prime Minister at the time, Harold Wilson, to consult the Matabele tribal chiefs.

All assembled in traditional dress, in a huge tent in the African bush, to hear him. Bottomley was to open his remarks with 'we are gathered here today ...'

'We are gathered here,' he declared, beaming, 'to die'. The chiefs assumed an ambush and rushed screaming from the tent.

But back to Mr Evans, who now quoted a survey alleging there were '15,000 bad teachers', (then, hastily) 'employed by the Labour Party'. It was 'loony Left councils' who hired these teachers, he added.

But ''Arriet 'Arman sent 'er son to a grammah school': proof that what 'that lot over there' (Labour) were saying to the voters was ... (he paused for breath, his face now puce) '*Get stuffed*!'

Miss Boothroyd's tremor registered 4 on the Richter scale. Evans subsided suddenly, before she could fell him. You could almost say he ducked.

By chance, the next question, from his colleague, John Butcher (C, Coventry SW), was about the Better English Campaign. With implied horror Butcher quoted a BBC sports commentator: 'The boy done great.' Catching the phrase, Evans looked chuffed.

James Paice, a minister, thought good English was the key. 'Nobody,' he cooed, 'is beyond redemption'.

Nobody?

27.2.96   Rotten Mackerel by Moonlight

The debate on the Scott report ...

Moments before the result was announced, John Major reached down and pulled up his socks. We know, from the knife-edge votes on Europe in 1994, that this means victory. And so it did.

The auguries had looked poor. The minister Roger Freeman, a sort of decaffeinated David Owen, had summed up for the Government from a sea of glum-faced Tories. As Betty Boothroyd called for the vote, a knot of Tories gathered around Quentin Davies, the would-be rebel, wagging fingers and shaking heads – but to no avail. Off he trooped into the Aye lobby. Moments later, all the Official Ulster Unionists followed him. All was lost for the Government.

Or was it? Next, Rupert Allason, whose speech had lambasted the Cabinet, rose, flanked by two fellow-backbenchers, both Tories: Andrew Robathan (Blaby) and Charles Hendry (High Peak). *Three* rebels? No. All three trooped into the No lobby, Robathan (a former army officer) all but clasping Allason's elbow.

Minutes later, Mr Major tugged at his socks.

At the beginning of the debate everyone was there: the whole of the Opposition front bench, back benches packed; almost all the Government; and most of the Ulstermen, looking inscrutable. Tony Blair, John Major sat impassively throughout. Ian Lang, President of the Board of Trade, who opened for the Government, and Robin Cook, Labour's chief foreign affairs spokesman, replying for Labour, adopted contrasting tactics.

Lang spoke fast and gave the impression that nothing mattered much. Cook spoke slowly, giving the impression that everything mattered a great deal. The Tories will claim a strong performance from Lang. The press will report a smashing victory for Cook. Your sketchwriter found both unconvincing.

Lang made the best of an impossible job. Mr Lang is the political equivalent of the aerodynamic car of the 90s, or the sucked lozenge. He is smooth all over. There are no sharp bits, nor anything which might resist airflow, or detain the tongue. His approach was 'safety first'.

To a House, a Press Gallery, and probably a nation already bored with the detail of Scott and interested only in the possibility of sin, disgrace and resignation, a speech which flatly ignored allegations of personal failure and concentrated on a score of modest procedural reforms, could invite only yawns.

Lang achieved a passable peroration, if only by dint of going back to the 1960s and Labour's record in arming Argentina. The Falklands campaign is now the last refuge of a cornered Tory.

He was followed by Robin Cook. Only David Mellor (interrupting) succeeded in tripping Mr Cook, and then only momentarily. Cook's was a brilliant, sparkling speech, but almost ostentatiously slippery.

In a media mood of Cookophilia this sketch risks with hesitation, but risks the thought that, even as they cheered, few missed the dishonesties in his argument. A very slight mental reservation about Mr Cook will persist long after the extraordinary, Alice-in-Wonderland fuss about Scott, is forgotten.

The debate put this sketchwriter in mind of a remark once made by one US congressman about another. Like a rotten mackerel by moonlight, it shone and stank.

6.3.96   **Two Species Pass in the Dark**

Bats on the opposing sides of the Pennines speak different languages, according to the latest research. Britain's most common bat, the pipistrelle, had been thought to form a single species, but a new study suggests there may be two.

To one side of the Pennines, pipistrelles communicate using a sound system based on 45 kilohertz. They have pointed snouts. On the other side, snouts are snubbier, faces are pinker and the bats pitch their voice at 55 kilohertz. 'We have an east-west divide,' an expert told the *Today* programme yesterday morning.

That afternoon, experts observing Prime Minister's Questions noted an even more striking dichotomy. MPs have often been thought to belong to a single race, the human race. But study on Tuesday of their snouts, squeaks and general behaviour suggests not only that they belong to two distinct races, but that these, too, are unable to communicate. Imagine a line drawn from the Speaker's Chair to the door, separating the two sides of the House. This is Westminster's Pennines. To Betty Boothroyd's right lies the land of the Tory bats. These have more pointed snouts and more tailored suits. They squeak at a lower frequency – often close to a grunt – and squabble ceaselessly among themselves.

Yesterday, their Prime Pipistrelle having flitted off to the Far East, they were led by his Deputy, a wily old bat called Heseltine. As so often with this tribe, opening hostilities involved a skirmish with awkward bats on his own side. John Wilkinson (C, Ruislip & Northwood) demanded assurances over Spanish fishing in British waters. Nicholas Budgen (C, Wolverhampton SW) delivered a menacing squeak on matters European. Heseltine, his radar system alert, took swift evasive action, dodging the question. Over to the left of the Pennines a large bat with a snubbier nose was checking out his flit path. John Prescott was preparing to fly. 'Ask about repossessions,' said his briefing note. Every bat behind him had the same instructions. Their leader was away making a speech about repossessions, and Chief Whip Donald Dewar had arranged that the Parliamentary Labour Party provide the mood music for Tony Blair's extra-parliamentary utterances. Labour fly in formation these days, controlled by high-frequency messages beamed from their leader but inaudible to the human ear.

Prescott asked Heseltine about repossessions.

This is where the expert from the *Today* programme would have been fascinated to note the parallels. One bat appeared unable to make sense of the other bat's audio-signals. Heseltine's response – 'Tory Government works!' – roused his side to an excited twitter, but hardly answered the squeak from over the divide.

Then Prescott did the same. Ignoring what he had just heard, he jabbered away angrily about the 'sheer misery' of homeowners. Those behind him squeaked a rising chorus of support, their faces pinker by the moment. Those opposite squeaked with equal passion on unrelated matters. Both sides twittered on until Madam Speaker called off the hopeless encounter.

'They have separated so much,' said the *Today* expert, 'that they simply don't recognize each other as the same species any more. One possibility is that at some time in the past, one species was divided by some kind of geological event.'

These events are called general elections.

For the Love of Little Children   *15.3.96*

MPs gather after the Dunblane massacre ...

Descriptions of the scene in the Commons chamber yesterday depend remarkably on the viewer. Judgment must be subjective.

The objective facts are these: that almost the whole of Prime Minister's Questions and the ensuing statement and interventions were given over to the expression by MPs, not so much of opinion or inquiry, as of grief.

John Major was at first subdued, then almost unable to speak; Tony Blair's voice quivered and broke as he spoke; Michael Forsyth, the Scottish Secretary, usually dry, sounded heartbroken. For Labour, George Robertson could hardly speak.

Many MPs came close to tears as they testified, as parents themselves, to the depth of their sympathy. For about an hour the Commons chamber became a place of public mourning. Nobody who witnessed this has the least doubt as to the sincerity of every Member. I have never seen the Commons more sincere.

The spectacle, however, affected different onlookers differently. Two utterly opposed views of the public display of grief exist in Britain. We should acknowledge each.

One – perhaps the more old-fashioned – is that grief should be private and that its display in public can border on bad taste. Many British people would not, if strangers to the deceased, wish to be seen crying at a funeral.

Unless we felt confident of being able to contain our grief on a public occasion, we would stay away or keep silent. We would not think anyone lacking in human feeling because he curbed its expression, nor assume that those whose sorrow is more public feel it more deeply.

Some who take that approach might have found something very faintly distasteful in the Commons scene, after Mr Forsyth's short statement. They would call it un-British. They could see that weeping MPs were overcome by genuine emotion, but will have worried that as the mood swept the chamber, MPs were unwittingly working each other up to greater public grief.

Responding to the Prime Minister, Tony Blair was so visibly affected as to start a sympathetic reaction in John Major who, responding to his response, found his own throat blocking up too.

Other MPs spoke of the loss of their own children; Ian Paisley (DUP, Antrim North) spoke of deaths in Northern Ireland and quoted scripture; Nicholas Winterton (C, Macclesfield) asked whether it was not wonderful that the House should be united through the love of little children; some called for a minute's silence.

The scene, though palpably sincere, did approach those meetings of the 'charismatic' type, where people offer public witness of their feelings. Some will not have felt easy with this. Some were saying so yesterday.

But there is another attitude to the display of grief, no less British for being more modern: that it is more honest to show what we feel, and there is nothing wrong with affecting each other by a genuine display of those feelings, perhaps touching off similar feelings.

Those who take that view will point out that such demonstrations can be very comforting to the bereaved; that when people have suffered an insupportable loss, they need others not just to state, but to show, their own sorrow. It helps them to bear the loss, even when it comes from strangers – perhaps particularly from strangers.

Such people will say that the MPs' response showed the House of Commons at its best, and kindest. Some were saying so yesterday.

Rash of Crafty Queries   *19.3.96*

Westminster watchers will have noted the birth, at Welsh Questions yesterday, of a new kind of 'open question'. The open question is the bland preliminary inquiry which conceals the backbencher's real question, his *second* one.

Backbenchers have to do this because they are obliged to give written notice of their first question. That threatens to spoil the fun because it gives the minister time to prepare his answer. So the chair (by custom) allows the backbencher to come back for a second bite at the cherry, catching the minister off guard with a question related to the first, but for which he cannot prepare. The open question must be so general that the minister cannot guess where it is leading; but it must relate to his responsibilities.

The favourite open question asked of a Prime Minister is whether he will state his engagements for the day. He duly states them. The MP then prefaces his second question with, 'In the course of a busy day, will he find time to tell us why ...'

To departmental ministers questions cannot be completely open, but almost so. MPs questioning the Transport Secretary can ask when he last travelled by train – leaving scope for any imaginable railway inquiry.

Of the Chancellor of the Exchequer, MPs can first inquire what are the prospects for the British economy. These opening gambits are rather like asking about the weather: they break the ice, but they are dull.

Until yesterday. Ministers from Wales were in the dock for questions. The first on the order paper was intriguing. Simon Coombs (C, Swindon) was to ask ministers for 'a statement on progress in reducing the incidence of coronary heart disease in Wales'. A junior minister, Rod Richards, replied with a volley of medical statistics. What, we wondered, would Coombs's supplementary question be?

Mr Coombs asked about last Saturday's rugby match between Wales and France. Was this not a magnificent victory? Would the minister join him in congratulating the Welsh team – and, incidentally, 'lending a helping hand to England, too?'

What, you ask, was the link with coronary heart disease? Apparently we were to understand that hypertension and heart trouble in Wales will have been reduced, as a result of the widespread sense of contentment which this sporting victory has brought.

The next backbencher on his feet, Labour's Allan Rogers (Rhondda), understood the link perfectly. If the minister wished to achieve further 'positive reductions in coronary heart disease' in Cardigan, would he please instruct the leader of the council there to drop his plans for a ban on all housebuilding which was not for the provision of dwellings for those within 25 miles of the town, or those born within its boundaries. Fury at this plan was giving the people of Wales heart attacks, implied Rogers.

Madam Speaker allowed the discussion to move to housebuilding in Cardigan. Readers will appreciate that the precedent now lets through a whole new range of googlies to bowl at ministers. 'What are the figures for insomnia, and will the Health Secretary make a statement?' – then ask about whatever it is that keeps you awake at night.

The possibilities are legion. If the Government gives you a pain in the neck, the head or the backside; if ministers drive you to drink, distraction, or a peptic ulcer; if the Tories bring you out in spots or a fit of the screaming abdabs, tell your MP and tell him why: you may supply the Commons's next open question.

Bringing Out the Beast in Dorrell

The curtain rises on the BSE crisis ...

Politics can produce the paradoxical situation in which it is the craven who plunge boldly forward, and the brave who drag their feet. Watching MPs yesterday as Stephen Dorrell, the Health Secretary, and Douglas Hogg, the Agriculture Minister, resisted advancing panic over BSE, and Labour's Harriet Harman went bananas, you could see it happening.

'Bananas' understates. Ms Harman threw everything she could find at the occasion. Public confidence had been 'hanging by a thread'. The thread had 'collapsed'. Public confidence (now unthreaded) was 'draining away'. Our confidence drained, collapsed and threadless, we were 'swept into a crisis' while ministers, 'fuelled by dogma', 'dragged their feet' as the 'nightmare scenario' loomed.

Ms Harman delivered her harangue in a breathless soprano which, hovering somewhere between Cassandra prophesying doom and a housewife throwing dinner at her husband, came to rest at a pitch reminiscent of the nanny near the end of her tether with a hyperactive child.

And Ms Harman achieved the impossible. In fact she achieved several impossible things. First, she roused Stephen Dorrell to anger, something that has never been seen before. Tories cheered. Dorrell is beautiful when he is angry. She also roused Tony Marlow (C, Northampton N) to call her a 'stupid cow', a remark he withdrew (at the outraged Speaker's command) while turning, smirking like a naughty boy, to his friends.

The second impossibility was to unite Dorrell and the right-wing Euro-renegade Teresa Gorman (C, Billericay) in a moment of unprecedented togetherness. After nine years in Parliament, Mrs Gorman has found something to agree about with a Tory left-winger. So emotional had Dorrell now become that he was temporarily unable to pronounce encephalopathy, and for Dorrell that's very emotional. When he accused Harman of 'ferreting around in the gutter for party advantage', doctors in the House prepared for Mr Dorrell's possible collapse.

The third impossibility was to produce in Labour a populist show so shameless as to embarrass even the Liberals. Simon Hughes, Liberal Democrat health spokesman, counselled caution; Paul Tyler, their agriculture spokesman, warned against heedless panic. Delicious to see Liberals trapped between their rural voters and their urban ones!

Finally – and this we thought we'd never see – Harman has made a statesman of Douglas Hogg. Our terrier-like Agriculture Minister can bark with the best but, following an hysterical Harman and facing an unhinged Gavin Strang (his Labour Shadow) he opted for the couch-side tones of a consultant psychiatrist.

In vain. To represent an English constituency is to know that the British all suspect, deep down, that someone is trying to poison them. They suspect, too, that somewhere hidden lie countless files of official information too hot for the public to know. Finally, they suspect that all politicians are at all times lying, probably compulsively, either for the hell of it or because it is in their nature.

Couple these primal insecurities with the rage and frustration an electorate is bound to feel towards a Government approaching its eighteenth year in power, and advice to any British cow reading this sketch must be to enjoy each day as it comes. Similar advice may be offered to Tory MPs.

29.3.96   # John Major's Birthday

Today is John Major's birthday. Yesterday was his last Prime Minister's Questions before turning 53.

Other birthday boys might have been waiting to celebrate. Mr Major was packing his socks for an EU meeting in Turin, where he will be shouted at by foreigners, badgered by officials and baited by British journalists following him there to make trouble.

Other birthday boys might have been planning an evening out, a quiet night by the fire or an exotic weekend break somewhere sunny with someone nice like Norma. John Major is planning a dismal Saturday outing to meet depressed supporters at the Tory Central Council in Harrogate, where it will rain, and where the prospective Conservative candidate is called Norman.

Other birthday boys might have been preparing yesterday by blowing up balloons, attending to the drinks cabinet or shopping for party poppers. John Major, guarded against being blown up by terrorists, spent his day attending to the dreariest kind of Cabinet, then being sniped at in the Commons by party poopers like Lamont.

Our birthday boy entered the chamber yesterday to the sound of Angela Browning, a junior Agriculture Minister, telling transfixed MPs that 'the whole head should be removed' (including the bits around the neck) 'but not the tongue'. She had already explained how to conduct a brain test on a dead cow's cranium, putting smears of brain 'on wax, then into a thin slide'. She regretted this could not be accomplished in slaughterhouses.

They had been talking about slaughterhouses all afternoon. John Major and Tony Blair came in, sat down, and then everyone began shouting about slaughterhouses again. What an eve-of-birthday! Mr Blair started on about slaughterhouses, Major replied on slaughterhouses, then read out an interminable Labour press release about slaughterhouses, with his comments 'point by point' on its contents: Blair told Major he had 'never heard anything quite so pathetic'; Major told Blair it was his reply which was pathetic; backbenchers kept shouting from their seats; Betty Boothroyd lost her temper and rapped, 'Members should learn to listen, not bawl out from sedentary positions' (some hope); Blair made as if to return to the fray, then slumped back in disgust; the Tory backbencher David Harris (St Ives) recommended 'selective slaughter'; Paddy Ashdown promised to support Major on slaughter; Norman Lamont kneed Major in the goolies; and Eric Illsley (Lab, Barnsley Central) accused him of 'total incompetence'.

Did anybody remember this was the eve of a special day for our PM? Dame Jill Knight (C, Edgbaston) surely did. Famed for her apparel, the retired actress, veteran backbencher and Birmingham dame yesterday surpassed herself.

In make-up of which Cleopatra would have been proud, she wore a silk dress in crazy-paved chips and swirls of blue-green and azure, a magnificent cape in purple, sky-blue and turquoise pinned with a huge silver brooch, and more chains and bangles around her neck than a caliph's concubine.

2.4.96

Gentleman John Kindly
Lifts the Tone

In these crazy, *fin de siècle* days, moods change so abruptly in politics without reason given. Last Thursday John Major, 53, sounded tired and exasperated; Tony Blair, shrilly confident.

Yesterday the Prime Minister, 54, came to the House as warm and funny as we have seen him. Mr Blair sounded cautious, measured and low-key. It was as though a quarter tablet of Ecstasy had been slipped into Mr Major's tea, while Mr Blair had come off the cocaine. (Not, we hasten to add, that the Labour leader ever was on cocaine: Blair snorts a mysterious new drug called Control.)

The PM was in the chamber to report on the European Council meeting in Turin. It was all very mellow. Mr Major had 'underlined' this and would 'pursue' that. He would 'outline' this, 'put forward' that and 'seek' the other. He would be looking for changes to the Article on Britain's opt-out from the social chapter.

We chuckled at the idea of our Prime Minister 'looking for' amendments to the Article, like a bunch of keys. Gosh, wherever did I put them? On the hall table? As to his chances of finding these mysterious changes, Major was silent. But it is comforting to know the search is on.

It was news about European help with the BSE crisis that had filled an empty Monday chamber. Here, too, Major's mood was new. He was doing his best (we were to understand) and was by no means pessimistic as to the outcome. He would keep us posted, but regretted that we might be on holiday by the time he had anything to report. Negotiation was to be conducted 'speedily'.

There is something crisply mannered about Major-speak; one gets fond of it. We proceed speedily rather than fast, using 'for' where others say 'because'. Where a Great Western Railway notice would print the advice Gentlemen Are Kindly Requested To Lift The Seat, our PM might actually say this. When Major says 'shown' one suppresses the instinct to write 'shewn'.

Tony Blair was conciliatory. Tory accusations that his contribution to the mad cow crisis has been inflammatory could hardly have been levelled yesterday. He could not, however, quite resist the temptation to moralize. 'Surely the lesson of the weekend,' he told Major, had been that being nice to Europeans pays. Mr Blair would not say Gentlemen Are Kindly Requested To Lift The Seat, but 'Surely the lesson of life is that we should leave this lavatory in the condition in which we expect to find it. To do less is to undermine those shared values in which each has a vital stake.'

Next, Major told Paddy Ashdown that 'being in a kindly mode' he would not quote Liberal Democrats. One imagines John cooing over the candlelight to Norma: 'Being in a passionate mode, my love …'

Answering questions, Major was teasing. He was examining 'some novel ways', he said in his Mystic Meg voice, 'of ensuring that we find the right beast'. He meant the right cow to slaughter. But he would not tell us what these novel ways were. Ducking stools? Is an equivalent of the medieval witchfinder to be hired?

A Lovely Little Runner

23.4.96

To the question 'Would you buy a used car from this man?' the answer is supposed to be 'No'. It damaged Richard Nixon. But watch Steven Norris at the dispatch box.

This former car dealer turned minister for London's transport is so deft that to hear him market dodgy Tory policies is to hear someone who could make a second-hand Reliant Robin sound like a Bentley. You really might buy a used car from this man.

Norris stands head and shoulders above the ranks of other junior ministers in his Commons performances these days: crisp, sharp, quick on his feet and more assured than many Cabinet ministers.

When Labour's Mike Gapes (Ilford South) asked what seemed a fair question – why had London's Crossrail project been sidelined? – most ministers would have spluttered. Not so Norris. Sidelined? Without actually saying that the project had *not* been sidelined, he blamed the rumours on 'disinformation'. Had the world not heard of the Government's achievements in London transportation?

What had Mr Gapes to say about the wonderful progress being made on the Jubilee Line? How could we overlook the two billion pounds to be spent on the Channel Tunnel rail link? Was it not time to sing the praises of ambitious new plans for Thameslink 2000?

Inspiring stuff! In our wonder we somehow forgot that Mr Gapes had not been denying the merits of these schemes, but asking about Crossrail. Of Crossrail Mr Norris said little. He had moved on.

'The rusty doorsills, sir? Ah, but may I draw your attention to the splendid chromework? Did I mention those turbocharged four litres of discreet power throbbing beneath the bonnet? That clunk as you shut the door, sir: sheer quality. Smell the leather; note the walnut fascia ...'

Nor are Norris's skills confined to burbling optimism. When the game gets rough he tackles ruthlessly. Clare Short, his Labour Shadow, was dismissed with supreme confidence – her anxieties over Crossrail 'about the most absurd notion' he had ever heard. He did not say why. When Paul Flynn (Labour, Newport West) suggested Norris was delaying legislation to curb dangerous bull bars on cars, Norris took only ten seconds to turn the attack back on Flynn. By the time he sat down it was Flynn who was in the dock: charged by Norris with cynically playing on public fears for children's safety to peddle bogus, worthless legislation.

Norris the Super-Salesman, Norris the Knife ... next came Norris the Wag. To the ever-earnest Nigel Spearing (Labour, Newham South), worried about declining maintenance for riverbus piers along the Thames, the man who once said of his Epping Forest constituency that it fell off the back of a lorry quipped: 'I thought it was Labour policy to abolish peers.' The laughter was so general that his failure to answer the point about piers was overlooked.

But for those moments when levity would be out of place, Norris the Sincere is on hand. Labour's Clive Soley asked about numbers killed in traffic accidents. The minister became quite moving on the subject of public unconcern for death on the roads, all but wiping away a tear. The feeling with which he spoke was genuine, but it is the *speed* with which Norris switches mode which so impresses.

Mr Norris has announced that at the election he will leave Parliament and return to commerce. For him, politics will have been a sandwich course, a mid-career training-break in the serious business of selling things.

Mad, Bad and Dangerous to Know

24.4.96

The event of the day may not be obvious. As heat-maps, registering infra-red radiation, highlight features which escape conventional notice, so a havoc-tracking satellite beamed to detect wickedness at the Commons yesterday would have mapped Prime Minister's Questions – boisterous though it was – in muted colours and blurred outlines.

But upon one quiet detail the satellite's mischief-scanners would have blown a fuse. Iain Duncan Smith's ten-minute rule Bill, mildly named the European Communities (European Court) Bill, leaps from that map: a scarlet stratospheric cyclone. The forces of anarchy came spiralling in. The vortex of all evil was gathering on the Tory backbenches. The mad people were convening. Briefly, the Dukes of Hazzard had assembled before dispersing to run like demons among us.

Mr Duncan Smith (C) represents the same Chingford that sent us Norman Tebbit. His declared aim was to 'amend' the European Communities Act. In fact it was to cripple the European Court, but, arguing with cool plausibility, Duncan Smith walked softly. Only the waistcoat and wild, penetrating stare gave him away.

John Redwood sat beside him, his face too thin and his eyes too wide. Norman Lamont slipped in and sat down between them, like Lucifer in grey flannel descended from the heights. It was chilling how many of them there were, beached by an ebbing tide, as good men and women, sensing something clammy in the air, drew their coats worriedly about them and hurried out. Redwood nodded as Duncan-Smith spoke. Behind them sat Tony Marlow (C, Northampton North), whose striped blazer and fluorescent opinions had lit the launch of Mr Redwood's leadership bid. Teresa Gorman (C, Billericay) bustled in with all the swagger of the Bad Fairy in a village panto. No child dared hiss.

And who was that, reclining palely in his usual place? John Arbuthnot Du Cane Wilkinson (C, Ruislip-Northwood) scrutinized the carpet for European micro spy cameras, sitting patient and motionless for a portrait in political alienation.

Sir Edward Heath rose to depart, his step slow and weary. At the Bar of the House he paused, turned and peered at the gesticulating Mr

Duncan Smith with a sort of dazed abhorrence, then lumbered out. Sir George Gardiner (C, Reigate), in front of Duncan-Smith, smiled a wan smile. Sir George always seems the wrong way up. Hanging upside down from a rafter he would look more natural. Nicholas Winterton (C, Macclesfield), in a tie of violent yellow, looked up attentively as Duncan Smith sneered, to titters, at the absent Sir Edward. To his left sat an animated Ian Paisley (DUP, Antrim North) and a bloodless Peter Robinson (DUP, Belfast East), like a ventriloquist and his dummy.

David Shaw (C, Dover), the only Tory ever to attack Queen Elizabeth the Queen Mother, kept his head still but flicked his eyes around the chamber. With Mr Shaw you half expect a long sticky tongue to shoot out and snap you up. Duncan Smith had all the best tunes. Charles Kennedy (Lib Dem, Ross, Cromarty and Skye), opposing, flailed about, a decent man somehow unable to marshal his case. Why, agreeing with Duncan Smith and disagreeing with Kennedy, would I fight on Kennedy's side? Because the argument is secondary. Ask first what kind of people are advancing it and why. Mr Duncan Smith and friends, more numerous by the day, are mad, bad and dangerous to know.

3.5.96   # Mad Conservative Disease

The cull of British cattle may remove up to 42,000 beasts from the national herd. Translated into Westminster terms, an equivalent cull of the Commons would condemn to the abattoir only two MPs. This is not enough. Mad Conservative disease, or BSE (Ballistic Scepticism on Europe) has taken deep root among the Commons herd, and the malady is spreading fast.

The first symptoms are a wild look in the animal's eyes. Doctors should have realized years ago that Bill Cash's unusually staring expression was an early warning: the full-blown condition reached the Tory MP for Stafford & Stone later. Sir Teddy Taylor (C, Southend E) looked like this as long ago as 1979, proving that incubation can extend to decades.

Iain Duncan Smith (C, Chingford) is beginning to stare, but then the disease is rampant in Chingford, where Norman Tebbit was previously the MP. Bernard Jenkin (C, Colchester N), too, has developed an intensity of gaze; as his father, Patrick (Lord Jenkin of Roding) was one of Mrs Thatcher's brave moderates, mad Conservative disease cannot always be an inherited condition. The eyes of Jacques Arnold (C, Gravesham) have begun to swivel only in the past few months, but the infirmity seems to be taking hold fast.

Interestingly, it was just after Christopher Gill (C, Ludlow) rebelled against a three-line whip for the first time, that his eyes began to bulge; but nobody yet knows whether it is the onset of mad Conservative disease which causes an MP to stagger into the wrong lobby, or whether incorrect voting patterns render an MP more susceptible to the anti-European prion.

After the staring eyes and the inability to select the appropriate voting paddock, further symptoms manifest themselves, most fearsome among which is a form of aggressive paranoia. The beast begins to suspect hostile plots, all attributable to Brussels, in the most innocent of daily events.

Some of the more common have been listed by psychiatrists in a booklet *Euromyths*. Bizarre beliefs, such as that Brussels wants to straighten our cucumbers, regulate our pizzas and put our fishermen in hairnets, haunt the afflicted.

There follows a selective memory-loss. Victims forget it was Margaret Thatcher who signed the Single European Act and Norman Lamont who helped to negotiate the Maastricht treaty. With this comes a sense-of-humour-blackout. In some (Sir Teddy Taylor is an unfortunate example) the symptoms approach those of rabies, the victim lashing out wildly at supposed aggressors and all but foaming at the mouth.

Most tragic of all, however, is a progressive and fatal loss of balance. Some sufferers convince themselves that if 'mad cow' disease had originated in Germany, Britons would have accepted a German demand that we eat their beef. Other victims become gripped by a kind of delirium, prey to hallucinations in which Britain leaves the EU and Europe reacts by lifting its ban on British beef.

Some students of the condition are reluctantly reaching the conclusion that the only way to eradicate mad Conservative disease is a cull of huge numbers of the Tory herd. The beginnings of such a cull took place in the local government elections yesterday. Tragically, this method of treatment is counter-productive. In their paranoid delirium, surviving Tory MPs convince themselves that Europe is the *cause* of the slaughter. The madness is reinforced.

There may be no hope.

16.5.96   # Merrie England

The President of France has a peculiarly Gallic smile, fastidious and slightly pained, like a cat with indigestion. To misquote, the French are so damned French it looks like an affectation. None more so than Jacques Chirac, whom peers and MPs welcomed to Westminster yesterday with a display of tin soldiers and top-of-the-range Merrie England flummery in best Ruritanian tradition.

All assembled in the vast Royal Gallery, which fulfils almost no function beyond these occasional VIP dog-hangings. A baroque frenzy of Victorian interior decoration – all display and no grace – it boasts enough gilt, oak, velvet and de-luxe wallpaper to furnish ten thousand curry houses.

An ermined George III gazed fatly from his frame through a phalanx of cameramen herded into a pen beneath. One wonders what he made of it. First came a disparate crew of MPs and peers jostling to their seats, inspecting headsets to translate M Chirac's French. French guests would be bilingual. We would not. Next came five creatures in scarlet and gold carpets and black hats with coloured frills, bearing pikes with tassels: hybrids of Tudor infantryman and Yankee drum majorette.

Cornet players in plumed brass helmets raised their instruments for an acid fanfare and in pranced a stately duo in black and gold: suntanned Betty Boothroyd with Lord Mackay of Clashfern; Betty out-brocading James, whose wig needs dry-cleaning.

Miss Boothroyd's silver wig is the more stunning for not being a wig, the Lord Chancellor's a lightly ruffled pond beside Madam Speaker's souffléd storm of curls. The carpets bowed. In paddled Sir Edward Heath, late, but entitled to be: after the carpets a dignified addendum to the Constitution, a portly afterthought.

Someone dressed like Colonel Gaddafi marched up to adjust the microphone: the Mike-Adjuster-in-Waiting, the carpets being too busy with their pikes. Another fanfare. In strode the French President, looking French.

The Lord Chancellor made a polite speech of no consequence, mentioning, as required on these occasions, the Second World War and the Channel Tunnel. He also mentioned 'reminders around these walls of when relations were less cordial,' which was cheeky considering that poor M Chirac was obliged to address an audience whose backdrop was two huge friezes, of the defeat of the French at Waterloo and Trafalgar. Both depicted scenes of indescribable carnage.

At Trafalgar (where the powder-monkey priming the British cannons was the spitting image of Teresa Gorman) Hardy was tastefully hanging back from kissing Lord Nelson, perhaps lest this reinforce in M Chirac's mind some French prejudices about the English.

The President spoke. Adopting a distantly thoughtful expression, he mentioned the Second World War and the Channel Tunnel. His remarks were punctuated by a polite cough. He said nothing, as was required. Thanking him, Madam Speaker mentioned the Second World War and the Channel Tunnel, then, in a moment of abandon, Eric Cantona. *Vive la France!*, she concluded, in merciful contrast to the 'tell Europe to get stuffed' she had had to take from one Conservative MP last week.

Another fanfare and out filed the carpets. President Chirac left, released from our barbarities, still looking French. We had warmed to him – 'that sweet enemy, France,' as Sir Philip Sidney wrote more than 400 years ago.

Plus ça change.

The Science of Topology   *21.5.96*

Michael Fabricant (C, Mid Staffs) knows a lot of words but sometimes has difficulty in using them. Meaning to be helpful yesterday, he chipped in after a question to the Heritage Secretary about television transmitters in Wales, from Cynog Dafis (Plaid Cymru, Ceredigion & Pembroke N). Mr Fabricant had advice on what you or I might call the Welsh landscape, but he solemnly called it 'the topology of the Principality'.

'*Ooh!*' chorused MPs in mock admiration, like a *Blind Date* studio audience. But wasn't their admiration misplaced? *Topology*? Topography, surely?

We fell to wondering what topology does mean. Speculating that it might mean the study of the top, I stared down aimlessly at the top of Tom Pendry's head.

Mr Pendry (Stalybridge and Hyde) is a spokesman on sport in Labour's Heritage team. Sitting, as he does, below me and a few yards in front, I have a view enjoyed by few outside the bird world of his bald patch. It is perfectly round and wonderfully smooth, just like that of the Heritage spokesman Mark Fisher. Is this monkish look a precondition for speaking for the Opposition on heritage?

But, as Mr Pendry spoke (on women's cricket), a more urgent speculation gripped me. 'A silly answer to a silly question,' he sneered at Sports Minister Iain Sproat, and each time he said 'silly', the skin around the back of his bald patch wrinkled. It wrinkled in tiny waves, like ripples along one bank of a pond: an eyeless scowl on the top of his head. But why only when he said 'silly'? Unable to see the front of Mr Pendry's head without crossing the gallery and losing sight of the back, I can only hypothesize.

I believe it is when he raises his eyebrows that the skin ridges at the back of his head. It takes up the slack. Thus were the Andes raised, millions of years ago, by a moving plate on the globe's pate.

For the next Heritage Questions I have arranged for a journalist colleague whose view is of the front of Mr Pendry's head to signal when he raises his eyebrows. Short of a system of mirrors this is the only way to check whether the phenomena are simultaneous.

But, as the philosopher David Hume taught us, where two events occur together, we can never know which causes which. We should not assume that it is the raising of Mr Pendry's eyebrows which is causing the ridging of the back of his bald patch.

It may be the other way round. The arena on which Mr Pendry's emotional life is played out may be the bald patch: he may be snarling with his scalp. It could be this which is tugging his eyebrows helplessly around – that famous Pendry quizzical look no more than what Mr Fabricant would call an epiphenomenon, if he could get the word right.

If this is the case then the television cameras are positioned wrongly, relaying surface movements on the part of Mr Pendry's head

with the eyes, nose and mouth in it, instead of zooming in on what –
as you, readers, and I, are among the first to realize – may be the seat
of an MP's passions: the bald patch on the top of his head.

'We want baldy justice!' shouted Dennis Skinner (Lab, Bolsover),
ten minutes later. His fellow heckler Andrew MacKinlay, the Beast of
Thurrock, was demanding of ministers that judges break with tradition
and abandon their wigs. Mr MacKinlay's question was signalled on
the Order Paper.

Moments before it was reached I saw an MP, one whom
sketchwriters have long suspected of wearing a wig, eye Skinner – and
slip prudently from the chamber.

Grande Dame Out-trumps Them

23.5.96

For the Baroness Trumpington to take her name from nothing more than
a small village outside Cambridge is unfair. An entire metropolitan
borough would hardly be substantial enough to serve as her namesake.

The noble baroness, winner of a *Spectator* parliamentarians' award
earlier this year, deserves at least a county and arguably an entire
mountain range for her name. Or perhaps a famous foreign battlefield:
'Lady Rourke's Drift,' or 'the Countess Agincourt' would do.

But fate has decreed that it is as Lady Trumpington that the great
woman, who is (unbelievably) 73, takes the dispatch box in the Lords
to answer questions, most weeks, as one of the longest-serving
ministers at Westminster.

She does so with rollicking good humour and an element of self-
parody that cries out, even this late in her career, for a casting in a
Christmas pantomime role pitched somewhere between Lady
Bracknell and the Widow Twankey.

'Ooh,' she once scolded a clever-clogs questioner from the Liberal
benches, 'the noble lord is just trying to get my knickers in a twist
again!'

Over on the red benches yesterday, as the Commons wound down
for its Whitsun recess with a riveting debate on the Civil Service, Lady
Trumpington took the floor to handle a question from Lord Eden of

Winton about proposals to site a waste-disposal plant on the Wisley Airfield site, in a greenbelt, in Surrey. She said the matter had yet to be determined.

Up popped Lord Finsberg, anxious to inform her that he had once been an Environment Minister in the Commons and knew something about greenbelts. Lord Finsberg has not been long in the Upper Chamber.

Lady Trumpington paused, as though drawing on a long black cigarette holder, then huskily observed: 'I'm very interested in my noble friend's background.' There drifted over the red leather a sound as of a gathering of very elderly seals, barking. Their lordships were amused.

'When I lived in Cambridge,' Lady Trumpington said, 'I constantly had a thing in the back of my car, saying "Keep Trumpington's Greenbelt".' The barking resumed.

The Countess of Mar rose. Though her pedigree looks very grand (*Dod's Parliamentary Companion* describes her as '31st in line, Margaret of Mar; created 1194, precedence 1404) Lady Mar, technocratic, with glasses, looks like a middle-ranking civil servant in the erstwhile Department of Education and Science. She told Lady Trumpington that, among the emissions given out by incinerators, dioxins generated by plastic waste were a serious problem. Could the noble baroness assure her that dioxins would be kept within a limit of 1 per cent?

Lady Trumpington looked at Lady Mar as though she had always assumed that dioxin was some kind of hangover cure, but now this awfully clever little person had brought her information for which she hadn't asked and which she could well do without. 'I'm not terribly good on dioxins,' she drawled, and referred Lady Mar to a government publication.

'And can I have her assurance,' Lady Mar had asked, 'that any waste disposal plant will have scrubbers in its chimney?'

Another pause. Trumpington peered at Mar. 'Very tempting, my lords,' she growled, in her large-gin-and-20-Gauloises voice. Basking on their red benches, all the seals barked.

A Fearful Symmetry

12.6.96

Bill Cash proposes a referendum on Europe ...

William, William, burning bright
In the forests of the night,
What immortal hand or eye
Could frame thy fearful symmetry?

It was apposite that Bill Cash chose Blake as the poet laureate for his referendum crusade yesterday, though that was not the verse he quoted. For there is a fearful symmetry about the Conservative MP for Stafford. His speeches are delivered rather than spoken, all in a strangely monotonous evenness of tone: declaratory, with just a touch of the trumpet, but weirdly passionless.

Mr Cash speaks as though sleepwalking. His argument walks somehow with its arms out parallel, straight in front of it, absolutely determined upon its course, guided by a greater force, curiously impervious to its surroundings. Watching a Cash oration (and they are the same whether made to an audience of one, over the teatable, or to an audience of 400, as yesterday, in the Commons chamber) one remains unsettled by the thought that all at once somebody might wake him up, and he would drop his speech-notes and fall silent, amazed at where he was, who he was, whom he was talking to, and what he was telling them.

Cash had arrived early, before Prime Minister's Questions. He sat down, fumbled in his inside breast pocket for his notes, pulled them out to check they were all there, returned them to the pocket, pretended to listen for a while, pulled the notes out again and checked them one last time. From the Peers' Gallery Lord Tebbit and Lord Bruce of Donington (Labour's 'Lord Angry,' an indomitable critic of the European Union) watched lovingly. The chamber was packed on both sides. All the Euro-sceptics were there: Redwood, Lamont, Gorman. Below the gangway sat Sir Edward Heath, unmoved and unmovable, like some huge malign doll: a curse on the House of Cash.

Mr Cash's speech began, continued and ended with a sort of automaticity, as might the liturgy in a Mass, the words and sentiments well known, but repeated as an expression of faith. Only when he mouthed the phrase 'German domination' did a sort of horror shine through with real and momentary passion. Dislike of something foreign breathed through the entire performance but never quite took visible shape, except here. It gave the game away. Odd, then, that the Blake which Mr Cash chose to quote was:

'A truth that's told with bad intent
Beats all the lies you can invent' ... for this was the thought which troubled those who found little in Cash's argument to dissent from, yet remained troubled by its expression.

The Bill was opposed by Tony Banks (Lab, Newham NW) in facetious and perfunctory fashion, his principal argument being that Sir James Goldsmith was a greengrocer and should therefore be thwarted. From Mr Banks's notional majority in Newham we may now subtract the greengrocers.

'Who will bring forward the Bill?' called Madam Speaker, after the vote. 'Mr Peter Shore,' declared Cash.

'Sir James Goldsmith' came a mocking call from dozens of doubters.
'Sir John Biffen.'
'Sir James Goldsmith.'
'John Redwood.'
'Sir James Goldsmith.'

Bill Cash had given us the end of a golden string. Who, or what, lay at the other end was less clear.

14.6.96   # Korky Major

Sometimes the Prime Minister reminds me of one of those kiddies' cartoon cats. Pursued by a ferocious dog he dives under a stationary steamroller, which then rolls, and flattens him.

As if by miracle he pops back out of two dimensions into three then pursues a mouse into the oven and is incinerated with the Sunday roast.

Singed hairless, he recovers for the next frame, in which the mistress of the house chases him with a broom.

He scampers over a cliff, running on air until – realizing the floor has gone – he plunges on to rocks below.

Still (incredibly) in one piece, he picks himself up and is swept by a wave into the mouth of a shark. The shark chews him up.

But in the next frame our cartoon cat has somehow stuck himself together, ready for the scene in which he mistakes a stick of dynamite for candy, and is completely exploded. Then, inexplicably renewed and refurred, he nips up a tree, where ...

You get the picture. Zapped by Bill Cash and his Referendum Bill on Tuesday, John Major, alias Korky the Cat, seemed to have turned the tables on his tormentor by yesterday, and stood confidently at the dispatch box to tell Labour smartypants Denis MacShane (Rotherham) that Mr Cash's group's funding by Sir James Goldsmith was unacceptable and he had banned it.

But by now Tony Blair (the cartoon dog) had arrived with a new torment.

Was it true that the Government had been forced by threats from two backbenchers into agreeing a new accident and emergency unit at Edgware? Pluto's supporters jeered. Pluto had dug a hole and Korky was in it.

'Well, what are we to make of this,' sneered the Dog (it is one of his favourite sneers), snapping at the PM's tail. Korky Major withdrew his damaged tail, recoiled from his pursuer and, climbing from the hole, told him his supposition was plain wrong. He had not been forced into any such concession.

Korky's supporters cheered. A Korky Komeback, no less! Pluto Blair yapped on but was thrown off balance, his soundbites biting only air rather than Korky's tail (miraculously recovered from the previous frame, of course). It was about to be tweaked. Jerry Ashdown, a sort of overgrown cartoon mouse, returned to the subject of Mr Cash's Bill, snapping shut on to Korky's tail a trap whose upper jaw was his troubles over Europe and lower jaw his troubles over Edgware.

Ouch. It hurt, but it was not fatal, and Korky had by now clambered most of the way out of the hole Pluto had dug.

Sir John Gorst (C, Hendon N) pushed him back in. This was not intentional. As one of the backbenchers alleged to have bullied ministers over Edgware, Gorst meant to offer Korky a helping hand. He had not demanded an accident and emergency unit, he said, and had not got one. He had been offered only 'a casualty unit ...'

Korky's side cheered. Their hero was climbing from the rim!

'... with doctors instead of nurses, on 24-hour duty'.

Thwack! Korky went spinning back into the hole. Labour cackled, Pluto snarled, Gorst gulped, and Korky fans' jaws dropped. End of cartoon episode. Next episode: June 18. We leave Korky bruised, tail shredded, fur singed, at the bottom of a hole.

But be sure that next Tuesday at 3.15pm he will be there, bright-eyed and bushy-tailed, miraculously restored for the next disaster.

26.6.96 # Team Captain Misses a Sitter

England face Germany in the European Football Champions …

OK, nobody expected John Major to stand at the dispatch box and shout 'Stuff the Krauts!' Nobody wanted him to sing ''Ere we go, 'ere we go.' No one was asking him to chant 'Two-nil/To the Ing-er-land!' From any Prime Minister, but especially this one, a shout of 'Away the lads!' would sound wrong in the Commons.

But was it too much to ask him to say out loud that he wanted England to win?

'I hope,' said the Prime Minister, 'they play well and have a satisfactory result.' *A satisfactory result?* Spit it out, John: *say* it for heaven's sake. *Win!* Three little letters, one little word: one plain, unambiguous hope; a firm coming-down on this side of the fence …

But no: something deep in Mr Major's peculiar psyche had gagged at the sheer, naked commitment of the word 'win' and, as the ball of his argument spun straight towards an open goal, headed it off sideways on to the post. Awesome words, those little ones, like 'win', 'lose', 'love', 'hate', 'reject', 'accept'.

Through the weird and fascinating marshes of John Major's unconscious mind cruise deadly, pith-detecting missiles, their mission plan: 'Seek and destroy meaning!' *Pith-warning! Pith-warning!* Danger lights flash and sirens wail. 'Red alert! The Prime Minister is approaching a definite statement! Mr Major is about to mean something! Avert! Evade! Abort!'

Even his own Cabinet colleagues could not conceal their mirth. Good-natured John McFall (Lab, Dumbarton) had offered up a patsy question, inviting Mr Major to wish England well tonight and to condemn tabloid xenophobia.

This offered Major two free kicks: the chance to say 'win', or perhaps even (snakes alive!) 'score' or (horrors!) 'goal', and at the same time to condemn the *Daily Mirror*, a Labour-leaning paper which would stamp on his neck if it got the chance. But could Mr Major hope for a 'win', or condemn 'the *Daily Mirror*'?

Could he heck. 'Win' became 'satisfactory result', '*Daily Mirror*', 'a certain tabloid newspaper'. We half expected him to wish England a staged framework for the achievement of goals.

This sort of thing is quite instinctive with Mr Major, whose prose I have been submitting to textual analysis for some years. It is absolutely not the case that his panic-stricken grasp for an ambiguous phrase whenever a plain-speaking word looms arises from any ambiguity in his own thought. He knows very clearly what he wants and thinks. The fear (which is unconscious) is of *saying* it.

Nor does this dislike of being clear arise from mendacity. Mr Major is more honest than his predecessor, but she would express herself punchily even when her intention was to mislead. Far from using ambiguity to further his own advantage, Mr Major sells himself short by hesitating to say what he could easily say and knows he thinks.

If, as this Prime Minister speaks, you follow the pre-released texts of his speeches, you will notice his habit of departing from the script wherever it contains a short, brisk, taut sentence. He snaps the backbone of his speechwriter's drafts by inserting dead phrases like 'now, in the past, or in the months and years ahead'. Required to read a three-word sentence – 'Nor will I' – Mr Major will find himself saying 'Nor will I, er, do so.'

He does this automatically, self-defeatingly. Even while acting decisively, Major is intuitively averse to the *sound* of decisiveness. It must reflect some deep, childhood terror of being pinned down.

MPs' Monkey Business   *2.7.96*

Hidden from this sketchwriter's view, Paul Flynn (Lab, Newport W) staged not one but multiple arrivals in the chamber yesterday. It was he who, hours earlier, had described the policies of his leader, Tony Blair, as 'timid and anaemic'.

His arrivals triggered strange and ambiguous body language in colleagues, some (I am told) shifting uneasily, faces twitching, others attempting frightened little pats to his shoulder or half-snuggles-up in his direction. Anthropologists studying such behaviour among baboons would note this tangle of admiration and anxiety, concluding that we were witnessing tentative early approaches to a junior ape who had dared challenge an unpopular but feared senior.

The small primate drama was played out against the background of Virginia Bottomley answering Heritage Questions. The apes were fawning on (or teasing) an influential lady baboon.

Among baboons an esteemed and beautiful female knows she is attractive to the troop and signals this in all kinds of small ways. She develops a self-confidence and poise and may indulge – for display only – in the faintest hints of coquettish behaviour. Even if she is in a permanent partnership with another baboon (in this case, Mr Peter Bottomley) she can be playful towards rival males.

Roger Gale (C, N Thanet) was sure the Heritage Secretary could help to promote tourism in Kent. It would have been inappropriate for Mrs Bottomley to lollop across to Mr Gale's bench and pick fleas from his thinning hair, so she flashed him a smile and told him how much everyone loved seaside holidays, especially in Margate. Mr Gale was in raptures. The pair looked ready to scamper off to the beach together with buckets and spades.

Tony Banks (Lab, Newham NW), the joker of the baboon pack, his rude capers much admired among apes, would ideally have wished to show his blue bottom. Instead he threw her the rotten fruit of a hostile question, gibbering derisively. A cross Mrs B gibbered back.

John Cunningham, Shadow Heritage Secretary, is a self-grooming ape who walks tall. Swinging from his seat he asked a would-be one-of-the-lads question about 'soccer'. Dame Peggy Fenner (C, Rochester and Chatham) asked about Chatham.

The dame, a majestic lady ape, is a grandmother now, fur greying, and removed from the daily nutcrack. She is revered by the troop, who take no notice of what she says. Then Robert Maclennan (Lib Dem, Caithness and Sutherland) rose. This sage but lonely baboon, isolated in his wisdom, quoted Voltaire without attribution. The troop scratched their heads. When you are part of an ape-pack it is no good quoting Voltaire, something Mr Maclennan will probably never learn.

Later, Tam Dalyell (Lab, Linlithgow) spoke. I once read about a rogue baboon who grew morose. He left the troop and sat permanently on a submerged rock in the middle of a lake. Mr Dalyell asked Gary Streeter (the youth fielding inquiries to the Lord Chancellor's Department) whether the trial of the Lockerbie suspects might be carried out in South Africa under the auspices of 'Mr Nzozo'.

South Africa's Foreign Minister is Mr Nzo. But Dalyell's solemnity is too vast for a word of such undignified brevity. With a roll of Tamtam's tongue it became Nzozo. Dalyellyell may be the librettist of *Wake me up before you go go*. Doubtless Nzo means something noble in Xhosa: buffalo, perhaps. Let us hope Nzozo does not mean buffalo-dropping.

Speechless if Not Penniless   5.7.96

Seldom has a silence spoken more eloquently in the chamber. It was Dennis Skinner who provoked (if we may put it thus) the silence. His was the first Question of the afternoon to John Major.

Mr Skinner has been an MP for as long as most of us can remember, but has only ever really asked one question: only really ever made one speech:

It's the same the whole world over,
Ain't it just a bleedin' shame?
It's the rich wot gets the pleasure,
And the poor which get the blame!

All Mr Skinner's utterances are a variation on this theme. And such was his Question to the Prime Minister yesterday. Would Mr Major confirm, he asked, that there was to be a new, increased minimum wage for MPs? And if it was good enough for MPs, then why not for everyone else in the country? Would this increased wage apply to nurses, manual workers, pensioners?

The sufferings of the down-trodden masses normally elicit sympathy from the Labour Party. Delivered with customary passion, Mr Skinner's little homily built up nicely to a rousing rant on a familiar and favourite theme. He could have expected a good cheer from his own side: he normally gets it.

Instead, silence. The Opposition front bench sat dumb, their faces like granite. Behind them the Labour back benches stared shiftily round, stuck for a response. Labour whips studied the carpet with impressive concentration. The silence gave way to jeers – from the Tories – who jabbed mocking fingers towards the sea of impassivity surrounding Mr Skinner, a sort of massive, mute 'no comment'.

The Prime Minister replied carefully. He was not sure Mr Skinner 'carried everyone with him'. The Opposition front bench, he said, had not been prepared to indicate their attitude to the proposals, but these would now be put to the whole House to vote upon.

So far so good. But what, we wondered, would the Government be recommending? What was *their* attitude? A host of hopeful little Tory faces looked up at Mr Major, still on his feet. 'The Government will vote for restraint,' he said.

Restraint? Now it was the Tories' turn to be silent. A sudden thoughtfulness descended from the Conservative benches. Cheeks were sucked, fingernails examined, ties adjusted. The silence gave way to a sort of grunting, rootling, interested sound. An invisible 'thinks' bubble hung above the back benches to both sides of Madam Speaker: *'If x is the total vote and p the Government's "pay roll" vote and assuming there's a one-line whip on both sides and if a half of the Opposition vote (l) plus (say) three quarters of the non-pay roll vote (n) on the Tory side is against restraint, then x minus p minus half l minus a quarter n is* probably *still greater than half x in which case ... we get the dosh! ... Or do we?'*

Nobody was sure. Tony Blair asked John Major about the slaughter of 190,000 cattle and the addition of £200 million to a sum of £2 billion, but few were really listening. MPs can do only one sum at a time. Another sum preoccupied them.

9.7.96 **Flying Off the Starting Handle**

It is hard to imagine Lady Olga Maitland succumbing to 'road rage'. Slim, poised and expensively dressed, the Conservative MP for Sutton & Cheam speaks in the cut-glass tones we might hear from the partially wound-down window of a well-kept (one careful owner), 1960s Mercedes convertible, asking the way to Ascot.

It was therefore puzzling that Lady Olga chose her Question to Transport Ministers yesterday to ask about road rage. Lady Olga – *road rage*? Chic-pique, at the very most. We soon discovered it was not road rage La Maitland really wished to discuss.

Glaring at Clare Short, Labour's Transport spokesman, she told the Minister Steven Norris, that if millions of unhappy motorists had been forced to take to London's roads yesterday, and tempers frayed, this was the fault of the rail unions who had brought London Underground to a halt, and the Labour Party who by their silence had condoned it. Fair-minded Lady Olga stopped just short of charging Clare Short with personal responsibility for the recent fatal stabbing on a motorway slip-road.

Ms Short glared back. One of the nice things about this feisty Brummie MP is that, whistled at by a smirking male driver, you can actually imagine her jumping out of her Transit van and biffing him on the nose.

Mr Norris told Lady Olga she was *absolutely* right about the Labour Party. Smooth-tongued Mr Norris is the sort of chap who would be more likely to *cause* road rage than exhibit it himself, slipping down the hard shoulder in his BMW, past solid lines of stationary traffic on the M1, chatting on his mobile phone.

Madam Speaker erupted. It was a hot day, black tights itch, buckled shoes pinch and Miss Boothroyd had had as much as she could take. They call it Chair despair. Would the minister please get back to the *question*, she barked, which was about motorists, not the Labour Party.

Norris obliged. He had tried cycling, he said, 'but all I seem to get are shouted obscenities from London taxi drivers'. Given that the two things most likely to provoke a cabbie to fury are the sight of a cyclist, and the sight of a Transport Minister, to see both rolled into one must be a provocation too far.

But – *beep-beep* – who was this beetling up behind us? It was Dame Elaine Kellett-Bowman, who still drives an ancient Morris Minor to and from her constituency of Lancaster every weekend. We can picture her: 40mph on the M6, middle lane, road rage all around her, unconcerned as she listens to *The Archers* on her valve-radio. It was Dame Elaine's 72nd birthday and she had chosen for the occasion a frock in a festive print resembling Euro '96 design.

What we now call 'road rage', she told MPs, would in her day have been called 'temper tantrums'. You can picture the scene: someone has spilt the travel-sweets all over the car-rug after the Morris Oxford boils over just south of Scotch Corner on the Great North Road. Steven Norris agreed – why, he said, even in the 1920s there were reports that angry motorists had attacked each other with starting handles. To this sketchwriter, who has heard Elaine Kellett-Bowman heckling the Labour Mayor of Brighton during his welcoming speech at a Tory party conference, the thought of the Dame wielding a starting handle – even at the age of five in 1929 – chills the blood.

Mr Norris wished Dame Elaine a happy birthday. We all do.

10.7.96   # Sir Edward Smiles

Sir Edward actually smiled. Independent witnesses attest to the fact. The previous confirmed sighting came in 1990, when Mrs Thatcher fell and he smiled continuously for a week. Then impassivity settled and the great statesman resumed his imitation of an unmissable bayonetters' dummy.

But now another verified instance can be added to the record. At 15.08 hours BST on July 9, 1996, the great man's lips parted slightly. A second later both corners of his mouth twitched, then pulled backwards and up. Tiny crows' feet, furrows unfurrowed for years, wrinkled into action by his noble eyes. Across that majestic visage spread what can only be called A BIG SMILE.

On and on it went. Up in the Peers' Gallery sat his friends: Lords Prior, Whitelaw, Pym and more. In the Distinguished Strangers' Gallery sat five Arab sheikhs, all in pink-chequered headdresses, all with moustaches, all with beards, and one with dark glasses.

Sir Edward Heath tried a small bow such as a retired circus bear attempting a comeback after stiffened joints and *far* too many buns might execute. Then, still grinning, he lowered himself into the usual place – front bench below the gangway – with the slow, gingerly movement, not unmixed with pleasure, we might observe in someone lowering his bottom into a hot bath.

It was Sir Edward's 80th birthday. Our most senior surviving former Prime Minister, Father of the House (the longest continuously serving MP), as well as the oldest Member, has been in the Commons for 46 years – as many as your sketchwriter has been in this world.

He had entered the chamber all neatly dressed in an immaculate charcoal suit, silk tie and shiny shoes, his white hair brushed up into a shimmering meringue, like one of those cumulus clouds catching the sun on a late afternoon. A great, dignified cheer had risen from all sides of the chamber. Beaming Betty Boothroyd, who discourages MPs from cheering, had made no attempt to stop them.

A man of Sir Edward's sublimity and renown does not need to *speak* on such occasions. If he had wished to put a Question to the Prime Minister he would of course have succeeded in catching Madam Speaker's eye. But such is his eminence that it would have been inappropriate for him to have uttered anything that ended in a question mark. It is a pity that Commons procedure does not provide for the Prime Minister to ask questions of Sir Edward instead. *Father of the House*'s *Question Time* would make a change.

But instead he simply sat, silent, for 17 minutes, in the place where he has sat for 17 years, occasionally resting his eyes. Voters who will soon vote for the first time in a general election were being born when he first settled there.

It was a Question Time like any other this last decade and a half. Miss Boothroyd ordered MPs to stop treating the session like a mob watching Roman gladiators, and MPs proceeded to treat it precisely thus. John Major was in confident, ranting drone, Tony Blair in powerful bleat, nothing was asked, nothing was answered, and a good time was had by all.

After it was over, David Shaw (C, Dover) rose behind Sir Edward with a vexatious little ten minute rule Bill to launch. Sir Edward twisted himself round from the torso, infinitely slowly, and, with a look of blank horror, stared at Mr Shaw as one might observe a beetle's presence on a rock. Then he rose as slowly as he had sat, and lumbered out. The smile was over, for now.

The Ann and Nick Show   *19.7.96*

Mr Nicholas Winterton is the Conservative MP for a Cheshire seat, Macclesfield. Mrs Ann Winterton represents a neighbouring constituency, Congleton. She, too, is a Tory. The couple are married.

Nicholas (if we may be so familiar) sits on the front bench below the gangway. Ann (if she will permit us) sits a couple of rows behind him. As a duo, they bring to the Commons a sort of Gothic version of the former daytime TV show, *Good Morning with Anne and Nick*, in which their guests are tortured until they surrender, beg for mercy, or weep.

Both were in their places for Agriculture Questions yesterday. Both wanted to ask about farming. They were not quite close enough to share a sofa, but ideologically they do.

Their special guest for the afternoon was the Agriculture Minister, Douglas Hogg. But unlike the other Anne and Nick, this Ann and Nick were not there to put their interviewee at his ease. Poor Mr Hogg had been knocked about a bit before he joined the couple, and subjected to jeers from much of his audience – the opposition side – from the start. There was no orange juice, no curtains, no pastel colours and no plants. Just Betty Boothroyd, looking grim, and a couple of uniformed men from the Serjeant at Arms department.

Anne and Nick would invite their guests to sit down. Ann and Nick made theirs stand up, facing in the wrong direction and obliged to crane round to answer. In went Nick, first, with the knee and boot: he is the hard man of the duo. He chose BSE and the European Court as his stick with which to beat Hogg, and began to shout.

Nothing is ever understated with this Nick. Every word, every 'it', 'an' or even 'the' is belted out. 'Is this not an AFFRONT to the SOVEREIGNTY and INTEGRITY of this PARLIAMENT? Does my Rt Hon friend not agree with ME that the EUROPEAN COURT is a court of VESTED INTERESTS?'

Mr Hogg, turning on the spit, begged leave to express himself in more moderate terms, as the audience jeered. And now it was Ann's turn. She is less brutal in her style – the soft cop: chillingly courteous at all times.

She chose the Common Agricultural Policy with which to abuse her guest: a cruel little inquiry about the relative sizes of agricultural holdings, Herr Fischler, and the British disadvantage. Ann said 'Herr Fischler' with special menace.

'Quite right!' shouted Nick, as Ann finished her question, further discomfiting their guest, who stammered out (to what Ann and Nick knew was an impossible question) the best reply he could. More jeers. Then the couple released their interviewee to be kicked around by members of the audience, their work done.

Watching Hogg's subsequent torments, Nick looked relaxed – sunk onto his bench with a jovial brutality.

Ann pursed her lips a little and watched tensely, like a bird of prey. Neither of them smiled.

Readers who have ever heard *The Jamesons* on BBC Radio 2 will understand this sketch's proposal that, beyond daytime TV, the Members for Macclesfield and Congleton might like to do a hard-core radio show, *The Wintertons*, later at night. Unlike Derek and Ellen Jameson, who only tease, Nick and Ann might aim to get their guests to cry, live and on air.

But they had better get their bid in fast. For the day is coming when, for sheer, creepy, flesh-tingling horror, *The Blairs* will out-chill every rival.

Titters Mar Hero's Welcome   *25.9.96*

Just before Paddy Ashdown spoke to his conference at Brighton yesterday I came close to joining his party. This was when its delegates began to giggle at their leader's own video curtain-raiser. To the strains of Elgar we saw Paddy on a building site; to the strains of Smetana we observed him in a cornfield; and Beethoven accompanied him into a conservatory. For five minutes Mr Ashdown bounced through the British Isles to gentle rhythms and in soft focus, looking tough but tender. His speech pledged to help his countrymen 'find the hero in themselves'. Happily for the Liberal Democrat leader, a camera crew, sound crew, producer, video-editor and PR adviser had helped us to find the hero in Mr Ashdown.

And his party tittered. There remains one party in Britain with its pap-detectors intact.

Unaccountably, Ashdown slouched in, chewing. What, and why?

'I want to take a long, hard look,' cried the brave marine, eyes narrowed to flinty slits, 'at some unfashionable subjects.' We wondered which. Flares? Kipper ties? But no: Courage, Leadership and Patriotism were his chosen taboos and the Liberal leader was about to appropriate all three to himself. In doing so, Captain Ashdown had the delicacy to observe that he was only embodying *our* courage, leadership and patriotism – doing it by proxy, so to speak, for the nation. Modestly he acknowledged that Churchill had had much the same thought. Deploring the debauching of patriotism by Tories he added that a true patriot would vote for the opposition parties.

Eschewing leader-worship, Ashdown subtly recommended it in his own case. An angry denunciation of 'phony figures' in politics drew support, while news that one 21-year-old in seven in Britain is now illiterate drew gasps. There was also a furious indictment of 'negative campaigning', sentiments applauded with a fervour otherwise accorded only to his harsh and personal attack on John Major, descending at one point to mimicry.

'My next wish,' he declared, 'is for Sally.' A nervous hush descended upon the audience. 'I met her on the Hartcliffe and Withywood estate in Bristol.' You could have heard a pin drop. 'She is a young mother.' A thousand Liberal Democrats groaned inwardly. This was taking honesty too far. Then it dawned on us that Sally was being cited only as an illustration of the benefits-trap. We breathed again.

A speech which began somewhat in the manner of Alistair Cooke's *Letter from America*, skirted the lower slopes of Martin Luther King, toyed with sub-Shakespearean soliloquy and lurched towards a Blairite barking of abstract nouns settled finally into a stale rant. Ashdown made much of his willingness to listen. Listening yesterday he will have heard his party's delight at every attack on the Tories. But did he hear their longing for a similar assault on Labour?

27.9.96   Elusive Butterfly of Power

All week at Brighton a late September butterfly, a red admiral, has been trapped within the hangar of a conference hall where Liberal Democracy has gathered for debate.

Sometimes it has fluttered above the heads of the delegates – a collection of good-hearted, free-spirited people such as no other party can boast. It fluttered energetically yesterday at the words 'the right to be different – the right not to conform – is the main reason we joined this party', from a lady from Taunton in a two-piece Marks & Spencer suit.

Sometimes it has fluttered around the lights of bored camera crews: representatives of a media crowd troubled, all of us, by the vague feeling that we ought to be somewhere else. For hours at a stretch, it seems, my eyes and attention have followed the butterfly. Whole swaths of key debates are, for this sketchwriter, memories only of a butterfly's aerial display.

Well into a good speech yesterday by Alan Beith, MP, the party's deputy leader, the butterfly had me transfixed again. Shockingly, Mr Beith actually used the word 'liberalism' – not the liberal-ism of brave moderns such as Tony Blair who gun down ideology with killer hyphens – and was cheered.

But it is hard to take the new Beith seriously. He has been got at by the image people. Someone has told him to look relevant. This being British Fashion Week, Mr Beith had discarded his funeral director's suit and tripped in wearing what looked like a Paul Smith design: three-piece deconstructed Edwardian. His delivery, too, aimed at the upbeat. Gone was his schoolmasterly drone; instead, he would suddenly and intermittently shout out passages of his text. The choice of passage seemed random. 'With the Liberal Democrats YOU KNOW WHERE YOU ARE,' he bawled, surprisingly. We felt embarrassed – like when granny suddenly rants at the dinner table. I stared at my Agenda – Motion F460: Stay Away From Myanmar (Burma), *this Conference urges the British people [to avoid Burma] from November 18 to the end of the dry season*' – then at the butterfly.

The butterfly was still there for Baroness Williams of Crosby's speech: Shirley Williams was the conference cigarette, as it were, after Mr Beith's climax. I was musing over a noticeable influx into the hall of a group who looked like thirtysomething gay men when it struck me that they had heard media talk of the arrival of Shirley, and supposed it would be Shirley Bassey.

The redoubtable and indefinably doolally Lady Williams, suited in buttermilk, delivered a heartening speech hardly a line of which bore any resemblance to the pre-released text. Perhaps she picked up the wrong valise at Heathrow after her flight from America yesterday.

Jane Ashdown, apparently in a crystal tiara but on second glance wearing her spectacles over her hair, applauded politely. Then her husband sprang upon us a little surprise soufflé of a final rallying call. It was scripted to end 'Good luck. And good campaigning,' but then Mr Ashdown sensed a dramatic hiatus and, unwilling to cry 'go back to your constituencies and prepare for government' added 'have a safe journey home!' In a year's time our political world may have changed out of recognition. A beleaguered Blair and Ashdown may be enmeshed in fruitcake plans for detribalizing politics. Squabbling about whether Mr Ashdown can be Education Secretary. A Liberal Democrat conference will then be a different affair. We may look back in disbelief at that anticlimactic 'have a safe journey home', amazed at our lack of any sense of an era closing.

I found the exit. So, I hope, has the butterfly.

2.10.96   Warning: This Body Language Could Offend

Tony Blair addresses the Labour Party Conference ...

Cherie Blair had tripped in for her victory kiss. She and Tony stood facing Britain, holding hands in a chaste but affecting stance, like Jack and Jill, her right hand clasping his left. More carried away than her spouse, Cherie swung her free arm across his body, meaning to touch his right thigh and pull him round to face her for an embrace. Tony did not co-operate. He preferred to stay facing Britain, with whom he has been having a separate affair.

Cherie gave up. Her hand trailed across the front of Tony's trousers, coming to rest for a second in an embarrassing place. This created a stance which was as surprising as it was unintended. It lasted no more than a second, and distracted only those few (perhaps) of us underwhelmed by that Billy Graham tone in the speech.

Of this it is hard to write without concern that many good people, moved for good motives by the speech, will not recognize the shudder it caused in others. Better judged, better crafted and better delivered than Michael Portillo's fiasco at the Tory conference last year, it still had something of the same faintly messianic ring. Grandiosity, especially when unaccompanied by any plan of action, can grate. Staking claims to larger things than politicians can command is a dangerous game, and perhaps one better left to prophets.

After telling us that the era he would usher in would be described by historians as 'The Decent Society', Mr Blair started to cry 'a thousand days for a thousand years' repeatedly. He probably meant the

31 months during which he believes he will be Prime Minister before the year 2000.

Perhaps, then, we should dub his tone yesterday 'millennialist'. On the morning of his speech this sketch had described Labour's stage-set as hovering between the Neo-Fascist and the neolithic. In fact the speech spanned both periods. Representing Mr Blair as an apostolic part of an unbroken line stretching from the discovery of fire, through the prophets then, by way of Wilberforce, to trade unionism, Nye Bevan, Alan Howarth ... and – you guessed, Mr Blair.

Apparently all these people share an ideal larger even than socialism: they want 'a better world'. Mr Blair did not explain which politicians it is who do not want a better world. The tone can best be described as 'Mosleyite without the anti-Semitism'. Oswald Mosley also christened his party 'new'. The language of regeneration characterizes both men, as Leo Abse remarks in a prescient psycho-biography of Blair.

The body language yesterday was remarkable. He swaggered on to the stage and swung round, jacket unbuttoned, like a male model. During the speech he repeatedly flung his arms out, stretched his hands forward, caged his fingers, cradle-fashion towards his heart and stared up at the sky – or was it the Union Jack projected chillingly on to a screen above him? After the speech he made a trance-like movement away from the podium.

To accompany part of a curtain-raising video, Blair chose the seductively narcissistic David Bowie. Abse wrote this: 'Roll on, Blair ... with David Bowie, each of you ... singing your bewildered androgynous anthem ...

'Rock on, Blair, with the moon dust and with the kids.'

'Labour's coming home!' shouted Blair, three times. Good. Can I suggest a mug of Horlicks and an early night?

Ruthless Street-Fighter   3.10.96

Have-a-go gran Barbara Castle, 85, on a seaside holiday at the Winter Gardens, Blackpool, yesterday, protested: 'I'm just a simple Yorkshire girl.' Castle, suspecting two other holidaymakers, Gordon Brown and

Harriet Harman, of stealing from her pension scheme, had attempted to mug the entire leadership of the Labour Party. 'Barbara meant well,' was the whisper among party managers at the Imperial Hotel last night, 'she was just confused.'

Baroness Castle of Blackburn, in scarlet, looked anything but confused, anything but simple and pretty mature for a girl, as she took the microphone that afternoon. Nobody knows better how to work a crowd and this wily survivor of Harold Wilson's Cabinets was milking her advantage at Blackpool for all it was worth.

As the debate started, Lady Castle was seated at the front, under the noses of the platform party and cool as a cucumber. In a ring around her were the nation's press photographers, sitting on the floor, snapping the variety of serene, defiant or thoughtful poses with which she entertained us. One moment it was head rested philosophically on chin; the next, chin up and eyes flashing; then she would study her notes.

She listened as a series of speakers praised her. 'Barbara Castle's done brilliant,' said Bolsover delegate Elton Watts, in broad Derbyshire. The Cockney tones of Dave Lawrence, from Poplar and Canning Town, were raised in her cause. And there was no mistaking the Scots accent of Jean Bishop, from Argyle and Bute, urging the Castle line: 'Conference, I appeal to you: you're Labour people! You believe in Labour values!'

It seemed that regional accents were mostly old Labour. When Matt Carter, a prospective candidate in the obligatory dark two-piece suit and bright silk tie, began his speech in a neutral BBC voice, you knew he would be supporting new Labour. From the platform, Ms Harman, in a pink suit squared with those graph-paper lines that warn enemies against messing with her statistics, watched with the remarkable calm which she had shown through a turbulent year. They called Lady Castle to speak. Everyone rose in applause as this tiny, birdlike figure in an improbable wig climbed the white stairs to the lectern.

She spoke well, adopting her usual informal 'Oh – and another thing ...' style. Opinion divides as to whether this was a well-meaning little old lady speaking from the heart or a ruthless street-fighter using audience appeal to maximum advantage.

Perhaps she is both. Declaring that 'a good debate strengthens democracy' and delivering a calculated kick at Mr Brown's shins, she stabbed the lectern, called Ms Harman 'dear', triggered applause skilfully, then protested that the applause was robbing her of time – which drew more applause, as she intended. In fact, nobody was trying to silence her.

Her descent from the platform, to another standing ovation, was masterful. Lady Castle is perfectly able to walk down stairs – I've watched her often – but on this occasion she hesitated, offered a frail elbow to a young chap who ran up to help, then descended ever so carefully.

Waiting below to offer her his arm was her adversary, Peter Mandelson. Old pro meets young pro. Wags joked that she'd better watch out in case his embrace concealed a knife. But I reflected that were it not for the cameras, Mandelson would have been well advised to guard his groin from an elderly, but still sharp, knee.

The Faces of Tony Stardust   *3.10.96*

A review of ...

THE MAN BEHIND THE SMILE
Tony Blair and the Politics of Perversion
By Leo Abse
FACES OF LABOUR The Inside Story
By Andy McSmith
NEW BRITAIN My Vision of a Young Country
By Tony Blair

To the proposition that Leo Abse is crazy, I offer my assent. So was Nietzsche. So was Dali.

To the proposition that old age is robbing the 80-year-old former Welsh Labour MP of his marbles, I return an emphatic No. Mr Abse's marbles have always been arranged unconventionally. He proceeds by the inspired rant. As a lonely crusader for social causes, almost all of which are now accepted as right, Abse ranted in his Commons days; he was ranting later when he wrote *Margaret, Daughter of Beatrice*, a psycho-political tirade against the mother-erasing Thatcher. People scoffed – then quietly acknowledged his insight. He was ranting when he wrote his tirade against the whole German nation, *Wotan My Enemy*. The day approaches when the work will be seen as visionary.

And Mr Abse is ranting now in *The Man Behind the Smile*. Its shocking assertion is that the leader of the Labour Party is androgynous – though mercifully the author stops short of suggesting that anything is amiss with Mr Blair's sexual apparatus. Age does not weary the exoticism of Abse's tirades.

Often heavy-going and in places – frankly – opaque, this book assumes the mantle of psychoanalysis. Examining Tony Blair's eccentric family history, Abse uncovers (he believes) a parenting which left the boy who, at choir school used to pray with his headmaster, emotionally incomplete: a young man with an unsecured personality, cleaving now to rock music, now to Christianity as he grasped at templates for his own identity which his upbringing never supplied.

He diagnoses in Blair's personality an hysterical rejection of challenge: scrambling for authority as a substitute for reason. His worshipping of authoritarian leadership is linked, Abse thinks, to emotional insecurity: and this is what underlies the 'consensus by diktat' he imposes. Abse finds Blair utterly different from Margaret Thatcher: she relished a scrap; he reinvents reality, writing conflict out of the script.

In the tense male relationships among the close-knit 'new' Labour gang encircling the leadership, Abse detects an unconscious homosexual rivalry he says can exist even between heterosexuals.

At this study's core are two linked assertions. Abse believes Blair's personality is – because not properly keyed into the male and female paradigms which parenting should provide – incomplete, androgynous, cold, coy, corrosively cute, and adrift: the David Bowie of Centre politics. This inward androgyny has invaded his approach to policymaking. Ruthlessly – desperately – intent on defining his own personality through Office, he is oddly flabby when asked what he would do with Office. That would be like asking the jelly what it planned to mould.

But what would he *do*? Blair retreats into an obsessive appeal to 'renewal', 'rebirth' and 'youth' – concepts in the deepest sense jejeune – as though they answer the question. 'New Labour. New Britain. The party renewed. The country reborn. New Labour. New Britain.'

This drives Abse, an old man of the Left, to a fine raillery. Sample his dense, weird, wild, intuitively persuasive style: 'As Blair and his impertinent young political pups wage war on Old Labour ... as they seek to kill off their fathers, these political adolescents boost themselves with a dangerous amnesic and, thus drugged, the courageous youngsters, manned with piss-proud erections, dare to obliterate the reality that the most radical and "regenerative Labour government", that brought us the welfare state, was led by old men ...'

In this, as in all Abse's work, I find the coupling of theoretical pretension with palpable spite an unhappy tangle. The whole endeavour is easy to dismiss. In the end, Abse can only be guessing. These guesses, however, seem to me to be touched by genius. Perhaps I am prejudiced. My own view is that Tony Blair is an alien from the Planet Vanilla.

Read the chapter on Blair in Andy McSmith's *Faces of Labour*. The scrupulous McSmith, whose notably cool biography of John Smith was unaccountably received as a homage, tries to be fair to Mr Blair and would be horrified to hear his book coupled with Abse's. But his attempt to describe where the Labour leader is coming from, where he is going to – indeed, where he might be at the moment, leaves the reader with a weird sense of vacuum. The chapter is one of seven readable and revealing studies of key or typical Labour figures, one of whom, Peter Mandelson, has described McSmith as 'one of the most biassed, ill-informed, malicious and unpleasant journalists in Westminster'. Coming from Mr Mandelson, such a citation would make a tolerably good library out of a library with only McSmith's book in it.

If you still think Abse absurd, read *New Britain: My Vision of a Young Country*, a collection of the Labour leader's speeches. It includes photographs of Mr Blair giving the blind David Blunkett an arm, Blair eating fish and chips in Sedgefield and John Prescott with his head in his hands. The speeches are unmitigated pap.

The note on the back cover begins, 'Tony Blair has nothing to hide'. After a day struggling with Abse's Freudianism, I cannot escape the secondary meaning of that sentence. Nothing may be precisely what it is that Tony Blair has to hide.

5.10.96

I Shot the Blonde with
Big Breasts

From The Spectator ...

Anyone who has endured, as I have, the cruel and unusual punishment of enforced attendance at every major political party's conference for each of the last ten years, has learned the myriad excuses a columnist can find for not attending the actual debate.

This dreadful process – you cannot dignify a conference debate with the term 'discussion', 'deliberation' or even 'conversation'; it is just a silly noise – occurs in a seaside hangar where a few hundred distracted souls stare blankly at a podium tacked together in plywood and covered in fuzzy-felt, polyurethane foam or quick-drying paint, upon which a score or more equally lost souls pick their nails and pretend to listen while some dry-mouthed wretch gibbers for his or her allotted time, and then is heard no more. It is a tale told by an idiot, full of pique and presumption, signifying nothing. Everyone applauds.

The press then announce what it 'meant', their commentary being the product of a creative tension between what the party's 'spin doctors' – careerist prunes – say it meant, and what the press wish to claim it meant. In truth, it meant little. Party conferences are a conspiracy between politicians and political journalists to hog the news media and fill them with stuff nobody would dream of entertaining in any other circumstances.

The parties make money and publicity out of conferences. The journalists make careers out of reporting them. And the secret of this happy symbiosis – the partnership of hippopotamus with tick-bird – is found in one tiny, key phrase, launch-pad to a million commentaries:

> At the [insert party name] conference in [insert seaside resort] yesterday, Mr [insert politician] said ...

It's 'news', you see. It 'happened'. It must have, because the modern media's equivalent of the Greek unities are all present. Brighton, 14.15, Ashdown speaks. Unity of time, place and action. His thoughts committed to paper and circulated to interested parties would have been the same thoughts, but unreportable as an 'event'. A conference is an event. Reporters report events. You read the reports. Why don't we all go home?

And so it came to pass in my hotel room at Brighton a week ago that I was roused from my slumber by a woman on the telephone who told me to wake up and reminded me that she was a recording. 'Thank you,' I said, then blushed because I had spoken to a machine, then reflected that you cannot make a fool of yourself to a machine and blushed out of embarrassment that I had blushed to a machine. I went to the conference centre and tried to be interested in the debate on gun control.

But it was no good. We've heard the arguments both ways a thousand times before and it was fanciful to suppose a Liberal Democrat would have thought of a new one. How could I find a new angle to this debate?

My friend Pete had told me that at the end of the pier there was a game called 'Drug Wars' in which you could shoot people legally, so, drawn by similar motives to those which impel other men to join the Metropolitan Police, I went to the pier to try my hand. By a big video screen were two revolvers, each sheathed in a leather holster, on either side of a control console.

The game went like this. You put 30p in the slot. On the screen a video involving a violent chase begins. You draw your revolver, point it down to load it, then aim it at the screen. You can shoot at the screen by squeezing the trigger. The 'shot' is a laser-beam. The screen displays a hole in whatever or whomever you've shot.

And they die. By electronic wizardry your laser bullet diverts the video story itself to a variant reflecting the new assassination. Thus, if you shoot a drugs baron he falls down dead off the roof and leaves the story. If he points and fires his gun at you first, you lose one of your five lives.

Spectator readers, people of alert moral sensibility, will at once realize that the idea is to shoot the bad people.

I suppose I did realize this too – at the level of the responsible, conscience-led part of my super-ego. But once I got that revolver in my hand, something wild lunged from my unconscious and gripped my trigger finger. I became strangely excited.

A scantily-clad blonde with big breasts ran towards me on the video, screaming. I shot her.

I am not proud of this. You must not suppose me to have made a conscious choice to shoot her. But she had become hysterical and I hate people who panic. Bystanders, families, nice people who had come to Brighton for the day, eyed me with concern.

Then I shot another blonde. There is no excuse, but truth to tell, I had rather enjoyed shooting the first. Another blonde went running along the beach, *Baywatch*-style. I hate *Baywatch* and I really don't think women should dress like that. I shot her, too.

Perhaps the reason I then shot the sheriff was guilt; perhaps it was fear of arrest; but, as he stepped from his cop car, I cannot claim to have examined my motivation. I simply thought, 'the Law' – and shot him.

Maybe the reason I shot my fourth blonde was that, having eliminated the sheriff, I no longer feared the law; and, having burned my boats with polite society, I was careless of public disapproval. Bystanders had moved away. Shooting the fourth blonde had ended the game. Sheepishly I replaced the revolver and left the pier fast.

Reader, the stress and frustration involved in reporting a Liberal Democrat conference is intense. Pity me, forgive me, and accept my pier-end story as a redeeming one. For, if I ever doubted it, I now know that the case for keeping firearms from the reach of apparently peace-loving citizens is extraordinarily strong.

5.10.96 # Blunder Makes Party Go with a Bang

It was a pretty loud bang and everybody thought a bomb had gone off. Or had someone been shot? The music stopped. Delegates dancing in the aisles froze. There was complete silence as people stared around in alarm.

Then from above came a rain of little leaflets – *Vote Labour* – fired from the Winter Gardens balcony. There was a brave 'three cheers'. Labour's composure returned but it took time. Until the music restarted, people milled distractedly around, the mood of celebration shattered.

It was the first and only big blunder in a week otherwise almost without incident, and it came in the closing minutes. As delegates and journalists left Blackpool, it remained unclear how the mistake could have been made. Why was the explosion so loud? Why did they halt the music?

Everything about the closing rally had been going so well. John Prescott had been welcomed with a standing ovation even before he spoke. After the now-routine video (the novelty of conference videos is gone and people are growing bored with them) he made a rousing speech with some good jokes, some bad jokes and some indifferent ones. All alike were greeted with gales of laughter from a rank and file in whose eyes Mr Prescott can do no wrong.

There were moments during his patter when we wondered whether we had wandered into the wrong arena at Blackpool and found ourselves watching Frank Carson, with Eddie Large's voice.

Labour's deputy leader did his best to keep to his pre-released text – Mr Prescott's controllers now steer him away from all unscripted encounters with Britain – but there was one stumble and it proved the bit delegates loved best. Losing the crib sheet of Labour's promises he had planned to hold up, Prescott exploded: 'I knew this would happen. You know me. I'm old Labour. Got to use my own words.'

Everybody cheered. Spin-doctors' video-pagers flashed 'off-message' warnings to new Labour's command-control centre on the Planet Vanilla. 'Off-message' is the PR-speak for signals out of line with the desired image. 'We believe in socialist principles!' declared Prescott. *Off-message – Beep – Urgent – Abort.*

Yet some of the best of Labour's conference has been off-message – or superfluous to the gloss which some want to project. For this is still a party with kindness and idealism in its ranks. The night before Prescott's speech I found myself in a room without videos or flashy displays, for a reception for Alf Morris, MP, who is retiring.

The compassionate and tireless Morris has worked for decades for the disabled; Sense (the deaf-blind association) together with Alzheimer's and muscular dystrophy groups wanted to thank him. Tony Blair, who must have been exhausted, took the trouble to come and made a moving speech.

Off-message or not, delegates gave Prescott a rousing ovation. But what a change that explosion wreaked! The edgy confidence the party has exuded all week evaporated instantly. One bang, one bad stumble, and it was as though delegates feared they had only been dreaming and the game was up. Would a giant spectre of Baroness Thatcher come winging, bat-like, through the hall, as everyone ran screaming for cover?

Confidence returned. Cameramen ambushed a toddler dancing to *Things Can Only Get Better*. Scared by the camera flashes, the child stopped and began to cry. Image of weeping babe. *Off-message! Off-message!* The toddler was hauled away.

Familiarity Breeds Tory Contentment

The Conservative Party Conference …

As at the Vatican, where ambitious cardinals crowd the corridors around an ailing Pope, so at Bournemouth do aspirants for the leader's crown linger by the bedside of a sick party, mouthing concern for the Prime Minister's political health.

The most honest bulletin we could issue from Bournemouth yesterday was that the patient's condition was grave, but stable. Bewildered Tories (the geek-quotient increases every year and this is the only party where you see conferencegoers attending with their mothers) met mixed signals on their first day.

They were confronted by a science fiction stage set: *Eurovision Song Contest* meets *Star Trek*. On to blank, futuristic screens, video projections remind us what the debate is about: for Farming we had combine-harvesters, ladybirds, par-baked buns, and a plum.

Platform parties float in space, safe within two lifeboat-like vessels. Between the boats a lonely speaker thrashes about like a swimmer in trouble. Bald heads peer over the boats' sides in concern. We half expect the occupants to start throwing each other overboard, or eating the cabin-boy.

Into one of these boats the Baroness Thatcher bustled before noon. Her familiar royal blue outfit and little partridge-like steps were reassuring. We held our breath, and – yes! – she kissed John *and* Norma Major. And sat next to William Hague, the Welsh Secretary. Could this be an omen?

Mr Hague gave the day's best speech. With conviction and fluency the young prodigy tore into devolution plans, Lady Thatcher gazing adoringly on. Hague's well-paced Yorkshire grind ('millions of uzz') verges on the robotic and comes oddly from a chap resembling a Cow-&-Gate baby competition winner – like one of those horror movies where the voice of an alien body-invader emerges from an abducted toddler – but the conference loved him.

They loved Michael Forsyth (the Scottish Secretary) too. Forsyth has a hunched, jagged delivery, faintly demonic, and played shamelessly to the gallery by waving altered images of the Union Flag. Finally he and Hague held a huge, real Union Flag between them: grinning poison-dwarf and alien body-invader, our poor flag stretched between.

The repellent spectacle was cheered wildly.

But then no conference speech succeeds, these days, without the gimcrack. Videos, postcards from old ladies in Liverpool, near-sobbing references to deaths in the family or among friends, politicians piggy-backing on to the emotional aftermath of national tragedy ... It is not enough to inform: we must be whammied.

Stephen Dorrell's whammy was to replace his speech with a marathon question and answer session. People could ask anything they liked. The ostentatiously competent Health Secretary coped well, so the session was without interest. Nobody asked the real questions: 'Why don't you get a suntan, you whey-faced bap?' 'Why do you scowl like a ghoul and shout all the time?' and 'Reincarnated, which animal would you choose?'

Still, Dorrell's gimmick succeeded, like Forsyth's flag. Soon will come the ultimate conference speech. A host of hologram angels flock from the ceiling, dry-ice puffs from the platform, lasers scissor, video-images dance around the walls and, to deafening disco music, politicians rollerskate around the conference floor, miming to quadraphonic repeats of a killer soundbite.

Douglas Hogg, the Agriculture Minister, did none of these things yesterday. He waved nothing, failed to sing – failed even to produce an anecdote about his dear old auntie. Instead he just explained doggedly how difficult it all was. Thus, Hogg missed the point. Some of us love him the better for it.

Nuts   *14.10.96*

With the exception of the Prime Minister, they all seem to be at it. One page of Michael Portillo's speech to the Tory conference last week contained little more than a hundred words, arranged in paragraphs, none of which contained more than one sentence. Only two paragraphs contained more than a dozen words. A week earlier in Blackpool, Andrew Smith, Labour's Transport spokesman, followed his Leader's lead into short, verbless sentences, one passage of his speech running:

'Traffic jams on the M1.

'Road congestion.

'Changing at Preston.'

As with so many attempts by politicians to be modern, the style is actually about half a step behind the times. You see the same grasping at what was modern yesterday in the design of today's conference stage sets, which ape the sort of look in vogue for the television set designs of the Eighties.

As in the visual, so with the spoken word. The modern conference speech unconsciously echoes the advertising copywriter's style of the 1980s. Advertising has moved on since then, the industry accepting that consumers can tackle sentences with quite complex structures; but to the politicians of the Nineties, the Eighties are still the latest thing.

It is time, then, for an all-purpose framework for the podium politician who wishes to impress. I have taken as my theme nuts, but for 'nuts' you can substitute almost anything … (*Party leader runs on, to disco fanfare, eyes burning …*)

'As I look about me, as I look around. Ahead.

'Forward.

'I see a vision.

'Let me tell you what I mean.

'I mean nuts.

'True nuts.

'New nuts.

'Not yesterday's nuts. No going back to the old nuts. No return.

'Instead, nut reborn.

'Young nut, shared nut, growing nut.

'Nurtured nut. Nuts fulfilled.

'Cherished.

'Nourished.

'Undiminished.

'Nuts' new dawn.

'Let me explain.

'Big nut.

'Not small nut.

'Huge nut.
'British nut.
'Yes, British!
'Strong.
'Tough.
'Tough nut.
'Not Brussels nut.
'Oh no!
'Caring, committed, community nut.
'Nut with values.
'Firm nut.
'Focused nut.
'Single nut.
'But never isolated.
'Oh no!
'Upright nut.
'Proud nut.
'Confident nut.
'Not timid.
'No bad nuts. Rotten. Soft.
'But firm. Uncracked. Unyielding.
'But we must have safeguards!
'My priorities – passion if you like – nut, nut and nut.
'Roasted nut.
'Nuts in every classroom.
'Nut superhighway.
'Trained nuts.
'Reskilled nut.
'Educated nut.
'Modern nut.
'Flexible, mobile dynamic nut.
'Nut for the 21st century.
'A thousand nuts for a thousand years.
'A nut on every street corner.
'Nut on the beat.
'Neighbourhood nut.
'Responsible nut.
'Decent nut.
'Principled.

'Three nuts and you're out!

'One nut: bold, courageous, firm.

'Tough on blight, tough on the causes of blight.

'No more lost nuts, spoilt nuts.

'Undervalued. Underfunded. Undermined.

'Seventeen wasted years!

'Integrated nut. Strategic. Global. Galactic.

'Proactive. Not reactive. Not negative.

'Positive.

'Open nut. Not closed. Honest nut.

'No sleazy nuts.

'I tell you this.

'Choice of nut.

'Real choice.

'Excellence.

'Honour.

'Excellence and choice.

'Choice and excellence.

'Diversity and choice.

'Diversity, excellence, choice, nuts, and honour.

'Opportunity nut. Fair, reasonable, reaching out.

'Nut 2000.

'Nut mission.

'Nuts for all.

'All our people.

'New solutions.

'No false promises. No betrayals.

'No lies.

'No letdowns.

'No more.

'No.

'I see aspiration. I see hope.

'Hopeful nuts, high-wage nuts. Skilled, sophisticated.

'Future nuts: limitless, optimistic and empowered.

'Stakeholding nuts, investing in nuts, partnership of nuts, nut potential, nuts anew.

'A force for good: for nuts unborn. So many nuts!

'A need for change.

'A fresh start.

'And let us now redouble. Let us now commit. Reach out, I say.
'Reach up.
'Down.
'Forward.
'A nutty covenant, I tell you: A nutty vow!'
(*Spouse of party Leader runs onto stage and embraces Leader passionately. Crowd goes wild. Press goes wild.*)

Cereal Stalker

15.10.96

'I'm only too easy to meet,' cried Virginia Bottomley to a crowd of startled MPs, regathered after the summer recess yesterday, 'in any number of settings!'

What could the fragrant Mrs Bottomley mean? What settings did she have in mind? Parascending? Boating on the Serpentine? Call me uninventive, but a cup of tea in her office would surely do.

The Heritage Secretary had been goaded into this surprising offer by her Labour Shadow, Jack Cunningham. At Questions yesterday, he asked her to confirm that for £500 one could have joined Mrs Bottomley at breakfast during her party's conference last week at Bournemouth. 'Is that proper?' In fact, Dr Cunningham was taking something of a liberty with these reports.

It seems Tories with funds to spare were being invited to sponsor the breakfast, but those with no more than loose change to offer were still permitted to approach the great lady at the muesli bar. Still, Cunningham decided to take a crack, and who can blame him?

Unable to decide whether to be indignant or dismissive, Mrs B decided to be coquettish. So cheery a picture did she paint of her approachability at breakfast, at tea-time or at any other time, that one wondered where she finds any time at all to be Heritage Secretary. This merry informality she contrasted with the '£1,000 Labour charge for nosh-ups with Tony Blair in Park Lane'.

It seems an odd reversal of the old certainties, much in keeping with John Major's attacks on the old school tie brigade on Labour's front bench. Time was when a Tory would have boasted how expensive they were to dine with, not how cheap. When Tam Dalyell returned to the subject minutes later, Mrs Bottomley went further. For most breakfasters at Bournemouth, she insisted, 'it cost only £7.50' to join her.

And there was more. 'I am available at virtually every major tourist event.'

Really? The Changing of the Guards *and* Mrs Bottomley? Bottomley at Stonehenge? Bottomley among the Crown Jewels? Bottomley at the Zoo? At your picnic at Henley? Leading the donkey rides at Cleethorpes? There can only be one logical conclusion to Mrs Bottomley's dash for crowd appeal. Can Mystic Meg's contract with the BBC be safe for much longer?

6.11.96 # Miss!

Nobody likes a tell-tale. With every parliamentary session, Madam Speaker grows more to resemble a kindergarten teacher driven to her wits' end. Now, to her despair, the kiddies have taken to telling on each other.

On a Monday, one of them tells Miss that someone else has been using Commons notepaper for unofficial business. On a Tuesday, another tells her that someone has used OHMS envelopes for party correspondence. Betty Boothroyd's patience grows more thin.

'Miss! *Miss!*' said Labour's Jim Dowd (Lewisham W) yesterday. (Well, that's what young Jim meant: what he said was, 'On a point of order, Madam Speaker'.) He complained that Tory ministers visited his constituency without telling him.

Wearily, Miss Boothroyd reminded MPs that it is a convention at Westminster that MPs inform each other when visiting each other's constituencies. Miss! Miss! *Miss!* ... this time it was the Tories' Graham Riddick (Colne Valley). The gangly child told Miss Boothroyd that it was Labour MPs who failed to notify others of their visits. He accused Labour's leader and deputy leader of this. Madam Speaker kicked at her footstool with elegant shoe.

Miss! Who was this ginger-mopped infant on the Tory benches? It was Ian Bruce (Dorset S). And what did little Ian want? To be excused? To complain that an older girl next to him, Elaine (Dame

Kellett-Bowman, 72), had shoved him with her elbow? No. Ian wanted Miss to know that Tony (Blair, 43) was talking too much. 'He used 342 words in his questions to the Prime Minister last Tuesday and 380 words on Thursday,' whined Ian. 'After 150 words, could you cut him off before his third question?'

Barely controlling her temper, Miss told Ian that she was perfectly able to find out for herself how much Tony was talking, and besides it wasn't just Tony. *All* the boys and girls talked too much.

European Power Surge   *7.11.96*

Animated exchanges took place across the Commons floor yesterday on how and where to plug in a vacuum cleaner. The discussion was prompted by a question to industry ministers from Sir Mark Lennox-Boyd (C, Morecambe & Lonsdale) about a mysterious body called CENELEC. From the answer given by the junior minister, Richard Page, it seemed this was the inter-European cockpit for discussion of electrical matters.

Page told MPs that CENELEC had decided not to harmonize plugs and sockets across the Continent. He supported the decision.

It was then that Mr Page revealed an unsuspected side of his nature. He is an easygoing rightwinger in the carpet-slippers-and-Viyella-pyjamas mould; few would see him as a New Man. But there he stood, admitting it was a pity you would remain unable 'to plug in your Hoover in Calais, and also in Dover'.

The minister did not explain why he or anyone else would want to plug in his Hoover in Calais and also in Dover. Many Tory MPs do expect to be looking for another job after the election, but the thought of Mr Page running some kind of cross-Channel domestic-cleaning service, lugging his Hoover on and off the Sealink ferry, surprised us.

Picture him in French maid's apron and feather duster on the Calais doorstep. *Est-ce que je puis passer l'aspirateur sur votre tapis, Madame? Où est la prise de courant? Zut alors! C'est une prise à deux fiches? Je suis désolé que ça ne va pas.*

MPs are never happier than when debate turns to something they actually know something about. Cycling, fishing, Hoovering ... such discussion being rare in our super-complicated high-tech world, it is seized on with pathetic relief. Quick to leap up next was Labour's Denis MacShane (Rotherham). The other MPs are jealous of MacShane because he spent some years working for the International Metalworkers' Federation and living (in style, they assume) in Geneva.

They call him 'the Member for Geneva Central'. With his rogueish grin, sharp intellect and faintly sneering debating style, MacShane strikes the Sir Buttons of this world as the sort of fellow who might wear red braces, and cheat at croquet. 'The hon gentleman lives in a cocooned world ...' drawled MacShane.

'Unlike you, in Geneva,' came the heckle, but MacShane persisted. European plugs and sockets should be harmonized, he said. When he travelled 'with my laptop, my mobile phone and my fax machine' he was continually frustrated by non-standard sockets. A faint hiss and scattered jeering could be heard.

Richard Page called MacShane 'an elderly, jetsetting yuppie'. Considering that Page is 55 and MacShane is 48, this was pretty rich.

Then came an unexpected newcomer to our debate on white goods and electronics: a Sheffield lawyer, Spencer Batiste (C, Elmet). To find a lawyer at Westminster who can switch an appliance on, let alone plug it in, would be unusual, but Batiste's knowledge goes wider. 'Madam Speaker,' he said, 'you can buy an adaptor.' With this, explained Batiste, MacShane could plug in his laptop anywhere.

But what about Mr Page's cross-Channel Hoover? As we go to print, this sketch's information is that some travel-plug adaptors, being fused, might not take the current needed for vacuum cleaners.

The Speaker, being a woman, was less interested in household trivia. She seemed to entertain some crazy notion that the Commons had more important issues to address.

13.11.96 # The Man Who Wrote it Down

Nothing is more fun than a public execution. Yesterday your sketchwriter took himself off to Committee Room 15 to watch the next instalment of the dismembering of the Tory whip who made the mistake of putting on paper what whips of both parties have always arranged in practice: David Willetts.

Were the cartoonist Bateman still alive, Mr Willetts would feature in one of his classic depictions of social gaffes: *The Man Who Wrote it Down*. One pictures the gawky confusion of the MP as older whips rush for the door while moustachioed colleagues raise eyebrows over the brandy.

At the start of the proceedings, a white-haired old lady was shown by the policeman on duty to a front seat in the public gallery, presumably to knit by the guillotine.

Mr Willetts looks like a giant, scraggy chicken. Yesterday he was set upon by the Dobermann-like Dale Campbell-Savours (Lab, Workington), who clearly sees himself as some sort of poor man's Perry Mason, interrupting the replies to his sneering questions. Mr Campbell-Savours became so obsessive that he helped rescue Willetts from his drubbing at the more polite – but deadly – hands of Quentin Davies (Stamford & Spalding), on his own side, on Monday.

Take it from an old parliamentary hand: this kind of investigation will never work. It runs right against the grain of the Commons ethos, as does the whole select committee system. The whips on both sides infiltrated select committee work from the start, and this episode throws a rare shaft of daylight on to the process. But nobody really wants to change it. Whether Labour, Liberal Democrat or Tory you simply do not attack your own colleagues in public unless you want to become a pariah. This is what Quentin Davies now risks. Each party has ways of disciplining, or even destroying, its own Members in private. But never in front of the children.

To watch the proceedings of the Standards and Privileges Committee yesterday was to observe the clash of two cultures. The culture of party, ancient and integral to the place, *versus* the culture of neutral inquiry, an uncomfortable import. Party will prevail.

Hot and Bothered Betty   *14.11.96*

Betty Boothroyd has beautiful feet. I can reveal this, having spent a fascinating half-hour studying her right foot.

In two centuries of *The Times*'s publication, no description of a Speaker's foot has ever appeared in this newspaper. Probably no Press Gallery reporter has ever seen a Speaker's foot. There is no mention of it in Dicey's *The Law and the Constitution*. Extended glimpses afforded to this Sketch must be unprecedented over six centuries.

The unshoeing of Madam Speaker occurred yesterday afternoon at 3.05. But first, a word of explanation.

An unusually boring session of Questions to Education and Employment ministers was testing the patience of even the parliamentary clerks, one of whom was scratching under his wig.

Barry Sheerman (Lab, Huddersfield) was determined to be cross. Describing an answer from the junior Education Minister Eric Forth as 'pathetically inadequate', he met clucks of irritation from the government benches. 'We have to say "pathetic" all the time this afternoon,' he protested. He did not say why. The Tories were equally cross. They faced another debate on BSE in which Labour's Robin Cook was to taunt the Government with a wit which had even civil servants, in their box, trying not to giggle.

Tory ill-humour had reached its nadir when, after a fair question about education from Labour's new recruit, the former Tory Alan Howarth, a young toff called Henry Bellingham (C, Norfolk NW) had risen. 'If,' he sneered, 'the Hon Gentleman had had a more fulfilling education himself, he might not have experienced the mid-life crisis he had this year.'

That raised eyebrows even among Tories. Bustling hotly to her feet, Madam Speaker protested that this was hardly the sort of thing Hon Members cared to hear. Miss Boothroyd was educated at Dewsbury College of Commerce and Art. Mr Bellingham is an old Etonian. Readers may conclude that the score so far was Dewsbury 1, Eton 0.

But the strain on the Dewsbury old girl was intense. It must be hot in those tights. The gown, though becoming, is a nuisance. And the shoes (Miss Boothroyd designed them herself: black patent leather with enormous brooches) appear to pinch.

Add to that the frustration a Speaker must feel as MPs squabble away the afternoon in pointless debate, and those shoes must pinch all the harder. Miss Boothroyd had placed both feet on the little footstool before the Speaker's chair. She was restless, fidgety. Slowly, the right shoe slipped its heel from under her own and slid forward until it lay beneath her instep, her regal toes slipped loosely in, only their tips sheathed. I held my breath. Would she?

She grew bolder. Withdrawing the foot completely, she brushed the shoe from the footstool.

Now exposed, Madam Speaker's foot lay delicately on the green leather, perfectly naked beneath the television lights, hidden from the House but visible to a sketchwriter perched above.

It was a fine foot, about size 4. Some women in their middle years suffer from corns or the deformation caused by ill-fitting shoes, but not Miss Boothroyd. At Ipanema beach I have seen worse feet on women half her age. Each toe was perfect.

Your sketchwriter became quite transfixed, his vision focused downward, the rest of the chamber and its graceless company fading into no more than a rude background to this elegant foreground: Madam Speaker's footstool: Madam Speaker's foot.

The Reply I Gave Some Moments Ago

20.11.96

Tuesday afternoon marked a significant anniversary for John Major. It was the 300th Prime Minister's Questions which Mr Major himself has taken: 300 sessions of nonsensical questions and nonsensical answers; 300 fatuous 15-minute spats which, laid end to end, would yield 60 hours of continuous babble.

Yesterday Major reached Question 6. The inquiry, like all the others, was whether he would state his engagements for the day. The reply, 'I refer my Hon Friend [Rt Hon Friend/Gentleman/Lady] to the answer I gave some moments ago,' was the reply he always gives. Only once does he actually state his engagements: a meaningless piece of non-information.

The pointless ritual arises for reasons it is pointless to relate. Along with the pauses and the getting up and sitting down, it consumes some 11 seconds. The initial diary-recitation consumes some 15 seconds. Simple arithmetic suggests that Major has now spent nearly six hours of his life in bland recitations of his day's diary, or referring his Hon Friends to the reply he gave some moments ago.

Prime Ministers are paid about £30 an hour. The skills needed to intone 'I refer my Hon Friend to the answer I gave some moments ago' can be hired for less. It is this column's modest suggestion – tendered as a small memento to the occasion – that if the British constitution absolutely requires somebody to recite these words twice a week, then an unemployed person might be taken off the streets and asked to stand in a small sound-proofed cubicle in the Palace of Westminster, out of earshot of serious politics, and intone the requisite mantra at the requisite hour.

Yesterday John Major did the honours. It was neither his nor Tony Blair's finest hour. For what felt like the 300th time, a Tory backbencher (Ann Winterton) brought happy tidings of a drop of unemployment in her constituency (Congleton) and asked, for the 300th time, whether this would not be imperilled by 'the minimum wage and the social chapter' (etc). For the 300th time, Major found himself 'delighted' with the good news, and in absolute agreement with his Hon Friend about Labour's threat.

Mr Major makes an unconvincing poodle-master and Mrs Winterton an unconvincing poodle. For the 300th time, this sketch asks: why don't they pack it in?

Then Tony Blair got up. His question about mixed wards in hospitals, on which he became puzzlingly insistent (returning to it three times) is the sort of thing which may sound logical when set out at a policy strategy meeting in a high-powered public relations consultancy ...

'You see, Tony, NHS *is* the message; market research shows we're ahead on health; health is on-message; economics is off-message. Look at these charts ... Peter, show him the charts ... We hit Major three times on health, *then*, in the final soundbite, we *link through* from unreliability on health to unreliability on everything else.'

'But there isn't anything to say on health.'

'Then we'll find something. Anji, dig up something on health.'

... but which sounded odd in the chamber. Blair sometimes gives the impression of having got a 'Be a Leader of the Opposition' kit for Christmas, painstakingly cutting along the dotted lines, working out which tabs have to be folded back and glued.

For his part, Major often speaks as though receiving instructions from an earpiece or perhaps from the spirit world. A bizarre duo. Three hundred PMQs down, how many to go?

Demons Gloat As Ill Winds Blow No Good

22.11.96

Describing Wednesday's Commons proceedings, this sketch reported the appearance in the chamber of an omen, and a sinister one: Sir George Gardiner (C, Reigate), a thin smile upon his lips, standing at the Bar of the House. We noted that when trouble for the Conservatives was brewing, Sir George was seldom far away. Yesterday the omens multiplied.

Three or four benches back from the front bench, below the gangway and somewhat to its end, lies the epicentre of an invisible zone. No more than six yards square, it is a zone of trouble and menace for Tory Cabinets: a vortex of the forces of mutiny.

It was from here that Geoffrey Howe launched his fatal attack on Margaret Thatcher; from here that Thatcher took aim at her successor's Maastricht agreement; from here that Norman Lamont described John Major as 'in office but not in power'.

The ghosts of such occasions still inhabit those benches. As unmarked on formal parliamentary maps as the Bermuda Triangle is unmarked on navigational charts, this small patch of green leather radiates spirals of stress, anger and treachery.

Positioned just off-centre in the Commons Triangle for Prime Minister's Questions yesterday was John Redwood. Pallid and unblinking, his silent presence was enough. It will have chilled Majorites as might the appearance of a death's head in their midst. And there was worse. In the Peers' Gallery above, the gaunt features of Norman Tebbit leered down like some malign gargoyle, gleeful witness to their discomfiture. Lord Tebbit had come for the fun – and to be seen there.

An observer who was profoundly deaf could have read the scene as accurately as we who could hear. What we heard was Tony Blair seizing the advantage and forcing the Prime Minister into an awkward defence of the Cabinet's decision not to allow a debate on European monetary proposals.

The subject may be arcane – the exchanges difficult (in cold print) to weigh – but there was no mistaking the Tory backbench anger, or the ministerial embarrassment. If meteorologists could weather-map political trouble, this morning's charts would show an area of intense pressure situated, not over the Azores, but over the Commons Triangle. Puffing an ill wind from the top right corner, like those cherubim on antique maps, would be the pursed cheeks of Lord Tebbit. The sea monsters such maps show would bear the faces of prominent Conservative Euro-sceptics, cruising around the Prime Minister.

27.11.96   # The Real Thing

The Budget ...

As Kenneth Clarke spoke yesterday, uninsured whisky-tippling Scottish dukes driving gas-powered Bentleys, who roll their own cigarettes, whose pay is not profit-related, whose wives do not work and who have a pathological fear of flying, will have raised their glasses in a grateful toast to a generous Chancellor. The rest of us scratched our heads and reached for the pocket calculator.

It was a brazen and stylish performance, containing many good jokes and washed down with nearly half a carafe of whisky and water. It met from an unusually well-armed Tony Blair the most crackling Opposition response in recent memory.

The Budget speech was heard, as ever, by a packed chamber. Standards of exotic garb for the occasion have fallen sadly over the decades and we had to make do with the knobbly knees of Bill Walker (C, Tayside N) in a dowdy kilt.

Mr Clarke was furnished not with the glass of whisky and water a Chancellor traditionally keeps at his elbow, but with a whole carafe. At one point he began refilling his glass at the same time as explaining how he was going to eliminate fraud. Warming to his fiscal theme, the Chancellor forgot his right wrist, still pouring the whisky. He remembered in the nick of time, just as the glass brimmed to overflowing.

Up in the Strangers' Gallery, Mrs Gillian Clarke, her hair in a neat bun, looked on with the resigned despair of one whose husband is forever burning the toast.

As an entertainer, Clarke showed the wit, timing and polish of a seasoned performer with a pig of a script to deliver – and pulled it off.

This Chancellor is not afraid to joke where others fear to tread. He began by chuckling that this was 'the real Budget', not the leaked one. He said this was his last Commons speaking engagement of the week – 'or so at the moment I expect'. He ambushed his shadow, Gordon Brown, by claiming that 'few serious commentators' disputed his forecasts, then (to Brown): 'I hear some mutterings from the front bench opposite. I said 'few *serious* commentators'. He giggled.

Revealing plans to raise taxes on alcoholic soft drinks, he explained this would put up the price by about 7p a bottle – 'for those of my honourable friends who have not yet tried them,' he added, grinning round at the Tories behind. Dame Jill Knight (Birmingham, Edgbaston), robed in a royal blue with the intensity of Quink, looked grim: 7p on a bottle of Hooper's Hooch or Two Dogs lemonade! Life in Edgbaston will hardly be worth living. 'Myself,' said Clarke, 'I haven't yet been converted to bubble-gum flavoured alco-pop.' He took another swig of whisky.

The Chancellor told us that the basic rate of tax was the lowest for 60 years, then translated this into terms John Major, sitting beside him, would take on board: 'not since Stanley Baldwin was Prime Minister,' he said, 'not since Wally Hammond scored a double century at the Oval.' At the mention of Baldwin *and* Hammond, Mr Major grinned affectionately.

As Clarke sat down and the cheers began, I looked up at Mrs Clarke. She had been watching like an anxious mum. As the cheering intensified she relaxed, permitting herself a small, proud smile.

Then Tony Blair rose. Moments before, Peter Mandelson had rushed in with an envelope on which was written the figure 2120. This was handed to Mr Blair. 'Two thousand one hundred and twenty pounds' worth of extra tax for the average family!' declared the Labour Leader, minutes later, with his customary supreme intellectual self-confidence.

Nigel's Empty Nest   *11.12.96*

They could call him the Clitheroe Kid. Nigel Evans (Cribble Valley) is the fresh-faced and winsome young Tory who represents that town. He has become one of Westminster's most frequent chippers-in. For

Madam Speaker, barely a parliamentary afternoon passes unlit by Mr Evans's engaging glance or toothy smile, no day closes ungraced by his Welsh lilt.

Unfortunately he always says the same thing. 'Does my Right Honourable friend agree that if Labour ever reached power the nation would be cursed with the minimum wage and the social chapter?' The mantra acquires a ritual quality: intoned more for sound than meaning. 'Minimumwage'n'thesocialchapter': this is young Nigel's song: increasingly his only song.

Does the afternoon promise Questions to the Scottish Secretary? Evans is ready. Where would Scotland be, beneath the yoke of the minimumwage'n'thesocialchapter?

Are MPs questioning the Agriculture Secretary? Evans is among them. How could farmers survive, ground down by the minimum-wage'n'thesocialchapter? Social Security Questions, Treasury Questions ... every session rings to the mockingbird sound of the Ribble Valley song. Ribble Valley is a beautiful place. Nigel Evans is a good-looking man. An MP makes a socially desirable spouse. This one is 38 and single. So Westminster-watchers have been saddened by Mr Evans's lack of success in finding a lady who might rejoice in the name of Mrs Evans and share his constituency nest. He is not, they say, unsusceptible to feminine charms. One wonders why womankind is proving unsusceptible to his.

Yesterday afternoon, Nigel encountered the Prime Minister. It being Prime Minister's Questions, and John Major having made some headway – turning the 'European splits' issue back upon a wary Tony Blair – Evans rose. Miss Boothroyd called him. As 1996 expires, here was his chance to ask something new. He asked something old. Did the Prime Minister comprehend the full horror of Labour's plans to introduce the minimumwage'n'thesocialchapter? Even kindly Mr Major looked bored. The Opposition looked nauseated. Evans's friends looked resigned.

And all at once I understood why Mr Evans has failed to score with women. Picture the scene: Nigel is entertaining a young lady to a candlelight meal at a discreet table in a small Clitheroe restaurant. Everything has gone swimmingly. Nigel and his companion sip the last of a dessert wine, exchanging glances over the guttering flame.

For reasons of delicacy the waiter has not disturbed the couple since topping up their glasses. Aware that her escort is a shy boy from the

Welsh Valleys and taking advantage of this pause in service, the young lady murmurs: 'Ooh, isn't the service slow, Nigel. My little flat's just around the corner. Why don't we slip back there and try my percolator? You could help me with it. I've never really known how it's done ...'

Young Evans's eyes light up. Go for it, Nigel! 'Service slow? If you think the service is slow now, just try eating out under a Labour government after they've brought in the minimumwage'n'thesocial-chapter. Slow service? There'll be *no* service, under Labour [*soundbite*]. The consequences for the catering industry of the minimumwage'n'the-socialchapter will be catastrophic. Restaurants will be shutting down all over Britain. Proof positive of new Labour's menace. Nor will restaurants be the only casualties. Small business as a whole will be devastated. Right across the board the dead hand of the minimumwage'n'thesocialchapter ...'

His companion slips sadly away. She must make sure coffee is served here and not *chez-elle*. The spell is broken.

Government By Confusion   *17.12.96*

In our frenzy over the detail of Tory policy, we are missing something more important: the creative genius of our Prime Minister. By stealth he is abandoning the ancient doctrine of collective Cabinet responsibility.

It is quite refreshing. Other leaders pretend they have a frontbench position on important questions, but John Major hardly bothers. Yesterday, quizzed by Tony Blair on the Government's latest cattle cull, Mr Major repeated what has long been his line: that BSE policy is led by 'the science'. He murmured something about 'changed scientific evidence' on maternal transmission to calves. 'The science' had changed, so the policy had changed.

Not many minutes later Douglas Hogg, the Agriculture Minister, was on his feet, offering his own explanation for the increased cattle slaughter. It had little to do with science, Mr Hogg said. 'The real justification for the cull is that unless we do the cull we will not get progress on lifting the ban. That is a political fact, not a scientific fact.'

Mr Major says one thing; Mr Hogg says the opposite. Mr Blair was vexed about the confusion and used it to some effect in the House yesterday, mocking what he called the 'serial incompetence' of the Government. But the chamber was half-empty and the press gallery listless. 'Hell,' we thought, 'this is all such a mess, and anyway it's nearly Christmas.' Pencils dropped.

If, in a through-the-looking-glass world, key figures keep contradicting each other, there is only so much mileage to be had from pointing this out. After a while we tire of demonstrating what has already been demonstrated – that different voices are saying different things – and give up. Mr Major just keeps throwing sand in people's eyes until they take their buckets and spades and quit the beach, leaving him alone with his sandcastle.

He seemed to be adopting this tactic on a broad front yesterday. Adopting his Mystic Meg voice and speaking in a strangely relaxed near-monotone, he told Euro-sceptic and Euro-phobic sleeve-tuggers (variously) that he would brook no fudging from Europe; that Britain's whole relationship with Europe was in the balance; that it wasn't; and that he absolutely shared the worries of backbench colleague David Wilshire (Spelthorne) about anti-European feeling.

Ray Whitney (C, Wycombe) is so Europhile that he sounds like a simultaneous translation from French. To Mr Major's delight he commended to him a mysterious 'middle way' called 'realistic British Europeanism'.

Sir Teddy Taylor (C, Southend E) is so rabidly Europhobe he turns up all but wiping the foam flecks from his mouth. He welcomed Mr Major's resolve to have no truck with EU demands. Mr Major agreed this was 'essential'.

Within minutes of each other, Sir Patrick Cormack (C, Staffs S) and Edward Leigh (C, Gainsborough & Horncastle) had congratulated him warmly over Europe. Sir Patrick and Mr Leigh do not inhabit the same planet. Either the Prime Minister has two European policies or one of these gentlemen has misunderstood the policy he does have.

In fact they both misunderstood. Mr Major may have a view, but none of us has the least idea what it is. We find ourselves confronted by him as in a canyon we might be confronted by the rock face. The rock keeps its counsel. We hear only strange, mocking echoes of our own opinions.

What Is He Doing Here?   *19.12.96*

Facing the Celtic music at Scottish Questions in the Commons yesterday was the ever-diffident, super-courteous junior minister, Lord James Douglas-Hamilton. Undoubtedly the politest politician at Westminster, Lord James is an Oxford (lightweight) boxing Blue.

His father, the 14th Duke of Hamilton, was the first man to fly over Everest, and the target of the Hess mission. In 1993 Lord James wrote a book about the episode, *The Truth About Rudolf Hess*.

Few are quite sure what a Lord is doing in the Commons in the first place. Some suppose it a mystery of the arcane rules of Scottish aristocracy; or has Douglas-Hamilton, looking for the upper chamber, wandered into the Commons by mistake and been too embarrassed to make his excuses and leave?

All enjoy the story about his first week as a minister, during which he had to be restrained from opening the chauffeur's car door for him.

But a new Douglas-Hamilton story has just reached me – from a usually impeccable source. Apparently Lord James was assigned the task of representing the Scottish Office at a symposium on the spread of Aids.

Conscientiously, he asked for a briefing and his staff provided extensive background reading material.

Lord James read carefully, until reaching a passage which appeared to trouble him.

With many apologies he called a private secretary to his side. 'Er, what does this word mean?' he said, pointing.

'Which word?' the secretary replied, for the minister seemed to be pointing at the word 'heterosexual'. '*That* one,' he stammered: 'het-het-heterosexual'.

The embarrassed functionary explained as best he could to Lord James, who is married with four sons.

If this story is true, he will be the modern counterpart of Molière's Bourgeois Gentleman, who asked his newly appointed tutor what the word 'prose' meant, and, on being informed, danced around in delight at the discovery that he should have been speaking prose all his life – but only now become aware of his capacity to do so.

Lord James had been a heterosexual for nearly half a century, without knowing it.

The Wittering Herd

A small technical slip during Foreign Office Questions yesterday spoke volumes. Something went wrong with the sound-amplification system in the Chamber. The fault was corrected in seconds, but it taught me something new.

Parliament's audio system is antique, but effective. Dangling from the high ceiling in the chamber are scores of small microphones, no MP's mouth being, at any one time, too far from one of them. On a lazy afternoon, as MPs shift and gape, the scene must be similar to the submarine view in a deep pond, as anglers' lines descend from the sky and dozens of old trout, opening and closing their mouths, eye the devices above with wary interest.

Boffins in a concealed box activate the microphones closest to whoever is speaking for as long as he speaks – then switch to the mikes nearest whoever replies.

Inset into the backs of all the benches, at ear level, are hundreds of small loudspeakers, recessed behind ornate circular brass grilles smaller than a soap dish. Individually they are muted, but the combined effect of some 500 of these is substantially to turn up the volume of the whole debate. When Stephen Dorrell, the Health Secretary, speaks – or rather shouts – the volume reaches a level capable of perforating eardrums, and all but the stone deaf reach out in panic to muffle loudspeakers.

Naturally, the automatic amplification of the MP on his feet causes those reacting from a sedentary position to shout their heckles or hear-hears all the louder, turning up the volume of the background hubbub to match the speaker.

The consequence of this louder background noise is that speakers raise their own volume to outshout their audience. This causes the audience to raise the volume of jeers or cheers by a competing notch. The result is deafening.

Yesterday, while Labour's John Marek (Wrexham) was in mid-inquiry about British relations with Indonesia, his amplification suddenly failed. All at once, the volume dropped. Dr Marek is not a ranter, and for a moment the background noise in the Chamber (still adjusted for amplified sound) completely drowned this unshowy, rather rational speaker. Without his mike, he sank.

But not for long. Once the background witterers realized the MP was now inaudible, they hushed their wittering. As our ears adjusted to the new, subdued volume, Marek's voice regained our attention. Everybody else shut up. For the rest of his question, Marek enjoyed what, in 14 years at Westminster, he may never before have experienced: the sensation of being listened to by other MPs.

And I realized that there is no need for sound amplification in the Chamber. It is an intimate and surprisingly small place, there is no echo and the acoustics are good. The whole debate – complete with heckles and cheers – can be turned down to about a quarter of the volume at which, with amplification, it normally takes place. We can still hear. Nothing is lost but the element of hysteria that goes with the shouting.

Perhaps the lesson has wider implications. If Tony Blair restricted himself to calling John Major disingenuous instead of 'knee-deep in dishonour', maybe Mr Major could describe Mr Blair as changing his mind instead of betraying his principles: in which case Blair could call Major overcautious instead of spineless, and ...

Just a thought; and one with not a snowball's chance in the months ahead.

Tory Ship of State   23.1.97

Michael Portillo announces a replacement for the Royal Yacht Britannia ...

'Although she is beautifully maintained ...' Two Tory dames, beautifully maintained and decked out for the occasion, raised their heads in pride as the Defence Secretary spoke.

'... she is old.' Both Dames, one of whom is standing down at the next election, registered shock.

'She is increasingly difficult to maintain.' The Dames looked indignant.

'She will not put to sea again.' The Dames looked disconsolate.

'We need to guarantee she will be kept in excellent condition.' The dames looked reassured.

'If that cannot be assured, it would be better to see her scrapped than to see her deteriorate.' The dames looked alarmed.

Michael Portillo looked anything but. He couldn't believe his luck. Rolling every syllable of his statement round in his mouth like an especially delectable piece of butterscotch, and speaking very slowly with vast pauses, he never *quite* allowed to cross his face that schoolboy smirk which says to the rival gang: 'You know and I know my gang cheated – but you'll never prove it.'

The Tory benches were like pigs in clover. 'Hear, *hear!*' they shouted, at every reference to Her Majesty's needs and Her Majesty's dignity: 'Hya, hya, *hya!*'

Poor David Clark, Labour's principal defence spokesman, panicked.

He complained that this was electioneering, he should have been consulted, and it wasn't fair. But everybody knew that. All's fair in general elections. Dr Clark just sounded plaintive.

Next he lurched into a complaint that private capital should have been considered. This caused one of the longest bouts of uncontrolled mirth the chamber has seen since Mark Lennox-Boyd (as Foreign Office Minister) tried to explain how the contents of the Canadian diplomatic bags had become lost in the Wandsworth Prison laundry. What? A Labour spokesman calling for the private sector?

And Portillo's luck held. Labour's Alan Williams (Carmarthen) offered a rant at royal extravagance which, from Labour, would not have raised an eyebrow ten years ago. Yesterday it raised the roof.

Hugging himself with pleasure, wrapping himself in patriotism, and slopping bucketfuls of loyal adjectives over the absent head of Her Majesty, Portillo stopped just short of questioning Williams's patriotism.

Next, Dennis Skinner (Lab, Bolsover) went into orbit: Stop gagging republicans ... aristocracy in death-throes ... sick kids on hospital trolleys ... pensioners robbed blind ... no pencils in schools ... four million unemployed ...

In vain did Kate Hoey (Lab, Vauxhall) and Peter Shore (Lab, Bethnal Green & Stepney) praise the plans. Portillo painted them as lonely monarchists among a republican rabble.

Then came a fleet of little Tory rowing boats, sporting their Union Jacks and escorting the new yacht. John Wilkinson (C, Ruislip) wanted a helicopter deck.

'And a casino,' yelled Skinner. Soames began to choke again. Portillo wanted a band. Soames looked close to asphyxiation. Robert Key (C, Salisbury) wondered what the new yacht should be named.

'*HMS Camilla*!' yelled Skinner's whole heckler's bench in unison. I regret to report that, among the Tory front bench, only Mr Portillo kept a straight face.

Election Fizz Crackles Through the Air

24.1.97

People say that you can tell whether it is going to rain by watching the cows. 'Ah, look at those cows lying down. Rain must be imminent: the cows are preparing a dry patch.' But it might just show the cows *think* it is about to rain. They may be wrong. One should not assume that because cows are *in* nature, cows understand nature.

A similar mistake is made by non-political people observing MPs. 'Ah, look at those MPs down there: they are behaving as though there was about to be a general election. It must be imminent.' They think that because MPs are *in* politics, MPs understand politics.

Not so. Most MPs have no idea what is going on. So to report that MPs at Prime Minister's Questions yesterday were behaving as though a general election were imminent does not mean it is. It means MPs *think* it is. They may be wrong.

Pre-election Pantomime

31.1.97

Weak! Weak! Weak! shouted Tony Blair at John Major. 'Silly! Silly! Silly!' shouted the Tories back at Mr Blair.

'Weak. [*pause*] Weak. [*pause*] Weak ...' barked John Prescott every ten seconds or so, like a rogue-male elephant seal in the fog.

'Order! Order! Order!' shouted Madam Speaker at the lot of them.

'Ha, ha, ha' shouted MPs.

'Hear, hear, hear,' shouted the Labour front bench.

How much more can we take? Madam Speaker had reached her limit. '*Order!* There seems to be a good deal of pre-election tension.' In the race for each day's top soundbite, Miss Boothroyd now offers Mr Blair serious competition. It had begun gently. Jerry Hayes (C, Harlow) asked his first question of Prime Minister's Questions since his recent spot of local difficulty with a Sunday newspaper. Mr Hayes chose Gibraltar as his subject, informing us that the Rock's inhabitants were 'fiercely proud of being British' and inviting the PM to give them his vigorous support. Hayes acknowledged the encouraging growls from colleagues around him. Patriotism is the last refuge of a *News of the World* quarry.

Prime Minister's Questions yesterday reached new heights of pantomime – or new lows of banality, depending on your point of view. Depending, too, on your point of view, John Major felled Tony Blair with salvo after salvo of withering commentary and devastating quotes, and left to a resounding cheer from the Tory troops; or Tony Blair needled John Major mercilessly with reminders of his recent policy wobbles, punched home the Tory confusion over a single European currency, and left to a resounding cheer from the Opposition troops.

So excited did both sides become that, by the end of the last of the three questions tradition allows an Opposition leader, the battle was still raging. Blair leapt up for another round and, being out of order, fell back, silenced. The Tories yelled 'More! More! More!' but Blair was gagged by the rules. So volatile was the mood that Paddy Ashdown was only halfway through his question when interrupted by Tory shouts.

Mr Ashdown: 'The Prime Minister has pursued a conscientious and honourable policy ...'

Hon Members: 'How would *you* know?'

Right at the end, John Hume (SDLP, Foyle) asked an anguished question about Bloody Sunday, of which yesterday was the 25th anniversary. Major gave a quiet, earnest, yet finely judged reply. In the 30 seconds this took he did more to demonstrate what most beyond the Commons would see as his strengths, than in all the shouting which had gone before. But in the cheer Tory MPs gave him as he left, there was no doubt which they had enjoyed best. It was not the thoughtful part.

The Meaning of Men in Wigs   6.2.97

This is a tale of three strange men in wigs. Everybody at Westminster has seen them, yet their identities are hazy, their function a mystery. So regular a feature are they that we hardly notice them, never study them, and never ask what they do.

Questions to the Secretary of State for Scotland yesterday, when MPs with funny accents shout at each other for an hour on complex matters, is an ideal time to concentrate on something else. So this sketch tried to answer the question 'what is a clerk?' and 'what does a clerk do?' After 60 minutes of intense field study, we were none the wiser.

Picture the Commons chamber. At one end sits the Speaker on a raised dais, her feet (often slipped from their shoes) on a footstool. At her feet is a huge oak table. At a big oak table before her, their backs just out of tickling-reach of her toes, sit three weird creatures, in a row. I shall call them (from her right to left) Creatures A, B and C.

All are of similar height in black suits, black gowns, black waistcoats with black buttons, white wing-collar shirts and white ties. Each wears a full-bottomed wig with a pigtail ending in a kiss-curl. Each wears gold-framed spectacles. In front of each a small drawer, and, on the table, a quill pen and ink.

Creature A wears a small Chinese beard and a faintly censorious expression. Creature B is somewhat portly, with a pursed face across which flits, from time to time, the ghost of a hint of owlish amusement. Creature C, the youngest, has a sharp nose and brow lined with studious concern. C fidgets a bit. A and B remain motionless.

At Madam Speaker's left arm stands a gentleman-in-waiting with iron grey hair and spectacles: Creature D. He wears morning dress with a white pocket handkerchief. This Creature has long, narrow shoes, like a clown. A blue clipboard on his knee carries the Order Paper on to which he marks a Member's name when he speaks. Occasionally Madam Speaker whispers to him. He appears to have no other function.

Creatures A, B and C have Order Papers too; and from time to time remove a *Hansard* from a green file and look idly at it. Mostly, though, they stare into space with strange expressions.

Once, when Michael Forsyth, the Scottish Secretary, accused Labour Glasgow of plans to pour red dye into the Clyde, Clerk B moved his left leg. When Anthony Steen (C, S Hams) suggested that new legislation for Scotland should be weighed, and remain inoperative until the same weight of old legislation had been destroyed, Creature A frowned. As George Robertson complained of delays to the Firearms Bill, Creature B opened his drawer, withdrew a pair of scissors and cut two pieces from the Order Paper. Might he make a paper plane?

Malcolm Chisholm, a Labour spokesman, ranted about '18 years of Tory failure'. Creature B pulled a blue book from his drawer, then returned it, unopened. Creature C then did the same. Creature A never did anything. We conclude that he was the senior Creature.

This was proved after questions were over. Madam Speaker called two MPs to table their Bills. These were handed to Creature A. He read out their names in a thin, piping voice, then handed them to Creature B. Creature C leant down and, picking up a water bottle and a glass, filled the glass. Creature D moved from the Speaker's side, took the glass, and offered it to the Speaker. She drank, returning the glass to Creature D, who returned it to Creature C.

That is all they did. The coming election may bring many changes but, after it, these Creatures will still be there, their habits unchanged.

So many of our European ...

14.2.97

A slight pause in Angela Knight's speech rhythm yesterday betrayed much. A last-minute change of vocabulary spoke volumes. The leggy Economic Secretary to the Treasury had been slightly disconcerted by the arrival of the Prime Minister, for Questions, just before the end of Treasury Questions where she was fielding the last inquiry. Wishing to explain the position on the Continent, she began her sentence: 'So many of our European ...'

But then she lost her nerve. John Major was almost beside her. Almost certainly she had intended to say 'so many of our European *partners*' (or 'allies' or even 'friends') – but, on second thoughts, was that the right word? Was European *courant* as an ideal these days? What was the Cabinet compromise on this? Had she missed an internal memo?

She could have tipped over the other way, and gone for 'our European *rivals*' (or 'enemies' or even 'foes') but this, too, might displease the Prime Minister, and would certainly displease her boss, Kenneth Clarke. What should Mrs Knight do?

'So many,' she said, 'of our European ... er ... countries ...' Especially in politics, there is refuge in gibberish.

The Marquis of Carabas   27.2.97

A by-election in Wirral South ...

Readers may remember the story of Puss in Boots, in which the Marquis of Carabas, through whose vast estates Puss travels, is spoken of everywhere but never seen. So it is here in the Wirral. Ben Chapman, Labour's contender for the prize of being an MP for three weeks, is as elusive as his party machine is massive.

The Wirral is all bits and pieces, the tatty and the genteel huddled together in the rain. Yesterday, street after street of Union Jack posters in windows and gardens met me. A late surge for the BNP? No, these are the Marquis of Newlabour's posters, boasting of his domain. 'Ben Chapman Means Business' each declared. But where was the subject of all this excitement? Where was Ben? Mr Chapman (said press releases) would be 'blitzing' at Old Chester Road. I arrived too late. The marquis was blitzing somewhere else.

Where? I asked the Liberal Democrat candidate: pleasant, accessible and secretly disconsolate Flo Clucas. 'We can't find him. The Green Alliance invited all candidates to a meeting last night. I went, but he never came.' 'Surge in support for Liberal Democrat Flo,' said a defiant freesheet behind her. But it looks like ebb, for Flo. 'I'll get you a taxi to the Labour HQ,' she said. 'They may know where he is.'

Labour has taken over a former Iceland superstore for its HQ. In the windows, where frozen fish fingers and deboned-cod posters were once displayed, photo-portraits of Tony Blair, and his pledges, now stand. Within, the whisper of NewSpeak replaces the hiss of refrigerant gas. There was a desk marked 'Reception' and another marked 'Enquiries'. Behind the shopfront was an operations hall whose scale would do credit to the commodity-broking floor of a secondary European power. But where was the marquis? 'Not here,' said Reception. 'Ben's canvassing. Out and about,' said Enquiries.

Could I join him, out and about? 'You've just missed him,' Labour's Barry Jones, MP said. 'Gone for tea.' After tea there would apparently be lunch. And that afternoon? 'Sorry, no. This afternoon he's preparing for this evening.' Ah. Of course.

Over at the Poulton Lancelyn Primary School, terrified teachers and insouciant tots were awaiting the arrival of Tory minister Roger Freeman, with candidate Les Byram in tow. They stormed in from the rain, trailing motherly Mrs Byram and her permanently apprehensive smile. 'I'm a native of the Wirral!' cried Mr Freeman, a U-certificate David Owen (airline version) with oiled hair and the manner of an ambitious undertaker's assistant. Mr Byram looked genuine, and weary.

'Hel-lo children,' he gurgled, in a peek-a-boo way, then (spotting a crayon picture) 'that's a bee-yoo-tiful butterfly!' Headmaster Wynn-Jones peeped nervously round the door, his busy, happy school invaded by monsters. Overwhelmed by the media excitement, one of the kiddies tried a Nazi salute at the occupying army. 'If you go down to the woods today ...' warned a wall poster. 'Nice to see you!' gushed Byram, with wolf-like grin. No child dared respond. 'What big teeth you have, Mr Tory Candidate!' 'Anything dangerous for him to be photographed under?' inquired a Tory minder, glancing warily at a coloured-in banana and plum on the wall.

'Bye bye children!' trilled the candidate, departing. 'That was a very interesting man!' whispered a relieved teacher to her puzzled class. On the table were three bears marked Baby Bear, Mummy Bear and Daddy Bear. Single Parent Bear is under wraps pending the appearance of the Marquis of Newlabour.

... Ben Chapman won.

7.3.97   # Bluster-bomb stuns beastly foe

The election looms

It's not that Labour's arguments are stronger than the Tories'. It is more that creeping feeling that nothing is to any avail. Mr Major is playing a children's computer game. An army of grotesque red cyber-beasties is advancing towards the Tory player, munching their way through walls, parachuting from the air and hang-gliding from cliffs.

For the Major player there are means of counter-attack – exploding tax-bombshells, whammies, double-whammies and killer-rebuttals – but these are in limited supply. Time, too, is running out. And still the Blairite cyber-beasties advance. *Munch-munch-munch* – here they come. They are through the battlements and waiting to storm the fortress.

Munch-munch … the beastie onslaught went into overdrive at Prime Minster's Questions yesterday afternoon. The cyber-assailants ambushed John Major over *E.coli* and a review of hygiene in slaughter-houses. Beastie Leader, Tony Blair, let fly a string of missiles concerning documents, civil servants and recommendations. Whether there was anything in these missiles was unclear, but Mr Blair munched his way forward with such confidence that the effect was to beleaguer the Prime Minister.

John Major appears to have become a Buddhist. In recent days he has faced attack with a Zen-like detachment, reciting his responses in a kind of trance, relaxed as you please. It would not have been out of place if someone were to have lit a joss-stick, or tinkled a little bell, in the breaks during his increasingly prolix replies. By the end of Prime Minister's Questions, Major's nerve remained steady, but the cyber-beasties and their Leader were swarming closer.

Munch-munch-munch. On the beasties marched. And then – a shock. An unexpected reverse for the besieging army! The Tories fielded their reserve cyber-weapon: the Heseltine bluster-bomb. A debate on puboic expenditure was opened by the Deputy Prime Minister.

Seldom in recent months has this weapon been deployed to such good effect. Blue eyes blazing and mane (slightly thinning) swept back, the blond bombshell gripped the dispatch box and chuckled as Labour's deputy-super-monster reeled. But behind the triumph, I could see fear in the Heseltine's eyes. Any day now, as, revelling in his old skills, he hits the controls, a message will flash on to the screen: 'GAME OVER!'

He fumbles for loose change for yet another game – one last game, please God. But his pockets are empty. *Much-munch-munch* … on they come.

Hogghunting

Even if it bans hunting, let us hope the next Government keeps what has become a Commons tradition: the weekly Hoggfight. The Westminster fiesta is similar to a modern Spanish bullfight. There is excitement, a great deal of action in the ring and much noise from the onlookers, but the bull (or, in this case Hogg) survives.

For the ritual, Agriculture Minister Douglas Hogg is dragged to the chamber, where he snorts and stamps his feet. The Hogg is then forced to read out an incomprehensible statement about hygiene in slaughter-houses. Then Miss Boothroyd allows Opposition frontbenchers to be matadors, and backbenchers picadors, infuriating the beast by waving brightly coloured distractions and spearing him with spikey inquiries. They insult the Hogg, call him incompetent and stupid, and ask complicated technical questions about E. coli viruses and meat pies.

Whatever the Hogg replies, MPs declare themselves totally dissatis-fied with it. Whatever MPs declare, the Hogg maintains an air of jaunty and bellicose confidence, charging around the ring, bellowing and butting people.

Chief matador during this season has been Labour's argiculture spokesman, Gavin Strang. Mr Strang has excelled for energy but disappointed those who look for nimbleness, stealth or grace. Racing back and forth, roaring abuse, pulling the Hogg's tail and enraging the beast, Strang's performance has astonished the crowd but never quite floored the quarry, whom his barbs often miss. Mr Strang trips himself up frequently, and keeps bumping into things.

After more than an hour of this sport the irrepressible Hogg, much fought but alive and kicking, departs. The irrepressible Strang, breathless but unhurt, departs too. The Labour picadors depart. The press depart. And everybody begins preparing for next week's Hoggfight.

Soapbox II

John Major calls the election and hits the campaign trail ...

After tea with the Queen it must have made quite a contrast. In Luton town centre yesterday John Major pitched himself into a walkabout which teetered perilously close to mayhem as a band of hard-core Militant-style mobsters teamed up with the usual spotty student-demo brigade – 'grants suck' – to offer the Prime Minister and the electorate a nostalgic reminder of the way we were 18 years ago. 'How much did Major pay these people?' I heard a BBC reporter asking colleagues.

There was something sweetly amateurish about the whole thing. To the trilling of a mobile phone and the heckles of beer-swilling English youths, an 18th-century kind of electioneering met a 20th-century election, perhaps our last.

As news of Mr Major's swoop on Middle England spread, more than a thousand had gathered. Leaping from his green Jaguar near a shop called Going Places, the Prime Minister was quickly engulfed in an extraordinary scratch-team of Tory ladies, gamely cheering 'Hurrah!', thin-faced yobs with shoulder bags, a posse from the Referendum Party – elderly women with sour lips – and a gathering mass of inquisitive shoppers.

Mr Major does what he always does in moments of tension. He started patting people. After a few introductory pats he stormed into a bank, inspected the cash machine and a share shop, and re-emerged, patting left and right.

This was 1990s Britain indeed. Along the first floor of the Woolwich, counter clerks gawped as Mr Major plunged past a baked potato stall, patting.

He then pushed hastily on towards Harveys solicitors, still patting, to a scattered cry of 'Five more years' and another of 'Give oop, John'. A tiny boy shinned right up a 'no-parking' sign as the Prime Minister struggled through to a terrazzo by a Burger King.

'You're out Bright!' shouted a pair of greasy anoraks as the sitting MP, Sir Graham Bright, took the microphone and declared 'Luton is now a prosperous town'. But the loudspeakers were faulty and most of the speech sank beneath the loyal cheers of Tory ladies and a chant of 'What do we want? More money for students!' Then the Prime Minister mounted his famous soapbox, There was a shout of 'ten more years', another of 'boring' and then a sort of hush. Mr Major began to speak. 'They won't stop the Conservative Party,' he declared.

'You're lying!' shouted a Geordie. Then he revised his heckle. 'You've got a nerve – but you're lying.' It was in some ways the most eloquent tribute of the afternoon.

Some of Mr Major's speech was audible. He looked at times rattled but always determined. As he made his way towards the waiting cars the police appeared to lose control and he was almost pinned against the Alliance & Leicester Building Society. 'More uniforms!' barked a slighly panicky police voice into a walkie-talkie. 'Eighteen more years!' shouted one brave lady.

Behind the Prime Minister, they retrieved the wooden soapbox which, should he win this fight, will be parcelled up and auctioned in bits as holy relics for centuries to come. At the bus stop outside the town hall, a little troupe of pensioners awaited their bus. Mr Major came, saw and patted. The crowds came. The police came. And, finally, all departed as the prime ministerial Jaguar sped off up the hill.

Previously engulfed, the bus stop came back into view. The pensioners were still there, waiting.

21.3.97   # End-of-the-road rage

John Major faces the Commons for the last time before the election ...

Just when you thought it was safe to return to Westminster ... They need to coin a new term for it – 'Mace rage', perhaps. As Parliament rises, the Prime Minister simply explodes. Like a bank manager driven beyond endurance, John Major flew off the handle during his final Prime Minister's Questions yesterday, lashing out in all directions. If it was less than statesmanlike, it was more than lively: it was awesome.

Major started hitting people almost before anyone had uttered. He took a swipe at Dennis Skinner, challenging him to quit. He landed a punch on John Prescott (who had not even spoken) accusing him of being in hock to the railway unions. And he accused Paddy Ashdown of finishing the session as he had started it, awash in piety and pomposity.

But it was Tony Blair who caught the full force. Needled by the Labour leader's accusation that he was conspiring to suppress a Commons watchdog report on alleged sleaze, the Prime Minister began a bombardment which threatened to keep Parliament stitting until Sunday.

It was like one of those domestic scenes in which some small but ill-judged remark sets a spark to the blue touchpaper – and bang. Everything Mr Major hates about Mr Blair came pouring out. Accused of sweeping corruption under the carpet, the Prime Minister angrily retorted that this was pretty rich, coming from a man who 'sells policy to the trade unions for cash'.

A sharp riposte. But getting it off his chest just seemed to get him going. Blair was someone who 'refuses to comply with the code of practice on party funding, who calls for party openness but won't publish the secret funds of his own office ...'

It all came pouring out. It was as though, having been the butt of personal remarks for more than two years of Tony Blair's opposition leadership, and having, night after night, lain in bed repeating and repeating, sotto voce, all the things he might have replied but had always thought better of before, he now let fly.

On and on he went: '... who attacks share options but takes money from millionaires for his own party; and attacks businessmen; and asks them to fund things for him; who flew Concorde and failed to declare it ...'

Was there no end to this?

'... who has a Deputy Leader [John Prescott] who spends a weekend at a five-star hotel and doesn't declare it and who flies to the other side of the world to do newspaper deals and never admits to them ...'

Finally, shortage of breath, if not material, brought his tirade to an end. But not before one final outburst: 'If there's any double standards, they sit there, on the opposition benches!' he yelled. The Prime Minister sat down to perhaps the loudest Tory cheers he has received all this session. Minutes later, he left to renewed cheers, as many government backbenchers stood in the aisles, waving their order papers.

In some ways those final 15 minutes encapsulated telltale elements of the strengths and weaknesses of all three principal party leaders during this Parliament. Fighting like a tiger when cornered, Major was well-armed in the detail but easily needled, losing stature and finding it hard to express anger while keeping his cool.

Tony Blair was poised, effective and controlled, but a faint odour of sanctity hanging over his words (he chose, yesterday, to talk of a 'stain' on government) left us uncertain whether this was a budding head-master or an officious head boy.

And Paddy Ashdown was well-judged, a little righteous, and completely ignored.